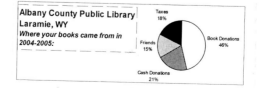

Albany County Public Library
Laramie, WY
*Where your books came from in
2004-2005:*

Taxes
18%

Book Donations
46%

Friends
15%

Cash Donations
21%

Ahmad's War, Ahmad's Peace

Ahmad's War, Ahmad's Peace

SURVIVING UNDER SADDAM, DYING IN THE NEW IRAQ

MICHAEL GOLDFARB

CARROLL & GRAF PUBLISHERS

NEW YORK

AHMAD'S WAR, AHMAD'S PEACE
Surviving Under Saddam, Dying in the New Iraq

Carroll & Graf Publishers
An Imprint of Avalon Publishing Group Inc.
245 West 17th Street
11th Floor
New York, NY 10011

AVALON
publishing group incorporated

Copyright © 2005 by Michael Goldfarb

First Carroll & Graf edition 2005

Library of Congress Cataloging-in-Publication Data is available.

ISBN: 0-7867-1515-4

9 8 7 6 5 4 3 2 1

Book design by Jamie McNeely

Printed in the United States of America
Distributed by Publishers Group West

For the family of Ahmad Shawkat
and Christin

Translation it is that openeth the window, to let in the light.
—Translators to the Reader, The Bible,
Preface to the King James Version (1611)

You've no idea of the country we almost made for you.
—*Fifth of July,* Lanford Wilson

Contents

بلا اتجاه
Bilattijah
اسبوعية ثقافية اجتماعية سياسية حرة

Without Direction - A Weekly Independent Cultural, Social & Political Newspaper

No.: (10) Wednesday 5th., Nove. 2003

رئيس التحرير صاحب الامتياز: أحمد شوكت

العدد (١٠) - الأربعاء ٥ - تشرين الثاني - ٢٠٠٣ - السنة الأول

صورة الشهيد البطل

مستمرون

Ahmad Shawkat, pictured on the cover of the tenth and final issue of his newspaper *Bilattijah*.

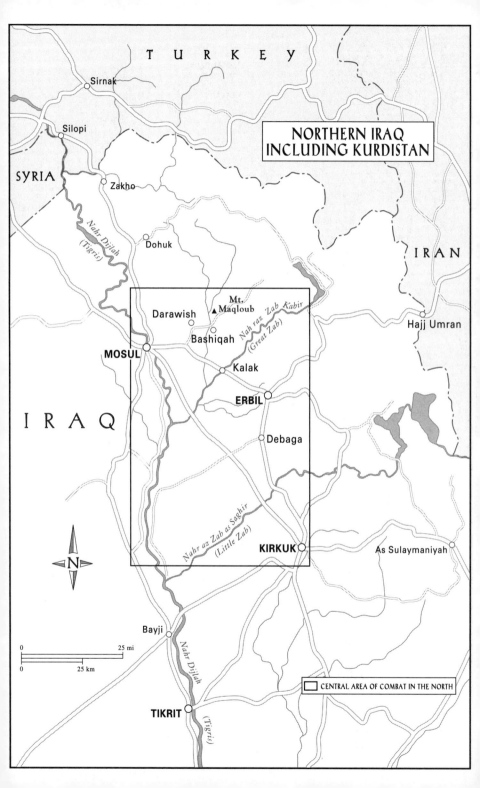

Ahmad's War

Prologue

Erbil, Kurdistan, March 19, 2003

Remembrance makes me sleepless at evening
But by dawn I am worn raw by my brimming disaster.

—Al-Khansa

IN A HOUSE that can never be his home, in a city that is not his place of birth, at the hour before daybreak, Ahmad Shawkat lies awake reviewing the disaster of his life. In his fifty-two years he has been awake just before the dawn many times. When he was young it was for happy reasons: he had spent the night talking about ideas with friends, or he had been with a lover. But for many years now he has been awake at this hour for different reasons: because he was in the physical pain that only the survivors of torture can know; because he was in the existential pain only political exiles can know; because in the hour before dawn he can no longer pretend he might still make something out of his life. All that he might have been in this world— teacher, man of letters, leader—had been taken from him by Saddam Hussein.

Lying still in the dark, Ahmad consoles himself that there are so many disasters to recall, more than could be contained in a single night's sleeplessness, that at least he is never bored. As in the poem by Al-Khansa, who wrote her verses in the time of the prophet Muhammad, he feels rubbed raw by his memories. He thanks the poet for the lines that go through his head as he lies on the floor. Her words have become his alarm clock; whenever those lines come to him he knows that the nighttime's painful ramble through his memory is coming to an end.

Beside him his wife, Afrah, stirs, and now he knows for certain the dawn is coming. Soon she will pray, he thinks. Afrah rises in the darkness and leaves the room, her tread light and anxious as if a teething infant had finally fallen asleep next to her and she doesn't want to wake him.

Ahmad doesn't move. He listens to the sound of her ablutions. Then the crackle of static as the muezzin at the local mosque turns on his microphone and begins to chant a sura from the Quran before the dawn call to prayer. Upstairs Ahmad hears heavier footsteps as his older children rise and join their mother. They go into a small room and quietly roll out their prayer rugs. The low hum of words, the wrinkling sound of skirts as the women fall to their knees and prostrate themselves before God, sound like thunder in his ears. He is a trained biologist and reminds himself that in darkness one's sense of hearing is more acute, so the sounds they are making are actually rather soft. His mind drifts to the war everyone says will start tonight or tomorrow. He still doesn't believe it will happen. Saddam will figure a way out. Then Ahmad notices that the wall in his living room is reflecting a grayish light. He gets up and walks to the front door, opens it, and looks up into the sky. It is no longer black. *Today I must try and find some work,* he thinks, although in his despair he fears there is no work to be found.

Chapter One
"I See You Are Well Cultured"

THE WAR STARTED bang on schedule. From the moment it was first mooted in leaks to *The New York Times* in July 2002 you could have predicted it would start around the end of February or middle of March 2003. After all, there was the precedent of the first Gulf War in 1990–91.

As happened then, there would have to be diplomatic shadow plays at the United Nations to cover the time necessary to ship troops to the region. Emissaries from the international community's organizations and self-appointed peacemakers from Britain's left would go to meet Saddam Hussein and treat with him. Then, when all the troops were in place, there would be a collective inhalation of breath and silence on earth for about the space of forty-eight hours. And in that time the final, predictable actions would occur. The United States would order Saddam Hussein to get out of Iraq. The dictator would refuse.

And the Kurds would take to the mountains.

Despite the establishment of a Kurdish safe area in northern Iraq after their failed uprising at the end of the 1991 Gulf War, very few Kurds felt that they would be protected from Saddam once this conflict began in earnest. As the deadline for the dictator to leave the country approached and the final countdown to war began, the Kurds of the northern city of Erbil loaded up their cars and headed for the mountains. Situated on the plain of the Fertile Crescent, with a division of the Iraqi Army deployed only a twenty-five-minute drive away, Erbil, with its population of more than half a million, was the most exposed large city in Kurdistan. With the expertise learned over decades of dodging Saddam and the Kurds' own occasional bouts of infighting, the cars and ancient flatbed trucks were packed with necessary household possessions, the kids finding places to sit where they could. Then the vehicles headed up toward the mountains, suspensions strained to the breaking point, undercarriages scraping along the bottoms of the switchback mountain roads.

The night before the war started, Ahmad Shawkat was seated in the Erbil Tower Hotel at the foot of the city's Citadel. Most of his neighbors had fled, but Ahmad stayed in town. Like most Erbilians who could string three sentences of English together—and he could do much better than that—Ahmad was hoping to work as a translator for one of the dozens of Western reporters who had come to the Kurdish safe area of northern Iraq to cover the war. He had had a bit of work during the few months leading up to the start of the conflict, but nothing proved steady. Reporters come. In the middle of the night they get a phone call from their editors. Reporters go. Now it was getting late to hook up with someone. Anxiety shrouded him. At home he had a wife and six children, but he was providing nothing for them, and as war approached he saw his opportunity for work slipping away. He had spent most of the day moping about the house until Roaa, his oldest daughter still living at home, urged him to go to the Erbil Tower one more time. He dragged himself from the house and went to the hotel and counted out more of his life passing away. Sitting quietly. Waiting. Smoking. Watching but not really paying attention to a Fox News broadcast playing on an ancient large-screen TV in the lobby.

A steady rain was falling in Erbil the day before the war started. Rain on the plain meant snow in the mountains. At the Iranian border, spring blizzards blew through the mountain passes, dropping weighty, wet snow on the trickle of late-arriving journalists heading down to Erbil through Iran. The border crossing at Hajj Umran is in a mountain pass almost a mile above sea level. As the road slid down from the pass, the snow turned to rain, and I could see the steady stream of heavily laden cars heading to the mountain villages or just pulling off to the side of the road, their occupants setting up camp in the mud. Men were putting up plastic sheeting for shelter, desperately grabbing at loose corners as sheets flapped in the wind. Women and girls in soggy burnt-orange and crimson dresses were down by fast-running streams drawing water for their families. Occasionally they looked up into the car headlights rolling by, dark hollows around their eyes and pinpoints of white in their pupils.

Their faces registered in my brain with the surreal clarity imparted by sleep deprivation. To get to Kurdistan before the war started I had been traveling for a day and a half without sleep. That was on top of the adrenaline-laced, sleep-deprived last few days I had spent in London getting myself ready, sweating out my Iranian visa—by then the only way into Iraq was to cross over at the Iranian border—packing, checking, and double-checking my recording equipment, and, finally, taking delivery of my body armor, which arrived just a few hours before I was due to depart on Monday, March 17. It was a good bet the war would start on Thursday. And once it started, the Iranians might also close their border with Iraq.

Tuesday night I flew hundreds of miles farther east than I needed to, to Tehran. Then, in the morning, I doubled back by air northwest to Orumiyeh, up in the Iranian mountains, then traveled by taxi due south to the border with Iraq. In Tehran, I had been kept waiting through the small hours of the morning while the local authorities fingerprinted me, a retaliatory indignity for the mass arrest of hundreds of Iranian men in Los Angeles the previous summer. Then, at the border, I was kept waiting in my car while a blizzard rolled in and one of Iran's local tyrants decided whether to acknowledge Tehran's authority over him. A fax from the government's Ministry of Islamic Guidance and Culture, giving me permission to go into Iraq, was on the desk in front of him. After a few freezing hours, it became clear what was going on. A hundred-dollar bill opened the gates to Iraq for me.

The Kurdistan Democratic Party (KDP) had handled my travel arrangements. Over the years the KDP, one of two main political groupings in the Kurdish north of Iraq, had put together a very effective media machine, facilitating journalist access to their hemmed-in, semiautonomous entity. On the Iraq side of the border, cars were provided to get us to Erbil. I piled my gear into a Mercedes and headed down the mountain. As the car flashed past the Kurdish girls, their raven hair washed out from under their head scarves by the steady rain, the tension inside me began to ease. I'd made it. I was in. I didn't even have to worry about finding a hotel. The KDP had booked me into a place with the magical name Dim Dim. "You will like it. It's a five-star hotel," their mustached representative at the border had told me. A five-star hotel sounded good, if unlikely. But at least I knew for certain I had a bed waiting. The war could begin now. All I needed to do was find a translator, though I figured that could wait until the next day. Now I needed rest.

By the time our little convoy of late arrivals got to Erbil, it was already evening. The Dim Dim was not quite as advertised, but by local standards it was quite grand. On my previous visit to Kurdistan, in the summer of 1996, the hotel I'd stayed in was so foul, I'd ended up sleeping on the roof under the stars. But the Dim Dim was reasonably well maintained. Its rooms were a decent size, and the bathrooms had sit-down toilets and a plentiful, if slow-arriving, supply of hot water.

The lobby of the Dim Dim was covered in marble and it was full of men. The lobby of the Dim Dim was always full of men: translators, drivers, bodyguards. In Kurdistan men are rarely at home. Home is a foreign, feminine country from which men flee each morning, return to briefly in the midday for a meal and a nap, and then run away from again. They return only when there is no longer an excuse to stay away. There would be plenty of translators to choose from in the morning.

In the morning I worked my way around the lobby and quickly figured out there was no one suitable. Most of the people in Erbil who spoke English reasonably well had already been hired. But I needed more than reasonably good translation anyway. My assignment for Inside Out, the documentary unit of WBUR, Boston's National Public Radio station, was to follow the war through an Iraqi's eyes. I had come up with the fanciful idea of finding someone who had suffered under Saddam's regime, documenting their liberation, then turning their experience into an hour-long program ready to air on radio within a month. All I needed to do was find a willing subject. That would be my translator's first task. He or she would have to know Erbil very well to help me find this person. Then we could proceed to the linguistic skill department.

What I needed from my translator, aside from grammatically

proficient English, was detailed accuracy. For a short daily news report, summary translations are okay. So long as the translator accurately and quickly renders the basic facts—what happened, when, how many people were killed, how many people fled— you have the information to fill up three minutes of airtime. But when a reporter tries to take people deep inside someone else's war-torn world, to keep listeners attentive the journalist has to offer clear details of what's being said.

For example, I interviewed a Muslim peasant woman in eastern Bosnia who was returning to her homestead five years after the conflict there ended. The last time she was in that place Serbs butchered her husband in front of her. The old woman was telling me the most intimate, heartrending details of her tragedy. A translator's natural tendency is to mediate and retell the story in the third person: "She says the Serbs destroyed her life." What I needed to hear was the direct, first-person story— "The Serbs came and destroyed my life"—otherwise the tape would not be usable.

Then a broadcaster needs the details. Conversation flows more freely when a reporter picks up on the detail of what's being said. The interviewee recognizes that the journalist really cares about what he or she is saying, and is inclined to open up even more. But to get all the details the translator needs to have an impeccable sense of timing. The translator has to know when and how to stop someone in mid-flow to translate what has been said already and not cause the interviewee to lose his or her train of thought.

I also look for someone who won't edit comments that he or she thinks reflects unfavorably on their country. In the Arab world this is a particular problem. Arabic speech is characterized by magnificent, allusive rhetoric. Expressions of criticism, anger, or hatred are never simple and direct, and they flow in torrents. If someone is angry about an American policy, the way in which that is expressed can sound offensive if translated literally, so a translator will tend to smooth the anti-Americanism out.

Then there is anti-Semitism. People in Arab countries often speak to strangers about Jews in the same way many whites spoke to strangers about blacks in pre–civil rights Mississippi. There is an implicit assumption that you, too, know they are an inferior, barely human group who really shouldn't be sharing space on the planet with you. Most potential translators in the Arab world are aware of the sensitivities of American reporters to such blatant anti-Semitism, and many will try to tone it down. But that takes a reporter further from the truth of what an interviewee actually believes. Usually, at some point in my reporting trips to the Middle East the subject of the Zionist entity—many Muslims will not say the name Israel, since that would imply that the state has a right to exist—comes up, and I will have to tell my translator to translate fully what is being said. I have to assure the translator that, as a Jew, hearing people express their anti-Semitism in an unguarded way is very useful. Bigotry is a subset of the category stupidity. It helps me gauge someone's intelligence.

I hear a lot of this hatred. Most of the ordinary people I talk to in the streets do not recognize me as a Jew. My looks don't conform to their stereotype. I don't have a beard nor do I wear a yarmulke. My name, which would cue most Americans or Europeans to the fact that I am Jewish, doesn't register that way either. The Arabic custom in naming is simply to give a child a single name. Then add on the name of the father, possibly grandfather, and perhaps an indication of tribe or village. So when I introduce myself as Michael Goldfarb, people in the Arab street hear my name as Michael. I am called, politely, Mr. Michael instead of Mr. Goldfarb. *Michael* has a generic

European sound to it. My translator in Jordan explained that most people in the Arab street think a Jewish name sounds like David Ben-Gurion or Binyamin Netanyahu or Ariel Sharon—Israeli names.

I have still more requirements of a translator. I need someone at ease with all strata of his society. This is not always possible, because in many places the person who speaks English to the standard I require comes from the well-educated upper classes and may not have a natural ability to talk to peasants or the working classes, the people who usually suffer most when the world is in upheaval.

Beyond linguistic accuracy I need a good companion. We're going to be together in a car for hours every day for weeks at a time traveling to wherever the news is. You need to be able to joke, talk about your families, and discuss politics without getting into arguments. I also need to be certain that the translator has a good work ethic. The harsh necessity of deadline overrides everything, even having lunch.

Finally, a translator needs courage, because in a conflict reporters have to get as close as possible to the fighting. We are required to see as much of it as we can ourselves, to talk to combatants and civilians on the front line, to be the firsthand source of information. If your translator isn't willing to go to the closest vantage point, you won't get the story.

It is almost impossible to find someone who meets all these criteria. It's very hard to meet someone who fits most of them. It is often a matter of luck whether a reporter scores a good one. When you are stuck with a bad one, the results can be painfully hilarious. During the war in Afghanistan to overthrow the Taliban, I was in Iran. My translator turned out to be an alcoholic, a neat trick in a country where booze is banned. It took me a while to figure out that he was a drunk. His breath certainly smelled of alcohol. And I noticed that sometimes people we interviewed in the street pulled back from him. He also hit on women we interviewed. I chalked it all up to rudeness and an embarrassing lack of social grace, until one morning, in the holy city of Mashhad, I walked into his hotel room and found him chugging back industrial-strength vodka from a can. It was 10 A.M. "To take the edge off," he explained when I confronted him about it.

In Egypt I worked with a son of the military upper classes. He had competed for his country in international martial arts competitions. One day, crawling through Cairo traffic en route to interview the head of the Muslim Brotherhood, a bicyclist who was from the lower orders of society bumped his car. My translator leaped out and launched a karate assault on him. By the time the police arrived and the fracas had ended, we were an hour late for the interview.

But when a reporter finds a good translator, it is a beautiful thing. You can feel the metaphorical walls separating reporter from interviewee being broken down. A good translator bridges two separate realities in the most extreme of circumstances. Sometimes you can actually see an interviewee's pupils widen in surprise that a foreigner seems to understand their culture, their particular circumstances. Sometimes a little black humor of mine, accurately translated, brings out a smile. From that smile, you are invited to probe deeper. The only way these moments can happen is because your translator is giving you a quick, accurate translation and sending back your English with equal speed, and has established rapport and trust with the interviewee.

The young men filling the lobby of the Dim Dim were doing what young men throughout the Muslim Middle East do: sitting, talking, smoking, and drinking tea. I worked my away around the few still available for hire. They spoke English with varying degrees of precision. None met my minimum standard. I visited a couple of other hotels around the city, but the situation was the same.

Now I was getting a little nervous. I still hadn't found anyone suitable, and it seemed likely the war would begin sometime in the night. As evening brought the conflict even closer, I decided to visit the BBC office at the Erbil Tower Hotel to see if they had the name of someone I might hire. The Erbil Tower had been turned into a fortress with a perimeter of roadblocks circling it. A couple of burly Kurds with Kalashnikovs manned checkpoints. On one of the upper floors the windows were filled with sandbags. An observer would have thought that an important Kurdish politician was headquartered there. But it was just Fox News' team taking no chances should Saddam single it out for attack. The paramilitary presence kept people away. The lobby of the place was nowhere near as full as at the Dim Dim. The half-dozen or so well-fed men who were hanging around watching Fox on a large-screen TV looked like bodyguards rather than degree holders in English literature. At the front desk I asked for the BBC office, and a few minutes later a young Kurdish woman came downstairs. I introduced myself and explained I was looking for a translator. She pointed to a small, quiet, middle-aged man I hadn't seen in this lobby full of bruisers. "He is a very good man." From the way she said *good* I couldn't tell if she meant "good for the job" or the deeper sense of *good* as in a morally correct person, reliable in a pinch. "He is the father of my friend," she added, which made me think it was probably the latter.

She took me over. He got up and with exaggerated courtesy shook my hand and made a little bow, as if we were meeting at an academic conference. He introduced himself: "Ahmad Shawkat." I told him my name, and we sat down. There was a little awkward silence. A bit of sizing-up began. He was a slight fellow, thinning hair going gray, and did not have a mustache, which in this part of the world was most unusual. His voice when answering simple questions about his translating experience was very quiet—not halting, but not confident either. My initial impression was this just would not work. Ahmad seemed a bit shy; more important, he was too old. At first glance he looked to be in his late fifties, maybe even sixty. Age mattered to me. If we came under fire and needed to run or were among a crowd of people that turned into a mob, I didn't want to worry that my translator was physically incapable of running away with me or, worse yet, was going to have a heart attack when the pressure was on. The other thing about hiring an older person is what any director of human resources will say: people get set in their ways and are very difficult to train when they get past a certain age. Then there was a corollary of the Groucho Marx axiom about not joining clubs that will admit you: This guy was willing to work with me, but if he was any good, why was he still available?

In the Middle East, good manners require that two men discussing business go through a period of small talk before getting down to the matter at hand. I was in a hurry, however, and went straight to the formalities: Had he worked for Western journalists? How well did he know the country? The local political leadership? Did he speak Arabic as well as Kurdish? He gave brief, satisfactory answers. Then he volunteered the fact that he wasn't actually from Erbil. He was from Mosul, over in Saddam regime territory. I asked if he was Kurdish. "Of course," he replied. "Mosul is a very mixed city." I asked him how old he was. There was a pause while he calculated what the boundaries of plausibility were. I know because, being past fifty myself, I've taken that pause when asked the same question. "Forty-five" was his answer. A wholly implausible figure. Before I could say anything, Ahmad changed the subject.

"Do you know William Faulkner?"

"Well, not personally. But of course I know his writing."

"I love Faulkner. The Compson family. I love *The Sound and the Fury*. I have read it many times. I love it, how he writes from inside the mind of the boy who is mentally ill."

I nodded. "Benjy. One of my favorite sentences in the English language is 'Firelight was still the same bright shape of sleep.' "

"Yes. He is a very Arab writer."

"I'm not so sure about that."

"No, really. We like him very much." Then he added, "I like the sentence 'They endured.' "

Now, this was not a conversation I expected to be having on the eve of war in Iraq. But I hadn't discussed or thought about Faulkner in a long time and I went along for the ride. We spent a few minutes trading Faulkner trivia: two middle-aged men competing like the smartest kids in the class about who knew more about a favorite author. Then he said, "I can see you are well cultured." It was an unusual phrase, one that required a bit of consideration; it seemed that meant I had met *his* requirements. He asked, "You understand that you cannot write about Iraq without knowing about the people and the history also?" I nodded. "I know these things very well. I will work with you and tell you about them. But you must agree that we stay together until the war is over."

It was an extraordinary demand. Still, it's not every day you meet someone in a war zone who speaks English as idiosyncratically as Faulkner wrote it. Ahmad seemed unlikely to meet my first linguistic criterion for a translator: simple clarity. But on the other hand, he would certainly meet my last: on a tedious three-hour drive through the mountains we probably wouldn't lack for conversation. So I found myself agreeing to his demand that we stick together, and decided to hire him.

Business finished, I said I was going back to the Dim Dim. I was tired and wanted to rest. But Ahmad decided for us that my education would begin immediately. He dragged me up the steep slope leading to Erbil's Citadel. By going up the hill we were going back to the beginning of civilization.

"They say this is the oldest continuously inhabited settlement on the face of the Earth," Ahmad explained. "Since 5000 B.C., maybe 6000 B.C., people gathered in this place. The Assyrian empire, the first empire on earth, was founded not far from here. But even before that there was a settlement here." Each millennium had added layers to the Citadel. The walls now towered nearly 105 feet above the town.

At the top of the slope, near the gate into the Citadel, a bonfire was burning. It was the start of Narooz, a festival that goes back to the founding of the Zoroastrian religion sometime in the first millenium before Christ and, like the origins of the Citadel itself, probably beyond that in time. Fire is critical to worship among the Zoroastrians. Natural fire, not the kind made by striking flints to get a spark, is a unique feature of this part of the world. Not far from Erbil, fire comes up out of the ground, great pools of it.

Ahmad began a little lecture. "Oil seeps out of the ground in this area. Sometimes it catches fire. There are many fire-worshipping cults. There is a place near Kirkuk called Baba Gurgur. . . . In ancient times women went there who could not have children. They bathed in the oil and became pregnant."

Fire and oil, oil and fire: the foundation of the world of men. As it is now, was then, and evermore shall be. Normally, on the eve of Narooz, Erbil would have been full of people dancing around bonfires, but on this night, with war soon to begin, only a small group of fellows was hanging around this solitary fire at the entrance to the Citadel. A crew from Syrian television drove up, and the Kurds began a desultory performance of a traditional dance for the camera. I recorded a bit of the singing. We watched for a while longer and then walked through the darkened complex.

Despite its grand name and the pride with which Erbilians speak about it, the Citadel is a wreck. Layer upon layer of human civilization has risen for eight thousand years to a topographical high point, but inside the walls development seems to have stopped a couple of millennia past. The interior was a mud-hut peasant village, the houses crumbling away, its higgledy-piggledy pathways unpaved. A single lightbulb illuminated a front room somewhere off to our left. It was the only sign of human life in the little village inside the wall. The residents had fled to the mountains, but their animals—dogs, cats, sheep, and chickens—wandered underfoot as we walked carefully through the darkness, talking about this and that.

Although the language Ahmad and I used was formal, there was an odd familiarity in our conversation. A couple of bookish men talking a bit about authors and local history, the subjects intellectuals all over the world use to feel out new acquaintances. But both of us were so advanced into middle age that we didn't express any surprise at having this conversation while wandering through an empty city on the eve of a war. It was a simple pleasure not worth remarking on. We moved from small talk to getting-to-know-you talk. We spoke of children. He asked me if I had any. "No." It's a painful subject for me, so I quickly shifted the question back to him. Ahmad was typically fecund in this area: he had eight; six children were living with him in a house not far from the Citadel in an "old quarter, very intellectual." He had two married daughters still in Mosul.

"Why did you leave Mosul?" I asked. "Politics?"

"Yes. Things I wrote. I have been arrested many times."

"Tortured?"

"Of course. When I released, I came here."

As we wandered through the ancient walls we later learned that American jets were striking "a target of opportunity" in Baghdad. This attempt to take out Saddam on March 19, 2003, would fail, and from that moment on a full-scale invasion was inevitable. We walked down a steep flight of stairs on the other side of the Citadel across from the shuttered-up bazaar. The empty city had lost its background din; a Kalashnikov fired for fun several miles away could be heard as clearly as if it had been fired around the corner. The thunking of an old taxi's engine caught our ears long before we saw it. We hailed the cab and jumped in. Erbil's main streets are laid out in circles around the Citadel. We swung around the great mound, and just by a dilapidated office building Ahmad had the cab stop. He pointed at the building. "Can you remember this place?"

"Yes."

"This is my street," he said, pointing down a narrow, darkened road. "If anything happens you can come to my house and you will be safe."

It was a polite thing to say, but if Saddam decided to launch a chemical or biological attack on Erbil, there really wasn't much we would be able to do about it. As Ahmad was getting out of the car, I realized I didn't have his phone number. I grabbed his arm and asked him for it. He took out his business card and handed it to me. There were three e-mail addresses but no phone number. I looked at him quizzically.

"These first two e-mail addresses belong to my daughter. This one is mine," he explained.

"Al-Fatih 51" I read out loud.

"*Al-Fatih* means 'the leader,' " he said. "It was my name in underground movement."

Interesting, I thought to myself, then I asked him where his phone number was.

He confessed he didn't have one. He wrote down a number and explained it was not his own phone. It was the number of his neighbor, and if I needed him for anything, anything at all, I was to call there and his neighbor would find him. If I had known that he didn't have a phone, I might not have hired him, but now it was too late. Besides, I had enjoyed our conversation. I already liked the guy.

He got out and the cab took me on to the Dim Dim. I kept thinking about something he said as we walked through the Citadel.

"When the U.S. gets rid of this bloody Saddam, I am going back to Mosul."

Mosul was just sixty miles away. There were two rivers, one ridge, and a single division of the Iraqi Army between Ahmad and home. It didn't seem like an impossible dream. I thought it might be worth following him home.

Chapter Two
"All Our Politicians Are Thieves"

"ALL OUR NIGHTMARES come from Saddam," Ahmad had said as we walked through the deserted Citadel our first night together. *Nightmare* was one of the key words in Ahmad's English vocabulary. The others were *despair, disaster,* and *monster.* All these words could be related to the bad dream that was life under Saddam.

When you fight your way out of a nightmare, sometimes the waking world gets mixed up with images and anxieties from the bad dream. For a while, the waking world seems surreal. Certainly the war in the north had its surreal elements. To begin with, there wasn't much war to be found, and hundreds of reporters were running around looking for what little fighting there was. For a very odd reason, most of them had been trapped in the north for a month before the war even began.

For reporters who wanted independence while covering the war the options were limited. The "embed program" offered a chance to observe combat, but from only one side and under tight supervision. There was also a lottery involved. If a reporter was assigned to a nonfrontline unit, he would see nothing more than desert and soldiers carrying out logistical activities. Alternatively, a journalist could go to Baghdad but, aside from the extreme danger, his ability to operate independently was nonexistent. The regime monitored and censored all foreign reporting.

Surveying the situation from abroad in the months before the conflict it became clear that the one place to be an independent reporter was going to be Kurdistan in northern Iraq. In addition to free access to the battlefield, Kurdistan offered journalists the prospect of being in position to cover the postwar political problems that many journalists thought had the potential to arise. Would the Kurds break away and form their own state? Would they make a grab for Kirkuk, the oil center of the region and a city Kurds regarded as historically belonging to them? Would the Turkish Army come over the border if the Kurds made a grab for Kirkuk? Would the U.S. Army turn on the Kurds, its only allies inside Iraq?

So some of the best war correspondents in the world decided to go to northern Iraq/Kurdistan. The problem was getting into the place. Kurdistan borders Turkey and Iran. The Islamic Republic of Iran was not the first choice for entry. The government was taking months to issue visas. I had applied for one in early January 2003, anticipating the war's start in mid-March. I figured it would take six or seven weeks to get it. I had been to Tehran just after September 11, 2001, and knew their system a little bit. But it was a risky and uncertain proposition. Many journalists didn't want to rely on the bureaucrats in the Ministry of Islamic Guidance and Culture, the people to whom you apply for a visa, to decide whether they got into Iraq or not. Another reason some colleagues thought Iran was not an option was that their reporting had offended the mullahs' regime over the years and they'd never get a visa anyway.

Newspapers and broadcast outlets from around the world brought pressure on the Turkish government to open the border crossing into northern Iraq/Kurdistan by the Habur River to journalists. The pressure increased in early February 2003. With war approaching, a meeting of the Iraqi exile leadership was called in Erbil. The international press clamored to get in to cover this event. In mid-February the word went out that the Turks would open the Habur Gate for five days to allow the press into the Kurdish safe area to cover the event. Several hundred journalists, among them John Simpson of the BBC, Judith Miller of *The New York Times,* and the great war photographer Don McCullin, who was coming out of retirement to shoot this conflict for *Harper's,* descended on Silopi in the far southeast corner of Turkey where the Habur Gate is located.

But just as in Iran, orders from the capital didn't have much meaning at the border. Silopi is in the Kurdish area of Turkey, and the whole region is heavily militarized. For more than a quarter of a century, Turkish Kurds had fought an insurgency against their government that had been brutally suppressed. Although the state of emergency had been declared over in 2002, military convoys still plied the crumbling roads of the region, making their presence felt. In this remote corner of Turkey, there was no doubt that the newly formed government of Recep Tayyip Erdogan's Justice and Development Party came a poor third in terms of authority. Reporters found themselves at the mercy of the Turkish military and local bureaucracy, a comically lethal combination. The border opening was delayed repeatedly while the Turkish authorities argued with the Kurdish authorities about who would be in charge of all the journalists. In a foreshadowing of the story that the reporters expected would unfold in a more dramatic and bloody way after the war, the Turkish military was insisting that it supply a convoy to escort the journalists into Iraq, "to guarantee their safety." The idea of elements of the Turkish Army coming down to Erbil was anathema to the leadership of the KDP, and the Turks knew it. The argument was just a little local chess match with journalists as pawns.

The teahouses in Silopi's hotels turned gray with the frustrated smoke of fuming reporters, while the arguments dragged on. Eventually a compromise was reached. The Turks would provide buses and escort the reporters into Kurdistan but would not go all the way to Erbil. The journalists would have five days there to cover the conference before the buses came back. Then the Habur Gate would be barred shut. Anybody not on the bus for the return trip would be stuck in Kurdistan until the war was over. That suited the hacks. Around two hundred went in. Perhaps twenty came out.

A few days later the Turkish Parliament did something most unusual. It accurately reflected the will of its people. Ninety percent of Turks were against the war. So Parliament voted against the Turkish government's plan to allow the Bush administration to use Turkey as a preinvasion base for the U.S. Army's Fourth Division. This effectively meant there would be no northern front led by the American army in the war to overthrow Saddam. Despite the changed circumstance, the Turkish government remained true to what it had told the reporters when they entered Kurdistan: the Habur Gate stayed shut. There was no way out for them. So some of the world's finest journalists said good-bye to the front page of their newspapers and prepared themselves for a comparatively quiet war.

As the fighting began in earnest down south, Ahmad and I tried to organize a work routine. The only warlike activity in the north took place at night, mostly American air raids. The routine was simple: around nine at night we would drive out to the front and hope for action.

In the first days of the war we worked with the husband-and-wife team of David Filipov of *The Boston Globe* and Anna Badkhen of the *San Francisco Chronicle*. David and Anna are avatars of a new kind of foreign correspondent. For decades, covering wars has been an absolute marriage killer. But as more and more women have started turning up on the story, it is becoming increasingly common for couples to form and to cover wars together. David and Anna were based in Moscow for their respective newspapers and had covered Russia's war in Chechnya and the war to overthrow the Taliban in Afghanistan. These married couples bring a level of domestic preparedness to the front line. David and Anna were hyperprepared for this one. They even schlepped a gas-fired electric generator from Moscow in anticipation of power outages in Erbil and all the other logistical inconveniences associated with war.

I first met Anna while running around Turkey just before the war. I had not gone into Kurdistan with the rest of the reporters. Anna had, and she was one of the few journalists to return from Erbil on the bus. In the few weeks between that event and the start of the conflict she had returned to Moscow, and then she and David had returned to Kurdistan via Iran. Anna and I stayed in touch and decided we might all share costs once the war got under way in earnest. On arriving in Erbil, the pair had found a wonderful driver, Sami Abdul Qader. Sami drove an old Isuzu Trooper. Each evening Ahmad and Sami would come to the Dim Dim. David and Anna would load the generator and satellite equipment for filing their stories into the Trooper, and off the five of us would go.

The front in our area was usually no more than a checkpoint or encampment with twenty or so Kurdish pesh merga fighters hanging around. The new bridge at Kalak, a town stretching out on both banks of the Great Zab, a major tributary of the Tigris, was the closest frontline point. A quarter of a mile away, on the Mosul side of the bridge, was an Iraqi Army checkpoint. In Mesopotamia, even at the new moon, the stars cast enough frail light to illuminate the landscape. When the clouds thinned out you could catch a glimpse of the army's fortifications atop a ridge on the other side and see their checkpoint at the other end of the bridge.

There was a small guardhouse on the Kurdish side. The first night of the war approximately twenty pesh merga were hanging around in the chilly, damp, spring night. We walked toward them. In Kurdish, *pesh merga* means "men who face death." It's a romantic turn of phrase, and the pesh merga do cut a romantic figure. They wear traditional Kurdish dress: military tunics tucked into baggy, multi-pleat, drawstring trousers called *shalwar,* wrapped tight at the waist by a couple of yards of light cloth. Many wear *smagh,* a keffiyah-like scarf wrapped tightly around their heads. Throw in a couple of bandoliers crisscrossed over the chest and a few curving Kalashnikov magazines of fresh ammo tucked into the belt and you have figures ready to play brigands in a Hollywood epic set in the nineteenth century. We greeted the pesh, and Ahmad debriefed them in Kurdish. "They say there has been no fighting and there will be no fighting."

"How do they know?"

"The Iraqi soldiers sent a local shepherd over today with a message saying they won't fire unless the pesh merga fire."

That first night, we stood around waiting for something to happen, but nothing did. From the bulrushes below the bridge came a din of frog calling, along with the occasional barking of dogs from the peasant villages strung along the riverbank. A couple of peasants wandered up and asked what was going on. It was all very relaxed and chummy, like standing around some suburban street corner with the neighborhood watch group. It didn't feel like we were standing a rifle-shot away from an army that had attempted genocidal war against the people with whom we were chatting.

The shepherd-borne mutual nonaggression pact held. The first night, we waited for hours for something to happen. Sometime after midnight David hauled the generator out of the back of the Trooper, fired it up, and plugged in his computer satellite phone. He read messages from *The Boston Globe*'s foreign desk, went through the wire service reports, and began to write. It really was as close to a frontline file as was possible. Sadly, there was very little happening at this particular front line.

While David and Anna worked, Ahmad and I wandered along the bridge trying to stay warm. He told me more about his family in Mosul. Two daughters remained there with their husbands and children. He had six grandchildren in all. I asked him again how old he was.

"Fifty-two. I was born in 1951."

He was a year younger than me and already had six grandchildren. We each smoked a cigarette, and Ahmad suggested we try and find out what was going on over in Mosul. I had a small Iridium satphone. He said he would call his brother-in-law. He gave me a number, but the dialing code was for Germany. I pointed this out to him. He said yes, it goes via Germany to Iraq. We tried on and off for an hour with no success while David and Anna got their first-edition stories finished. They packed up their equipment and put it in the back of the Trooper. It was now around 2 A.M. We had a brief huddle and decided it wasn't worth waiting in the chill any longer, so we left.

But in the morning we heard that Iraqi artillery up on the

ridge had shelled the old town of Kalak just beneath them sometime around 4 A.M. No buildings were hit. It was just firing to remind the town's residents that the regime was on the ridge above them. So the second night of the war we went back out to the bridge in hopes of seeing some artillery fire. We left around one o'clock. Again there were reports of artillery fire after we left, but no damage. By the third night, the absurdity of going without sleep to see a couple of shells launched into some fields finally struck us, and so we left a little before midnight. In three nights of waiting at the bridge we had seen only one glimpse of war: a video-game view of a fast-moving flashing red light—an American jet—followed by the forlorn white tracer streaks of outmoded antiaircraft batteries shooting at and missing the plane. The sound of the bomb striking its target somewhere between the ridge and Mosul was carried on the wind. In Ahmad's war, you heard the blasts more often than saw them. In Erbil, you could tell when a bombing raid was going on because the ground concussion rolled up through the Dim Dim and made the roof rattle. It was like the vibration in a Central Park West apartment when the New York subway's A train rumbles underneath.

We changed our routine. Ahmad came to the Dim Dim each morning after having checked the bush telegraph for word of actual fighting. "In this place there was striking last night." *Striking* meant *bombing* in Ahmad-speak, a dialect I was rapidly learning. We then sat in the lobby drinking chai (Kurdish tea), reviewing his findings, and discussing an itinerary. Then off we went to the site of alleged combat. First inspection site was just past Dola Bakir on the road to Kirkuk. There was a little encampment by the roadside, surrounded by modest breastworks. We spent a pleasant afternoon hanging around, interviewing the pesh merga commander. Reports of fighting proved accurate. In the middle of the camp was a crater that had been created by an incoming artillery round. The pesh had an ancient Soviet-issue antiaircraft gun trained on the green plain in case the Iraqi hordes launched an assault. We hung around waiting for action. Nothing. We were interviewing the camp commander when a convoy of late-model SUVs pulled up and a bunch of bouncers, a cameraman, and a long-legged blond model got out. The model turned out to be a reporter. Fox News had arrived on the scene. One of the bouncer types came over and spoke quickly to the commander. The pesh merga officer terminated our conversation and said he could no longer speak to us. Apparently there was an exclusive arrangement with Fox for his time.

We returned in the night. Fox had left. There was quiet singing going on in a tent at the back of the camp. I went over to record it. The young fighters seemed giddy, if not completely high on drugs. My tape recorder came out and so their singing got louder. Then they invited me to start singing. One of them asked if I had some whiskey, Black Jack, a local rip-off of Jack Daniel's. I professed amazement that, being good Muslims, they drank. Yes, yes, they assured me. In Erbil they have whiskey. The singing got rowdier. Ahmad came over and suggested the commander was getting a little angry about my disruptive presence. I said good night to the pesh and followed Ahmad to the other side of the road and continued to wait for action, although I doubted if the slightly out-of-it young men I had just been recording could fight very effectively if the Iraqi Army turned up.

Ahmad pointed to the southern horizon. It was glowing orange. He explained that the light came from natural gas being burned off in the oil fields of Kirkuk. It meant the oil installations were still operating. David and Anna flipped open their laptops and began furiously writing copy for their newspapers. The evening was cold and clear. An occasional gust of wind deepened the chill. We all had had enough of this nighttime stuff. So we walked back toward the car. As we did, a real skirmish began on the ridge, which we turned to watch. Tracer fire poured out from one of the Iraqi Army forts. It stopped. Then, from what seemed like a distance of a hundred yards, a stream of bullets went back toward the fort. For five minutes or less, the two sides traded fire. Who was up there on the ridge, attacking what, we had no way of knowing. But we had finally seen what we came for: war . . . real war.

In the long hours of waiting and driving I found out more about Ahmad. He was an old-fashioned intellectual, a man with a scientific vocation and a deep cultural avocation. In the nineteenth century through the mid-twentieth, it was a not uncommon combination of interests in the West. But after World War II this survived mostly in the Eastern bloc and third world countries. Postcolonial regimes steered their bright young people into the sciences regardless of the individual's passion for them. Artistic interests were pursued in one's spare time. Ahmad had studied biology at the University of Mosul and, after graduation, became a lecturer in anatomy at the university's medical school. Meanwhile he also ran a literary magazine and held lectures in a teahouse in Mosul's Old City. These weren't just book club meetings. They also had a political agenda, because, Ahmad said, "You cannot separate literature from politics. All fiction is an expression of the political system in which it is written."

Literature dominated our conversation. Sometimes conversation *was* literature. Ahmad's first language was Arabic, Kurdish was his second, English his third. You could see him translating a thought through the first two to get to an English expression. Because his English vocabulary was acquired through reading, not via conversation, his usages were unusual, occasionally archaic, frequently incorrect. But if you did a little retranslating of your own, what he was saying was always comprehensible, in a poetic way. "In Mosul, I had a house in a very aristocratic quarter." I knew he wasn't the son of a sheikh or tribal leader, the local aristocrats in Iraq, so I pressed him a bit about who lived in the neighborhood and figured out that "aristocratic" meant "wealthy"—full of doctors, lawyers, and leading professors at the university. About his time in prison he said, "They practiced every kind of violation on me." Violation of the body is another way of saying tortured. "I know village-ian life very well." A village-ian was someone who lived in a mud hut village, a peasant. "He is my intimate friend," Ahmad said, introducing me to someone in the street. The first time he said it I thought, What? Are they lovers? Then I ran through my own internal thesaurus: *intimate* means close. So he meant close friend, not lover.

He decided it would be good for my continued education into his society to meet some of his intimate friends. First we went to Mechko's teahouse. Mechko's, carved into the base of Erbil's Citadel, was a place for teachers and journalists and political exiles to hang out with other men in the late afternoon, in the space on the clock between the end of work and returning for supper to the women's world of home. We sat down with some men from Kirkuk. They were in the same predicament as Ahmad, living in internal exile so close to their homes that every piece of gossip in their old neighborhood could find its way to their ears. But they could not take part in the conversation. They might as well have been ghosts. The years of ghostly eavesdropping had removed much of their vitality. I noted this to Ahmad as we waited for chai. He whispered back, "In Kirkuk these were important men, but here they are not important. There is an Arabic phrase: *Man tarak darah/Qualla Miqudaraht*. It means 'He who leaves his home behind/no respect will find.' "

Introductions were made. By now I had improved at performing a simultaneous internal translation of Ahmad-speak. "These men were dismissed from Kirkuk, and Saddam engaged their lands for people planted in Kirkuk," he said as we shook hands all around. This meant "These men were exiled from Kirkuk, and Saddam had their houses confiscated and given to Arabs transplanted from the south."

The old brick walls of Mechko's teahouse were framed with fading pictures of local writers and their heroes, mostly French existentialists. The famous photo of Jean-Paul Sartre standing with striking workers outside a Citroën factory in 1968 had a prominent place on Mechko's wall of fame. More even than in the United States, 1968 was a critical year in Ahmad's country. It was the year the Ba'ath Party seized power and intellectual life in Iraq became frozen in time.

Chai was brought and the conversation continued, its frame of reference suitable to any café in Europe in that hopeful year of student uprisings. Existentialism, absurdism, Marxism were still big ideas among these intellectuals. I pointed to the pictures on the wall and said Mechko's seemed frozen in time. They all agreed. Time stopped when Saddam took over the country. People simply ceased to move forward. They grew older but they did not progress. One of the exiled fellows from Kirkuk said, "That's the victory of Saddam. He made us to gaze and stare without meaning. Waiting, waiting without any hope. Like Godot."

"What?" I asked. I couldn't understand what he had said.

"Like the play *Waiting for Godot*. For us, America is Godot
. . . the end of the first act was 1991. Godot didn't come."
The men laughed softly; Godot was coming now.

Ahmad kept using *quietly* as an adjective. That took some figuring out. At least once a day, as we confidently looked ahead to
Saddam's overthrow, the name of Iraqi exile leader Ahmad
Chalabi would come up and my translator would say, "Ahmad
Chalabi is quietly stupid." Did Ahmad mean he keeps his stupidity to himself? Or, more poetically, that Chalabi's stupidity was
like a person within a person, keeping quiet so that the would-be
ruler of a new Iraq didn't know just how stupid he was?

"I was quietly despairing after I was released from prison,"
Ahmad said. I thought I understood that. He meant "despairing
in silence." But I was wrong. The word was Ahmad-speak with
an accent. He pronounced the word *quite* with a "y" sound
between the *u* and the *i,* so it came out "qui-yit." So "quiet-ly"
actually meant *quite,* or to a great degree. "Quite-ly despairing"
meant very despairing or in great despair. But I preferred "quietly" stupid to describe most politicians, because their stupidity
is so often unknown to them.

Sometimes Ahmad would just drift off into his own world.
He would stare out the car window looking "quite-ly" sad.
Only one other person I know could just drift off and stare
like that. She was a Holocaust survivor. When Ahmad
looked into the open spaces of our war zone, I assumed he
was back in one of Saddam's torture chambers or perhaps
that he was feeling the existential despair of the torture survivor: knowing that there can never be proportional justice
meted out to those who inflict the worst pain on people,
because you would have to become an animal to do to them
what they have done to you.

While Ahmad looked into the distance quite-ly sad, I stared out the car window quite-ly in awe. Kurdistan's beauty is raw and epic. Here the earth is in agony, tectonic forces scarring its surface. Just underneath the ground the Arabian plate, shifting north and east, grinds into the Eurasian plate, driving Kurdistan's mountains up toward the sky. You can feel the pressure just by looking at the rock formations squeezed up out of the earth along the side of the road In the distance, the razor-backed ridges march toward Iran, each a little higher than those in front, snowfields glistening into the distance. You measure your driving time not in minutes and seconds but by the number of mountain ridges that must be crossed. The long narrow ridges are separated by wide valleys. In the spring they are as green as any pasture in Ireland, by midsummer they are roasted to the golden color of a lion's pelt.

Birds of prey swirl about surveying their dominion. Black kites, harriers, and the occasional golden eagle go about their predatory business oblivious to the human conflicts that agonize the ground beneath them.

This was the second time I had been in Kurdistan. The first was in September 1996, when the two main Kurdish factions, the Kurdistan Democratic Party (KDP) and the Patriotic Union of Kurdistan (PUK), had begun a bout of internecine bloodletting. Like an unhappy family, they were fighting over money. The border crossing into Turkey was in KDP territory, and the leadership of that group was keeping all the entry fees and smugglers' taxes on trucks ferrying out black-market oil. The PUK didn't like this at all, and fighting flared up.

The KDP's leader, Massoud Barzani, asked Saddam Hussein for help. The dictator obliged, sending troops into Erbil over the cease-fire line that was established at the end of the Gulf War. This was a major news development. At the end of that war, after Saddam's army had been rousted from Kuwait in four days, the first President Bush urged Iraqis to rise up against the dictator. The Kurds had needed very little encouragement. Since the end of World War II, they had been fighting an on-again, off-again insurgency for complete autonomy from various Iraqi governments. In the decades of Ba'ath Party rule the Baghdad government and Kurdish parties had gone through periods of conflict and negotiation with some regularity. But at the end of the Iran-Iraq War the conflict had taken on a new intensity. Kurdish pesh merga had fought beside Iranian troops. When the war ended in 1988, Saddam turned on the Kurds with genocidal ferocity. He unleashed the "Anfal campaign." *Anfal* in Arabic means "spoils," as in "to the victor goes the spoils." The spoils Saddam claimed from the Kurds were the villages in the most fertile parts of Kurdistan. He drove them out with great violence. Poison gas was one of his weapons of choice against the Kurdish villages. At Halabja, a town of forty-five thousand not far from Sulaimaniyah, Saddam's commander in charge of the Anfal campaign, Ali Hassan al-Majid—Chemical Ali—unleashed every gas and nerve agent in Saddam's arsenal. More than five thousand people, mostly women and children, were killed in the attack.

This memory was fresh when the first President Bush called for an uprising in March 1991 at the end of the Gulf War. Despite their history of rivalry, the KDP and PUK formed a united front and swung into battle against Saddam. The dictator's elite Republican Guard forces were suppressing a Shi'a uprising in the south. When they had polished off that uprising they turned to the north. The pesh merga were able to fight them off on the ground, but the Kurds had no aircraft. For some reason, while negotiating the terms of the cease-fire, which included no flights by Iraqi fighter planes, General Norman Schwarzkopf was convinced by his Iraqi counterpart, Lt. General Sultan Hashim Ahmad, that the Iraqi military should be allowed continued use of its helicopters. The Iraqi negotiator told Schwarzkopf the choppers were necessary for transport purposes, and the American commander gave his permission for their continued use.

But the helicopters were immediately thrown into the battle against the Kurdish insurrection. The gunships broke the back of the uprising in a matter of days. A million and a half Kurds from the plain stretching from Kirkuk to the border of Turkey fled to the mountains. As the uprising collapsed—despite having encouraged it—the Bush administration offered no military assistance to the Kurds. The president now called the uprising an "internal matter" for Iraq. Saddam's helicopters continued to attack refugees as they struggled from the plains and up into the mountains.

Finally, the United Nations Security Council passed resolution 688, requiring Saddam to end internal repression of ethnic groups. That resolution, combined with earlier resolutions forbidding the Iraqi Air Force to patrol the skies north of the 36th parallel, belatedly created a safe area for the Kurds. The no-fly zone was patrolled and strictly enforced by the United States, Britain, and, initially, France. Kirkuk and Mosul were outside the safe area, but Erbil, in KDP territory, and Sulaimaniyah, headquarters of the PUK, were protected. With this arrangement in place, the Kurds began to take tentative steps toward their longed-for autonomy. Elections were held and an assembly was set up in Erbil to house the nascent government. But the rivalry between the two groups always threatened the experiment. By 1996, the physical skirmishing reached a critical point, and in late August, the KDP's Barzani asked Saddam for help in getting rid of the PUK's pesh merga.

In those days, before satphones and the Internet were common in Kurdistan, it took a while for word to get out that Saddam's army had come across the cease-fire line. That was news in itself, but when it was learned that his army had been invited by the Kurds themselves—people he had gassed—it became a huge story. Add in the fact that Erbil had an office of the Iraqi National Congress, Ahmad Chalabi's CIA-sponsored exile group dedicated to overthrowing the dictator, and you had a story for the front page. So off the press went to the Habur Gate. Turkey provided special credentials: reporters could go to Iraq but were not allowed to do any reporting among Turkey's Kurds.

By the time reporters got through Turkey and into Iraq, we were a day or so behind the action. When the press corps arrived in Erbil, scene of most of the fighting, the PUK's forces had been routed. The Iraqi National Congress offices had been looted and a number of their staff killed, and the rest had fled on foot deeper into Kurdistan. The press followed the PUK fighters to their stronghold in Sulaimaniyah, a decent-sized city up in the mountains. But by the time we arrived, the PUK pesh merga had fled farther east into the mountains on the Iranian border. With a colleague I drove to the camp they had set up there. The defeated fighters and their families were strewn along a narrow mountain road somewhere off the map, per-haps even in Iran. Panic and violence surrounded us. Some Red Cross workers were in a mob a hundred yards away, being held hostage. They were physically abused but eventually released. My recounting of that story got all of three minutes on NPR. As we chased after the fleeing PUK, we passed Western mine-clearing teams removing the deadly presents left behind in the fields by Saddam during his successive wars against Iran and the Kurds. They hardly looked up as the losers from the latest skirmishes in the area raced by.

It had been a wild, weird story to cover in 1996. But Kurdistan stayed with me. Empty, connected to the modern world by a couple of satellite dishes and third-hand cars, the Kurds lived in a poverty I had never before encountered. Their society offered glimpses of peasant life no longer lived anywhere in Europe. Speeding through the long valleys, I effortlessly passed time following spots of color—young women and girls wrapped from head to toe in blood-orange or aquamarine dresses, their mothers in black abayas. I watched the cloth billowing and followed their progress into the brown flatness and began to notice the villages—one-story mud huts with ancient iron beds on the roof. In the late summer bedrooms here are outside. Boys herded goats, sheep, and cattle over the road, completely oblivious to the taxis, Japanese-built flatbed trucks, and old buses full of men rushing off to fight.

And the fighting had peculiar rules.

The last significant PUK resistance was at the bridge of Degala, a couple of trestles over a deep, narrow gorge. The bridge was on the only open road between Erbil and Sulaimaniyah. The PUK tried to defend the bridge, but when they were about to be overrun, the fighters fell back behind it. For some reason, they failed to blow up the bridge. That simple action would have halted the KDP advance and given their own PUK pesh mergas time to regroup. Instead I traveled with a small column of KDP fighters over the still-intact bridge. A couple of kilometers down the road we stopped just as an offensive operation was getting under way. A group of approximately thirty KDP fighters had fanned out in a line and were slowly walking up a steep rise in the middle of an open pasture about three hundred meters away. Some PUK fighters were on the other side. About ten or fifteen yards from the crest of the rise they paused briefly, then broke into a run. As they reached the top they opened fire and disappeared charging down the other side of the hill. The shooting went on for a little while. About twenty minutes later one of the KDP pesh merga came racing back in a flatbed Toyota to announce that the road was now clear to the intersection with the main route to Sulaimaniyah.

If the PUK had blown up the Degala bridge, their fighters on the other side of that hill would not have met whatever fate had befallen them and the drive to Sulaimaniyah would have slowed significantly. I was puzzled by the PUK's failure to blow the bridge up and asked one of the UN soldiers stationed in Erbil why. He said it was the nature of the fighting among the Kurds. They don't destroy things as they retreat because the side that is losing always figures it'll be coming back next week and resuming ordinary life.

Which is exactly what happened. Within weeks, the heat of the bloodletting had cooled. The PUK fighters had come back from the mountains and retaken their headquarters' city, Sulaimaniyah. The status quo ante had resumed in the Kurdish safe area . . . minus the lives of a thousand or more pesh merga. So the KDP's leader, Massoud Barzani, and the PUK's chief, Jalal Talabani, accepted a summons from the Clinton administration to the Turkish capital, Ankara, to negotiate a settlement. Two years later, in 1998, they traveled to Washington and signed an accord that guaranteed the KDP would share border revenue with the PUK. It also set up a mechanism to guarantee equal distribution of the UN's oil-for-food money and established a democratically elected parliament. The United States resumed financial support for the Kurdish safe area. This support later accelerated as the second Bush administration prepared for war to overthrow Saddam.

Erbil in 1996 was just an aggregation of two- and three-story buildings, many unfinished or in a state of collapse—after the fighting it was difficult to tell the difference. But clearly some of the American funding in the previous half-decade had trickled down to the street. On my second visit, Erbil was in substantially better physical condition than before.

There was an additional, ironic reason for the improvement. Many Iraqi Kurds, like our driver Sami, had fled the country in 1996. They sent money home from their exile. This added to the newly prosperous surface of the city. Sami had made it into the Netherlands, where he worked as a fruit picker. He lived in a hostel, wired money home every month, and saved more. After he'd been away for five years he had enough put aside to buy a used Isuzu Trooper, and he drove it from the Netherlands across Europe through Turkey to the Habur Gate and back to Erbil. He had also saved enough to build a modern three-story house on a small plot of land on the north side of the city.

One day we drove over the Degala bridge and I excitedly told Ahmad what I had seen there in 1996. He spun around from the front seat and shook his head, saying, "All our politicians are thieves. This is the disaster of the Kurdish people."

We were on our way to Lake Dokan, site of Jalal Talabani's personal compound. During "major combat operations" Ahmad Chalabi was staying at the compound, and we were going there to interview him.

"Chalabi is a bigger thief than anyone." Ahmad laughed. "Tell me, does Bush really think he can lead this country?"

"No. Look, it will never happen."

"But this is what they say. I'm telling you. Iraqi people will not allow it."

"That's why it will never happen," I assured him. "When the war is over that message will get through to Washington. They will want this to succeed and they won't let Ahmad Chalabi stand in the way."

We got to Dokan and parked outside a massive house. We had no appointment with Chalabi; we were just going to "doorstep" him. As it turned out, we didn't get our interview, although a very pleasant young man seconded from the Washington office of the public relations firm Hill & Knowlton gave us Pepsis and let us watch Fox News, the channel of choice for the would-be ruler of Iraq. But I did have a chance to see what Ahmad meant about Kurdish politicians being thieves. Talabani's compound was as magnificent as the setting, a glistening man-made lake surrounded by mountains. It was quiet and peaceful, no Jet Skis, no noisy motorboats. We went out on the terrace of the guest-house where Chalabi was staying, and Ahmad the translator became Ahmad the networker. He took the young man from Hill & Knowlton aside and gave him a small lecture on the politics of the north, and suggested the names of some people he might want to try and contact to get a "real" understanding of the place. They exchanged business cards.

As we drove away, Ahmad returned to the Chalabi theme. It wasn't just that Chalabi had a reputation for dodgy financial dealings—the Jordanian authorities wanted to put him on trial for his role in the collapse of the Petra Bank—but he had been away from the country for decades. Ahmad felt that anyone who had not suffered and survived under Saddam would find it hard to gain the trust of the nation.

"The Americans don't really think he can be the leader of Iraq. It will be disaster if they put him in charge."

"I know, don't worry. They're too smart for that. Bush knows that if Iraq doesn't work it will cost him the White House. Failure is not an option."

Chapter Three

"My Smoke, My Tears, My Breaths and My Words"

"I AM WRITING again," Ahmad announced one morning with satisfaction as we bounced along the road to Taqtaq. In the night, in the front room of his house, after the television was turned off and the children sent to bed, and while his wife, Afrah, slept, Ahmad was snatching a few hours to write by candlelight. Lying on his stomach, a pillow doubled up on which to rest his chin and arm, a swimmer stroking toward his words, he wrote himself to sleep until Afrah rose for the dawn prayer.

"Doing this work has shaken loose ideas," he said.

"What are you writing?"

"Fiction."

"What kind?"

"Short stories" was his answer, written in a style that seemed to conflate all the trends in world literature around 1968. Magical realism, in other words, but Ahmad refused to acknowledge that he wrote in the magical-realist style. His uniqueness as a human being was very important to him, so of course he would not write in a style used by others. But whatever phrase he chose to differentiate himself from Gabriel García Márquez and others, what he wrote, as he described it to me, still boiled down to magical realism—with a tendency toward grand, overblown Arabic poetics. "Oh. . . . ! what a silly world! How small a planet and how great a disaster!!" is a line from "Mr. Key," the story that led to his exile from Mosul.

It was about a key that developed a mind of its own and would not open the door into the author's private room, his past. The room contained all that was most precious to the narrator: "I had in my lovely room all my accessories: my history, my perfumes, my gazing, my smoke, my tears, my breaths and my words. My room is the only world where I can hang my ankle-length shirt, my dishdasha, encrusted with sweat and remember my nonsense, my love fables and my ravings."

There is a character in the story called the Abbasid Donkey, who might be able to help the author make his key work, to unlock the room holding his past. But, as in a dream, the donkey is always just out of reach and of no help. As Ahmad explained the story, it seemed both willfully obscure and allegorically obvious in an undergraduate sort of way. The Abbasids were a Shi'a group that overthrew the original caliphs, the Umayyads, back in the dawn of Islamic time. They then took over the caliphate. That much I knew. But the donkey I didn't get.

"Oh, that's Saddam," Ahmad explained.

"How would anybody know that?"

"Believe me, it is clear to everyone who reads this story."

In Arab culture, to call someone a donkey is more insulting than calling someone a jackass is in English. It is considered a very rude term. To print this and have people who read it know that the Abbasid Donkey is meant to be Saddam was to court disaster, and, of course, disaster is what befell Ahmad. He self-published the story in 1995 and was dragged away by the Mukhabarat, Saddam's secret police, for another bout of torture. I was losing count of how many times he had been imprisoned.

This time he was a guest of the state security apparatus for six months. When he was released he took the hint and fled for his life to Erbil.

Ahmad was becoming my "Mr. Key." But unlike the tool in his story, he happily opened the door into his society and its past. He was an excellent tour guide. Each place we visited was the subject of at least a brief lecture. Through these seminars I learned that Iraq was composed of a wide range of communities with few clearly defined ethnic or sectarian boundaries like Sunni, Shi'a, Kurd. In Ahmad's world, communities were interwoven and not easily picked apart.

Ain Kawa, a suburb of Erbil, was a Christian town, therefore a place where alcohol was easily obtained. That's one reason the UN and NGO offices were there. "Saturday night all the boys from Erbil go to look at the girls," he said. "Because they are less wrapped up than Muslim girls." Shaqlawa, spread down the side of a mountain ridge on the way to Harir, used to be a Jewish village.

"Are there any Jews left?" I asked, thinking I might go and meet them.

"No, no. They gone before I born. In the night the Jewish people disappear." He remembered something else about the place. "They made excellent wine here. When I young I drink this wine."

"But, Ahmad, you're a Muslim."

"Yes, but I wish to experience many things."

Language was another seminar topic in the Isuzu Trooper. It was a car full of multilinguists. David Filipov is a linguist by training, a specialist in Slavic languages and fluent in Russian. Anna Badkhen is Russian by birth, and in a single university year abroad in America she had started from an academic knowledge of English and transformed it into perfect, virtually unaccented fluency. Ahmad spoke Kurdish, Arabic, and English, plus a smattering of classical Persian, learned so he could read and translate the great romantic poets of that country. Sami spoke Kurdish, demotic Arabic, Turkish, and Dutch. My high school conversational French consigned me to the sidelines in these talks. So I just listened.

Often, after a visit to a village, David would review Ahmad's translations. David might mention a word he had heard a "village-ian" say in Kurdish and offer his own translation of it. Ahmad and he would debate the precise English meaning of the word. This would lead to a more general discussion of the language. Kurdish is part of the Persian branch of Indo-European languages. Persian-derived tongues are spoken all through the mountainous regions from the Hindu Kush westward. In northern Afghanistan and the western part of the country adjacent to Iran, people speak Dari, a language almost identical to Persian. While covering the American invasion of Afghanistan in 2001, David had picked up some Dari.

Ahmad and David traced out sounds and meanings across the languages, and this would flow into a conversation about ethnographic history. A discussion about the number four— *chitere* in Russian, *çar* in Kurdish—led to speculation about which language influenced which and the migrations of people through the massive mountains that separate Russia from Persia.

Ahmad explained that Kurdish is a flexible language. This reflected the history of its people over the last thousand or so years. The Kurdish nation has been split up among the many empires that grind together in and around its mountainous heartland. Being ruled at various times by the Ottomans, Persians, Russians, and Arabs—and frequently being divided among those empires—has created a language of many dialects with odd distribution patterns. When a group of Kurds created trouble in an empire, they would be forcibly relocated to another part of the kingdom. They took their dialects with them. The Kurds of Mosul in general speak a different dialect from the Kurds in the surrounding towns and villages. The place with the highest concentration of people speaking a similar language to Mosul's Kurds is hundreds of miles north, through the mountains in Turkey. The Kurds have adapted their language to fit the alphabet of each country where they live. Kurdish is written in Arabic (the alphabet of Iran, Iraq, and Syria), Cyrillic (the alphabet of Armenia and Azerbaijan), and Roman letters (the alphabet used by modern Turkey).

Finding the most accurate word in English, when it had to be filtered through so many variables, was not easy. David and Ahmad had an ongoing argument about the words *upper* and *greater* and *lesser* and *lower*. There are two Zab rivers in Kurdistan. The bigger of the two, the Great Zab, flows in the lowland plains between Erbil and Mosul near Kalak. The Lesser Zab flows in uplands near Sulaimaniyah. On some maps the words have been completely mixed up; and in my companions' minds as well, the rivers and their names had become jumbled. The Great Zab is geographically the "lower" Zab; and the Lesser Zab, coming out of the mountains, is actually the "upper" Zab. On some maps the lower of the two Zab rivers is marked "Lesser Zab" and on others the same river is marked "Great Zab." Ahmad must have learned the names of the rivers from one map and David from another. Once a day, it seemed, David would ask Ahmad the name of the river near Kalak.

"The Zab," Ahmad would tell him.

"There are two Zabs. Which Zab is it?"

"The Lesser Zab."

"No, it's the Great Zab." David would take out the map, and Ahmad would point out where it lay geographically, down on the low plains.

"Lesser Zab!"

"But it's the Great Zab," David would insist.

"Yes, it is also called Great Zab, but it is in lesser place."

"Lower place, not lesser place."

"But lower Zab is here," Ahmad would say, pointing to the smaller or lesser of the two Zabs up there in the mountains near Iran.

"That's not the lower Zab, it's the upper Zab."

"But it can't be upper. Upper means 'greater.' It is not Great Zab."

Neither Groucho Marx nor Samuel Beckett could have resolved this language problem satisfactorily.

The war was unfolding in the south very slowly. The bad weather that had brought heavy snow and wind-driven rain to the north was whipping up sandstorms in the south. In Erbil, with several hundred reporters looking for a war that wasn't happening, the KDP began laying on events for us, press conferences to provide a quote or two for hacks desperate for something fresh to put in their stories. One morning we were summoned to the Chwar Chra Hotel for a press conference with the KDP leader, Massoud Barzani, and President Bush's special envoy to the region, Zalmay Khalilzad. A half-hour after the conference was to begin we were told there was a delay and were invited to step out into the Chwar Chra's lovely garden. The bad weather had finally broken; it was the first really glorious day of spring since the conflict began. As the hundred or so of us mingled, I heard a soft thump. A few others heard it as well. About a mile away a plume of bright white smoke lifted up into the sky. Attack! *News!* We raced back inside and demanded that Fawzi Hariri, the KDP's press spokesman, find out details. This he promised to do. A short while later he summoned us for a briefing and claimed that white smoke, as opposed to black smoke, is usually associated with a chemical attack and the KDP was checking into it. We never heard about the incident again, although a rumor later went through the press corps that within days of the "chemical attack" the United States had issued nuclear/biological/chemical suits to the leadership of the KDP and their families.

Over in Sulaimaniyah, about a three-hour drive away, there was real fighting to report. Ansar al-Islam, an Islamist group based in some villages in the mountains near the Iranian border, was being attacked by a combination of U.S. Special Forces and pesh merga. In the propaganda run-up to the war, the United States pointed to this group as the contact point between al-Qaeda and Saddam. The link was tenuous at best. What was true about the group is they had been terrorizing villagers in that area for several years with their Taliban-like grab for local power. This geographical area was under PUK control. The PUK managed to convince the United States to wipe Ansar out as part of the wider war against Saddam. U.S. Special Forces hooked up with PUK pesh merga and went into the mountains and cleaned out this nest of vipers, at least for a while.

Since hanging out with the pesh merga was yielding very little combat to report on, Anna, David, and I decided to go looking for American Special Forces. They were out there. We knew that from the fighting with Ansar. Ahmad and Sami went to work tracking down rumors. They were told Dolaman, a small village on the plain, was where we could find them. The front in Ahmad's part of the war was a wide-open plain. Pastures and fields and small peasant villages were scattered throughout its gentle rises and folds. A low, flat-backed ridge overlooked this plain, a fifty-mile-long speed bump running from Kalak down to Kirkuk. Along the ridge at regular intervals were fortifications manned by the Iraqi Army.

Dolaman was in a slightly elevated position near the ridge. We drove out on an unpaved road in filthy weather. The track had been reduced to muddy ruts, which reduced our speed to a notch above crawl. It took an hour to travel what was no more than a few miles. Dolaman was a primitive place, and in this weather it didn't even have romantic charm. There were no sewers, and after the steady rains the smell of human waste overwhelmed even the barnyard smells. I commented on how primitive things were here. Ahmad laughed. "When I was a boy I lived in a place like this."

"I thought you grew up in Mosul."

"When my father died we left Mosul for some years. I went to live in a village with my uncles. I know very well village-ian life."

He asked one of the "village-ians" in Dolaman what was going on. The peasant pointed to a little mound about half a kilometer away. There was a small camp dug into the side of the mound facing away from the ridge. There was no road between the village and the camp, just a quagmire of fields. Anna, David, and I looked at each other and shrugged—anything for a quote. We trudged out through the mud, which sucked us down past the tops of our boots with each step. On the side of the hill one soldier stepped out and watched us slogging through the rain and mud. From two hundred yards away we could see him shaking his head, although it was hard to tell whether he was shaking his head in warning or in disbelief at our progress through the mud and farm shit. Another soldier came out and was talking on a satphone. Within minutes some pesh merga appeared out of nowhere and escorted us out of the field, away from the little observation post the soldiers had built on the hill.

When we returned to Dolaman, Ahmad was debriefing a couple of the men about the military activity that had been going on in the vicinity. David and Anna took down notes greedily; a couple of hours had been spent getting to the village and there had been no interview with American Special Forces. It would take a few hours to get back to Erbil through the mud. This was their reporting opportunity for the day, and they needed something original to fill out their stories.

That first week of the war we were no closer to seeing combat firsthand than the rest of the world was. Like everybody else, we watched it on TV. At the Dim Dim there was a massive satellite dish on the roof, and in our rooms reporters had a choice of CNN, BBC World, and Sky News. In the lobby, the translators and drivers flicked between al-Jazeera, al-Arabiya, MBC from Lebanon, Syrian state television, and local KDP TV. Over chai, Ahmad and I would compare notes about what Arab television news and Western television news were reporting.

One week into the war I awoke in the middle of the night to the bass-note rumble of C-130 transport planes flying overhead. I didn't bother to get out of bed to look for myself. I figured I'd catch it on the news later. In the morning CNN and FOX were full of green-tinged night-camera footage of the 173rd Airborne para-chuting into the north to "secure" the airfield at Harir, the sheer audacity of the act extolled by breathless embeds with the 173rd. In reality, Harir was two mountain ridges north of Erbil and about fifty miles away from the nearest Iraqi with an inclination to fire in anger. The security of the airfield at Harir where they landed was not in any doubt. In the months before the conflict started, private military contractors had overseen the runway's lengthening and reenforcement in anticipation of its use someday in a war to over-throw Saddam. The C-130 could have simply landed there. But the footage looked wonderful, it has to be said. And now at least we knew where to find American soldiers.

We went over the two ridges from Erbil to Harir and combed along the airfield for troops to interview. The rain had been steady for days in the long valley, and the poor paratroopers had landed in thick mud. They were "securing" their perimeter in a quagmire surrounded by dozens of reporters pestering them for a quote. For daily journalists like David and Anna, the situation was difficult. They were filing a minimum of a thousand words every day, and there simply wasn't enough news to make that an easy task. We worked every little village around Harir, with David and Anna interrogating the local peasants about what they saw or heard during the night, and Ahmad translating as quickly as possible. But it was clear that Ahmad-speak wasn't helping David. Tension had crept into the day's routine. David found Ahmad's occasional "quite-ly" sad moods disconcerting.

There was also a bit of cross-purpose in our work routines. I was trying to get to know Ahmad intimately and I had no dead-line for that. David and Anna needed speed and the simple clarity of fluency. Retranslating the translator took time that working on deadline simply didn't permit.

The dilemma came down to this: Ahmad was a good trans-lator and a brilliant interpreter. The daily journalists needed more of the former. I needed the latter.

A couple of days later, David announced they had found another translator. It was not an easy thing for him to say. We all were aware that we were getting close to Ahmad in a way that none of us had ever experienced with a local hire. There are sharply drawn lines in the field that prevent friendship in the usual sense from developing. Cordiality can flourish but real friendship is withheld, because the basic unalterable fact of our work is this: reporters are visitors, and when the news moves on, so do we; for the translators it is their country, and whatever mess is being made of it, they will have to stay behind and be among those who clean it up after the bloodletting stops and we move on. But with Ahmad something different was going on, and breaking up our little partnership was quite emotional. David was upset after making his announcement and went back to his room at the Dim Dim to work on a feature.

Anna and I went to a refugee camp on the outskirts of Erbil. "Refugee camp" was a bit of a misnomer. The houses looked permanent and the streets were laid out on a planned grid. But they were poorly paved or in some cases not paved at all. Most of the people here were Kurds from Iran who had drifted into northern Iraq during the late 1990s. In a field at the edge of the settlement were rows of neatly laid out tents. These housed more recent arrivals. Most were from Kirkuk. They had been straggling in during the months leading up to the war. The story they told, as Ahmad translated it, was of a city held in fear by the Fedayeen Saddam. These ultraloyalists had begun commandeering houses in residential neighborhoods before the war started. They set up watch points on the roofs and kept a tally of people coming and going. The refugees described Kirkuk as on the edge of rebellion but that people were unable to meet and plan because the Fedayeen were watching everything and everyone. Their very presence kept the city's population in fear.

Ahmad was not at his best in this environment. These new refugees seemed to speak a Kurdish dialect he did not know. There were details he was missing. Sami kept correcting the textbook Kurdish that Ahmad usually spoke. Ahmad and Sami were arguing over meanings, when all of us, refugees included, had our eyes drawn to the sky. We heard B-52s but could not see them. We scoured the sky for the contrails and found them. Then, in the distance, a couple of plumes of smoke rose up near Kalak. It was the first daytime bombing run we had seen in the war. We jumped in the car, leaving the refugees and their untranslated tales of misery behind, and, like wayward Israelites, headed toward the pillars of smoke.

We drove to just before the Kalak bridge. The excitement was over by the time we arrived. A small hill a half-mile before the bridge had been turned into the press's observation post. Camera crews were posted all along the summit. Reporters were stretched out in the spring sun. Ivan Watson from NPR had his shotgun microphone pointing desultorily toward the ridge in case the Iraqis decided to open fire. Field glasses were handed to us and we were able to assess the damage for ourselves. Nothing had been hit; the slope of the ridge that came down to the Zab had a couple of massive divots kicked up by the bombs. It seemed like the mission had been to deliver an explosive calling card from the U.S. Air Force. There was nothing to report, so we hit the road and headed back for Erbil. Ahmad was trying to reexplain something that one of the refugees had told us about the way the Fedayeen Saddam kept control of Kirkuk, when Sami casually said, "American soldiers."

"Where?"

"Back there."

"Sami, Jesus Christ. Turn the car around."

We cut across both lanes of traffic and the grass-covered median, driving back toward Kalak, then cut across the same two lanes of traffic and the median over to an SUV parked on the shoulder. The hood was up and the soldiers and their driver were doing what men all over the world do when their car breaks down:

stare at the engine, as if just looking at it would somehow bring it back to life.

Two of the soldiers were American. They had to be Special Forces, because their mud-spattered uniforms bore no names or insignia. They were the ghosts we had been chasing for the last week. One was tall and redheaded, the other short and dark-haired. As we slowed up by the SUV, a Kurdish officer raised his rifle—American issue, not a Kalashnikov—and growled at us to get away. I yelled out the window in my broadest American accent, "Hey, guys, you need any help?" One of the Special Forces guys brushed past the Kurdish officer, came around to the window, and said no, the car was just overheated and they would wait it out. I offered them a lift. "No, we're okay." "You sure?" "No, we're good." Anna had brought some Pepsis along and she offered the soldiers a drink. That seemed to break the ice and Sami got out to give a hand.

Sami had some experience with vehicles in wartime. He had done two tours of duty driving an armored personnel carrier during the Iraq-Iran War. Sami joined the team staring at the engine, then he took over the situation, putting his head under the hood and sticking his hands into the engine block, feeling around among the wires and hoses. After ten minutes Sami's diagnosis was that the ignition system was completely shot and the car needed to be towed to a garage. He had a rope in the back of the Trooper, so we offered to tow the soldiers back to their base. Even if the Special Forces guys wanted to maintain operational security by staying away from us, they couldn't do it now. We asked them where they wanted to go and they told us: a base on the other side of Erbil about twenty minutes away. So they got into their car and, yoked together by a frayed yellow rope, we set off.

We drove slowly through the potholed streets of Erbil. The city was beginning to fill up. People were returning from the mountains as they realized Saddam's army was not going to attack up here. Our little yellow-roped convoy didn't stir up too much interest. We got the soldiers to their base without incident, and I figured, having done a favor for them, I might get some exclusive information. Before I could even ask, our Isuzu was surrounded by half a dozen very angry Kurdish pesh merga, and we were cordially told to get away. While Sami was unhitching the SUV, I got my exclusive interview. I still have the tape. Here is a full transcription (there are no names because no names were supplied):

Tall Redhead: Hey, thanks. Where you from?

Me: WBUR, the NPR station in Boston.

Tall Redhead: Cool, I'll watch for you.

Me (thinking to myself): *Watch me? Don't you mean listen?*

Me (seeking operational info, speaking out loud): It must be pretty muddy in Dolaman.

Tall Redhead stares through his sunglasses for a long beat, then extends his hand for a bone-crunching handshake.

T. R.: You be careful out there.

Me: No, *you* be careful.

The smaller guy then comes around.

Me: Stay safe.

Small Guy: We're good (his voice inflected to imply "we know what we're doing"). *You* stay safe (his voice inflected to imply "you don't").

The war was now ten days old. In the south of Iraq, the bad weather had lifted and American forces were finally rolling. The war's effects began to ripple through the north. The Iraqi Army pulled back from the plain near Dola Bakir. We went out to see how far. When we got there the ever media-aware KDP were organizing a photo-and-sound opportunity for broadcast journalists. Some pesh merga were demonstrating mine clearing, Kurdish style. They had dug up and defused dozens of the lethal packages and put them in a shallow pit. They waved us away, poured gasoline on the mines, lit a match, and ran like hell. The explosion sounded wonderful on my tape recorder. It was the first sound of war I had managed to record in the ten days since the conflict started.

Ahmad convinced a pesh merga officer to take us to their most forward position. We drove a few kilometers down the road and then walked through a field toward a shallow trench. Halfway into the field it occurred to me that the area looked a lot like the place we had been watching "mine clearing" operations being carried out. I asked the pesh merga whether this area had been cleared of mines. He simply replied, "Walk where I walk." Ahmad and I looked at each other and shrugged. A bit of Muslim fatalism goes a long way in these situations. If it was our time to die . . .

From the little observation dugout we could see a two-lane blacktop road slicing toward Kirkuk. A car carrying a Japanese TV crew went down the road and disappeared from sight down a little dip. Watch this, our pesh merga guide said. About one minute later, from the dip in the landscape a puff of smoke went up: a mortar round. A minute later the Japanese crew's car came tearing back up the road significantly faster than it had been traveling two minutes before. Having seen that the Iraqi Army was still around, we tiptoed back to Sami.

There was a small family graveyard by the side of the road. The gravestones were covered in Arabic script. I glanced at them and didn't give them a second look. Ahmad took me over to them. "These are Kurdish graves, but the inscription on them is in Arabic language, not Kurdish," he explained. "That is Saddam's law. Even in the grave he touches you."

Chapter Four

"Our Real Identity Is as Iraqi People"

SOMEWHERE ALONG ONE of Kurdistan's roads, I realized I was no longer seeing Ahmad as a subject for a documentary. We were becoming friends, close friends. The closeness was possible because of his openness. No subject was forbidden. Any question I asked received an honest answer. He was doing more than just opening the door into a society, he was opening himself to friendship.

It may have been near Sulaimaniyah, after we tried to find Ahmad Chalabi. It may have been at a checkpoint where we had stopped to stretch our legs and get an assessment of the security situation on the road ahead. It may have been in a mud-hut hamlet where we were debriefing the "village-ians" about some "striking" the previous night. We were making small talk. I don't remember the topic. It could have been politics or sex. But I do remember a gesture. Ahmad reached for my hand and drew me to him so he could say something sotto voce. We had a low chuckle about it. As we walked back to the Isuzu Trooper he kept hold of my hand. My instinct, based on my society's taboos, was to withdraw it. I had to remind myself that in the Arab world men hold hands when they stroll and have conversations.

Ahmad's Arab gesture was unself-conscious and natural. So I left my hand in his. We continued to talk. Then he said, "You are my intimate friend."

You are my intimate friend. It wasn't so much a declaration as a statement of surprising fact. We don't really make close friends after a certain age. Life teaches us to wall off certain parts of ourselves. If we reveal a little too much of ourselves in the playground we might get teased. Reveal a little too much on the job and we can get fired. We may become "friendly" with new neighbors when we move house; children might widen our circle of acquaintances as they go through the school system; we can become "friendly" with colleagues in a new job. Acquaintanceship, collegiality, friendliness are what we expect in the friendships we form in middle age, not intimacy.

One part of intimate friendship is admiration. We allow ourselves to grow close because our friend has qualities we admire and aspire to. The more I found out about Ahmad's life, the more I admired him. By now I knew the broad outline of the story and its constantly repeated cycle of frustration, risk, torture, and survival, but he still had not been beaten down. *Despair* was one of his favorite words. He knew despair often, but somehow always returned to a place where he was willing to risk everything to be his own man. Iraq is a society whose every aspect works against individualism. The government at the time was totalitarian. Its religion, Islam, emphasizes the collective at the expense of the individual. The obligations to family supersede all other social obligations, acting as an enormous gravitational field, preventing individuals from flying away from the group. The pressures to conform are enormous, but Ahmad was unwilling to surrender his uniqueness. Not even under torture. Nor had torture robbed him of his sense of humor. And family responsibility had not taken away his exuberance. He was the father of eight and the grandfather of six, but he hadn't grown that paterfamilias veneer that turns so many of his age into pompous old men before their time.

In addition to admiration for a person, another characteristic of friendship is recognizing what you have in common. However, Ahmad came from such a different place; speaking through the filter of two different languages, it seemed presumptuous for me to say we were becoming friends because we were alike. How could we be alike? I hadn't been tortured. I hadn't spent part of my childhood living in a mud-hut peasant village. I've never had to fight to be able to speak my mind in public. But there was something connecting us. It was like pulling petals off a daisy: He's like me . . . no, he's not like me. He's like me, no, he's not like me.

He's like me. Ahmad was part of the universal fellowship of smart-asses: the clever kids in high school who prove their regular-guy credentials by verbally making life hell for teachers and keeping people amused in the playground with cynical commentary on the idiocy of adults.

He's like me. There was the freemasonry of 1968. Anyone who entered university that year is a member. Ahmad entered the University of Mosul in 1968. I started college that year as well. We were the shock troops of change in that time of hope and violence. A shared nostalgia washed over the car as Ahmad reminisced about the political hopscotch he played back then. We all did, promiscuously flirting with political ideologies, holding them to a standard of purity that could only lead to disappointment, then licking our wounds and moving on. In his time Ahmad had joined pan-Arab political groups, then the communists—practically every political party available except the Ba'ath—before coming to the realization that "all the ideologies are going to be something like nonsense. We don't need ideologies. We need to be sure that our real identity is as Iraqi people, not as Arabs or Kurds and Turkmen."

Iraqi identity was his frequent theme. Like most journalists, I assumed that the war would unleash Kurdish nationalist feeling, yet as we worked our way around Erbil and the surrounding villages, I did not hear a lot of separatist talk. When I asked villagers about independence, their answers indicated to me that it was an aspiration, not a demand for the day after Saddam was overthrown. The people I spoke with acknowledged the country's ethnic and sectarian complexity but also expressed a real sense of pride in being Iraqi. It was surprising to hear, and I asked Ahmad about it. He was adamant that this was a view shared all over the country: people thought of themselves first of all as Iraqi citizens, not as members of distinct ethnic or sectarian groups.

Another reason we grew close is that the atmosphere in the Trooper was incredibly relaxed. We were having a good time. Ahmad's pleasure at having a ringside seat for the fall of Saddam was palpable. The signs were in the sky. The war had started at the lingering end of winter under lowering skies and rain. Now the weather had cleared and spring had come all over Iraq. American forces were on the move. With each passing day it became less likely that the dictator would try to get his last licks in against the Kurds by using chemical or biological weapons against them. Soon the dictator would be gone.

Ahmad wanted me to meet his family. He also wanted his family to meet Americans. Lunch at his home was arranged.

Ahmad's house had a typical layout for this part of the world. A high wall separated it from the street. Metal gates opened into a courtyard: a small bit of paving to park a car, then a patch of dirt with a couple of orange and lemon trees. A living room and kitchen and two small rooms were on the first floor, two more rooms were on the second, and then a large flat roof, where Ahmad, his wife, Afrah, and the six children still living at home could sleep during the hot summer months. The physical layout may have been typical, but inside his gates Ahmad's home was full of surprises, the place where Western preconceptions about his country and his culture were challenged.

Preconception one: Iraq is not really a nation but simply borders drawn up after World War I. Inside these borders three different, irreconcilable groups are forced to be part of the same country: Kurds, Sunni Arabs, and Shi'a Arabs. These groups could only be held together by a dictator. Yet Ahmad was a Kurd, Afrah an Arab, and they had bridged the ethnic difference to achieve the deepest, quietest kind of love, the love where one person inhales and the other exhales the breath, where one person has a thought and the other person speaks it.

Preconception two: Modern Islam is a radical political force, unable to live side by side with other beliefs. Yet Ahmad was secular, his wife extremely devout. His children also prayed regularly. Religion and rational secular thinking coexisted harmoniously in his home.

Preconception three: In modern Islam, women's roles outside the house are diminished. In Ahmad's house, his daughters were educated and encouraged to speak their minds and have professional lives.

Finally, Ahmad's house was a place of laughter. The public face of most Arab societies is relentlessly sullen. In Ahmad's house, the cure for all the suffering he and his family had endured was humor.

Some of the laughter came from the fact that there were so many kids underfoot. There were six children living in the house. Sindibad, the oldest son, was twenty-six; Zainab, the youngest, a girl, was six. Two more boys and a girl—Rafat, Shawkat, and Rasha—were high school students. The oldest daughter in the house, Roaa, twenty, was the brightest source of laughter. She was clearly the favorite. She said so, and Ahmad did not deny it. Not because she was very pretty, although she was, but because her mind worked like her father's. She, too, was a journalist and a political skeptic.

Inside the gates everything was hustle and bustle. The rustling of the women's long skirts as they finished cleaning floors and began washing food in preparation for lunch was very loud. Ahmad gave a brief guided tour of the house, which ended up on the roof. When we came back downstairs, the women were in the courtyard making dolma, stuffing minced lamb into peppers, cabbages, and aubergines. They were chatting and laughing with a bearded young man, clearly a good friend of the family, who had been invited round as part of Ahmad's "continuing education program for Western journalists," namely me.

He introduced himself as Abdussalaam al-Medeni. Abdussalaam was Sindibad's and Roaa's tutor in Islamic studies. It was clear why Ahmad wanted us to meet. In the West, when we think of Islamic politics we often think of al-Qaeda, the Taliban, and jihadists. But Islamic politics is more complex than that. We went back upstairs to one of the bedrooms, and I interviewed him. His English was exceptionally good. The young man said he was an Islamic, as opposed to Islamist, politician. Through teaching and political activity, Abdussalaam was thinking his way to a political program that would satisfy the growing need in Kurdistan for Islamic politics that did not succumb to the dark simplicities of the Wahhabi creed, which had originated in Saudi Arabia. Wahhabism, espoused by Osama bin Laden, the Taliban, and other radical groups, was sweeping across much of the Muslim world.

"This is not part of the Kurdish personality," he explained. "This jihad, this kind of hatred between East and West."

His courses dealt with the dilemma of reconciling modernity with the Koran: "How to deal with the role of women; how to deal with new thoughts. There is some thinking that says we have to make our territory like it was before, fourteen hundred years ago, as it was at the time of the holy texts." This he dismissed. "It is so difficult. How to deal with the music, for example, with others who have another religion in the Islamic community. The Islamists try to tell us that we have to get rid of everything that came from the West"—including the concept of democracy. "We think that's a great mistake in Islamist thinking."

Abdussalaam was head of something called the Islamic Studies Bureau. He was brought up, like everyone in his community, as an "ordinary Muslim." It was only at university that he had made the decision to make Islam his "aim, to live for it."

His commitment to both Islam and democratic politics was absolute. His study center was funded by the Kurdistan Islamic Union, a political party. Before I could question him about his connection with a political party, he explained, "Everything in Kurdistan is partisan. We are not independent." What he meant was that no one and no institution in Kurdistan stands on its own. In Kurdistan every aspect of life, from education through business, flows through political patronage. One way or another, everyone has to be tied into a party. In the ultraloyal world of Kurdish politics most people belong to the parties that grew out of the Kurdish independence movement: the KDP and PUK. These parties are avowedly secular. Abdussalaam claimed the Kurdistan Islamic Union was becoming the alternative choice, particularly for young Kurdish professionals who, like many young Muslims around the world, were seeking a more overt Islamic element in their political life.

The current situation posed a conundrum for the Kurdistan Islamic Union: the party was against the invasion but it was against Saddam as well. "We should stand against Saddam ourselves, to make a union with the Iraqi population and here in Kurdistan," said Abdussalaam. "We can't and we don't, however, because our problems with each other are bigger than our problems with the regime." He sighed. "America will do it instead of us, and she will drink the oil."

Afrah poked her head into the little room and asked whether we wanted to be served in there. It was an oblique and polite way of saying it was time to eat and we were delaying everyone's lunch. We made our apologies. Abdussalaam did not stay for the meal. He had come to be interviewed by a Western journalist, and that mission was accomplished.

Lunch was served in the living room, which doubled as Ahmad and Afrah's bedroom. For the duration of the conflict it was also the family's safe room. A double thickness of plastic sheeting to protect against chemical or biological attack was taped over the big picture window that looked into the courtyard. The space was empty except for some pillows scattered around the floor and a cart with a television and VCR. We sat on the floor. "In Mosul, I had furniture," Ahmad apologized. "But Saddam took it all. So now we eat like Arabs."

A plastic mat was brought in and lunch was served on it. The room filled with the smell of meat simmered in the spices of Arabia: cardamom and cumin. The meal consisted of a mountain of stuffed dolma; two soups, one made out of tomatoes and okra, and the other a light chicken broth; a plate of kubba, fried cracked wheat cakes stuffed with minced lamb; and a couple of roasted chickens, plus plates of chopped tomatoes and cucumber . . . and rice and bread . . . and more rice and bread. Arab hospitality is a very real phenomenon.

Before we tucked in, Afrah made a little speech of welcome, saying she wanted Americans in her house because, "We would like to have in the near future an American president. So we have to like Americans and know them very well."

Then we got to work on the food. Everyone but Roaa ate themselves into a sated silence.

It was time to do a little business. I had recorded the preparation of the food as well as some of the chomping and chewing of the meal, and then I had shut my machine off so I could get my share of the grub. Now I turned to Ahmad and put the recorder back on. The sheer artificiality of interviewing someone who had become a friend made me feel awkward. We had had a lovely meal, but the first thing I asked about was his time in prison. I knew he had been tortured, but he had never gone into much detail. Ahmad's willingness to perform, his pleasure at finding someone who understood a little of what he wanted from life, made him quite happy to sit back after a good meal and remember something hellish. He began to describe what happened during his last imprisonment, after the publication of "Mr. Key." "They burned my back, they used electrical cables to bite me" (Ahmad-speak meaning they clipped cables onto his genitals and gave him electric shocks). The torture that stayed with him was one that was unique: "They had an electrical chair. This chair is like a cage. When you sit in the chair, they switch it on. The chair makes you like a small ball and press your body inside until you become the smallest size. . . . One giant guy hold me in that chair and say, Well, I hope you are comfortable there. And I lost my conscious."

As happens to almost everyone who is tortured, Ahmad broke down. Whatever questions they asked, he answered. "But after a few days, when they got everything from me, I told them there is no need for all these things. I am talking faithfully and I have nothing to hide. Yes, I wrote that story and I meant that thing. I can sign you whatever you want. Just don't hurt me. So they said, No. We have to know everything about your background, who obliged you, who is with you."

While Ahmad spoke, his family sat quietly. Most of the children had some knowledge of English, but I don't think they could follow our conversation. I think they were simply being polite; their father was being interviewed and they were quietly watching the scene. When Ahmad finished his story, I was stumped for what to ask next. "Ask anything you want," Ahmad urged. "No subject is forbidden in this house." I moved the interview onto ground more appropriate for the setting. How did Ahmad meet Afrah?

"She was my neighbor and my student. I was giving classes in my house and she attended. We recognized each other and loved each other for two years. Thereafter we get married."

"Would you like to see the pictures?" Roaa asked. Out came the photos. The most compelling showed them on their wedding day in 1975, stepping into a 1960s-era convertible, the bride in a Western wedding dress, looking dark and beautiful, Ahmad in a tuxedo, smiling with a peacock's preening pleasure in the whole scene.

I asked, "Ahmad, did your wife understand when she married you that you were the kind of man who didn't know when to keep his mouth shut?" Afrah, a small woman, who since her little speech had been sitting impassively, now became animated . . . or at least her face did. She chuckled as Ahmad translated, then she answered. "Yes, I know very well because I knew that he was a politician and writer."

"One of my friends told her I am going to make her very tired in her life, but she insisted to marry me," Ahmad added.

Then his wife sighed. "Life without problems is not interesting."

I asked if they discussed religion these days. There was an explosion of laughter. The visitor had found the family joke. Afrah made a little fist and shook it at her husband. "We disagree completely and always we are fighting. Alhamdulillah," she said. "Thanks be to God. Ahmad is better now than he used to be." Then she gave him a knowing look. "Because he went to prison." And had learned some humility. She smiled and sighed. Ahmad had come home alive, and the only explanation for that was that Allah had heard her prayers.

The conversation turned toward reminiscences about the older children's life in exile in Erbil and their embrace of Islamic political ideas. Being a true liberal, my friend gave them a free hand to find their own political credo. "I don't like to oblige them to believe in my ideas. They have their own freedom to believe what they like."

Neither Roaa nor Sindibad held their tutor Abdussalaam's skepticism about the war, but neither did they have their father's optimism about the new day dawning for Iraq. Sindibad looked at the future with trepidation. Since the family had fled to Erbil in 1997 he had been the main breadwinner. He had given up his engineering studies at the University of Mosul and taken up tailoring. At a little shop in the bazaar he made bespoke suits and had a nice line in embroidering the black abayas worn by Kurdish women. He did not share his father's desire to return to Mosul as soon as possible. Sindibad wasn't sure what his father would find there except danger. "The great problems are going to arise after the war. Not now."

Ahmad shook his head. "They have no hope. They first opened their eyes on a disastrous situation." He nodded toward his oldest son. "More than twenty-six years old but he always suffers of war, and war and war after war and losing his father and losing his family and stay alone several times and facing problems how to be the responsible man in the family." Ahmad believed that these great difficulties leech hope out of a person.

While we spoke, chai had been served and drunk. The women had rolled up the plastic mat and cleared away the debris of lunch. We went back out to look for war. In the Trooper, I picked up on a point made at lunch.

"Ahmad, Afrah said she wants an American president. What does she mean by that? Does she want Iraq to be the fifty-first state?"

"No, no." He laughed. "She means she wants America to be in control for a while. She does not think Iraqi people are ready to be democratic people. So America should appoint our ruler."

"What do you think?"

"It may take some time, but we will have a democratic society."

Ahmad changed the subject slightly. He was surprised and a little hurt that so many people in the West, particularly on the left, seemed to be against the overthrow of Saddam. "Why they not want the war? Don't they know our suffering?" he asked.

We had had this conversation several times. It was a repeated riff in our friendship. Why were so many people in the West— particularly progressives, who had much in common with Ahmad—not clamoring in support of a war to overthrow a fascist dictator? It was not the first time I had heard the question "Don't they know our suffering?" During the Bosnian war, when I was in Sarajevo, and later, among exiles from the Balkans who were living in London lobbying for Western intervention during that conflict, that question came up over and over. My answer to Ahmad was a variation on a theme I had been developing since the breakup of Yugoslavia.

When wars end you have to clean up the battlefield. After

World War II, warships were mothballed and the California desert filled with old warplanes. After the Cold War, the situation was different. The Cold War's infrastructure was human. The war was fought in the third world by proxies: tyrants created and sustained in power by the Soviets or the Americans. But when the Cold War was over, America did nothing to decommission its proxies. Now it was paying a price. The mujahideen of Afghanistan morphed into the Taliban and al-Qaeda. September 11 had been the result. Saddam Hussein, who had been sustained in power as a bulwark against the ayatollahs next door in Iran, had become a mass murderer and destabilizing influence in the Middle East. The worst aspect of this failure to decommission tyranny was that the people who lived in these countries continued to suffer. Ahmad and I agreed that intervention to remove the most egregious dictators was the right thing to do. We also agreed that given its failures in Bosnia and Rwanda, the United Nations could not be relied on to save people suffering genocidal attacks and extreme political repression. America alone had the power to intervene, but this posed a problem for the liberal left in the West, I explained to Ahmad.

"I think for many on the left there is a difficult choice to make," I said. "They hate fascism, but they fear an American empire. They would rather let you live under a fascist dictator than see America use its military power unilaterally—in an imperial way. So they don't want the U.S. to overthrow Saddam. They didn't want the U.S. to go to war in Kosovo, even if it led directly to the fall of Milosevic. They didn't want the U.S. to intervene in Bosnia, and so on."

"But what they want?" Ahmad asked. "Only America has the power to do these things."

"I know. I know. It's a strange world where the left would prefer to see fascists in power. I argue with my friends. I tell them: if for once in our lives the American government chooses to overthrow a real tyrant, then this is a good thing."

Mosul began to dominate our conversation. In one week, two at the outside, the war would be over and Ahmad would be back home. Each day the enthusiasm would bubble out of him. He would turn around in the front seat and describe the things he would show me in his hometown, and every fantasy ended the same way. We would go to one of the fish restaurants on the banks of the Tigris and eat lunch. "The best fish in the world," he promised me.

There was still the business of journalism between us, and with the war reaching its inevitable climax, a lengthy interview session was required. A few nights after our lunch, I went back to his house. We sprawled on the floor in the "safe" room and watched CNN for a bit. Baghdad was surrounded. Like people all over the world, we sat transfixed, looking at the Iraqi information minister, Muhammad Saeed Sahaf, lying for Saddam to the bitter end. Comical Ali, as he was dubbed, was claiming that American troops were at least twenty kilometers away while CNN was showing pictures of U.S. tanks in Baghdad's streets. My friend shook his head in disbelief.

"Doesn't he feel shame?" Ahmad asked.

"Who? Him? Of course not."

In one corner of the room Rafat and Sindibad were playing chess. Sami sat against the wall watching the news, sipping a Pepsi. We lay across pillows, relaxed, letting the furious pace of the previous weeks slip away. Then Ahmad, with very little prompting, began to unfold the political story of his life to me, a story that began in a middle-class neighborhood in Mosul and that was beset by trouble from the time of his adolescence.

"In my life I faced many problems socially and politically.

Socially, because I belonged to a Kurdish family; politically, because I was involved with many national movements."

Even before he started university, Ahmad was active in politics. Like many young men in the Middle East in the mid-1960s, he idolized Egyptian president Gamal Abdel Nasser. He became part of a group that espoused the Egyptian president's pan-Arabism. "They believed in Toynbee's lie. You know, Arnold Toynbee, the historian? He writes the Arabs are a single nation." He shook his head. "Arabic unity. So they believed that Arabic union is coming. For this reason they tried to make everyone believe the Arab nation is one nation."

But he soon discovered a flaw in the organization, an authoritarian strain quite at odds with its democratic principals. There was also a bit of racism. Ahmad was elected to the local leadership council. But the national leadership of the movement removed him because he was a Kurd. Ahmad told them, "Fine, I'll go start my own party." Then he found out how treacherous Iraqi politics could be. One of his former comrades denounced him to the Ba'ath Party. Ahmad, just twenty, was arrested and held in prison briefly, then released.

He finished university and became a lecturer in anatomy and histopathology at the University of Mosul's prestigious medical faculty. In his free time he lived the life of an old-fashioned man of letters, writing fiction and criticism and giving lectures to his medical students on literature. These extracurricular classes gave him the greatest pleasure. "The relationship between me and my students was very intimate. Because my dealing with them was like a brother talking, like a friend." It was in these talks that he indulged his need for politics, interpreting Iraqi literature from a political perspective. "It was forbidden to discuss such affairs in Iraq. It was something like a sin." The Ba'ath's gatekeepers at the university pressured him to stop these courses, and eventually their threats drove him into exile. He left Afrah and young Sindibad behind and went to Cairo for a year and worked as a journalist.

When things had cooled down for him in Mosul he returned, but almost immediately Iraq entered a new era. In 1979 Saddam Hussein, the puppet-master of the Ba'ath Party, stepped out from behind the curtain and took over absolute power. Within months he launched a war against Iran; its impact on Iraqi society was no less than the impact of World War I on Britain or France. The fighting quickly ground down into trench warfare that would last for eight years. All able-bodied men were subject to call-up. Ahmad was assigned to a medical battalion. By 1984 Saddam had run out of money to fight his war. As Ahmad told it, the dictator demanded that his people give up all their gold to help pay. Ahmad refused. He was sent to a military prison in Kirkuk. This time he encountered real torture. Six months of it. The interrogation was constant, although he had very little to reveal. "They discovered that I had nothing to say. I wasn't guilty. I am not useful for them. They returned me back to my hospital. They said, 'Excuse us. We misunderstood. Come on, go, continue your service in your military hospital.'"

His tour of duty over, he returned to the university, where the regime did the one thing that could break him. "They obliged me to retire." He was forced to resign his lectureship. No torture was greater than being separated from his students.

We shifted about on our cushions. Up to this moment Ahmad was reporting on his past, not reliving it. Now his speech changed, slowed, the pain palpable in his mouth. "I became very sad. I told you my relationships with my students were very intimate. I was thinking to make those students enlightenment points." This was a bit of Ahmad-speak I couldn't immediately translate. "Enlightening people. I thought that they could be good members of a political party if I decide to practice politics again. I considered them as a storage in Iraqi people." In Basra and Hillah and Ramadi he hoped his students would go on with their lives and remember the lessons about an Iraq that could someday throw off the Ba'ath and be more like the countries he read about in Western literature.

"I lost the dearest relationship in my life. I was proud of this relationship because there was a great response to my ideas. I could see the response in their eyes."

Listening to this story, I found myself thinking again about admiration as an element of friendship. There he stood, that seeming rarest of things in the Arab world: an individual, a man in and of himself. Americans have the luxury of being able to take individualism for granted. That individual effort will be rewarded is a cornerstone of the national myth. If he had been born in America or Britain or most anyplace in the European end of the first world, his individualism would have been the key to his success. Ahmad would have become, by dint of his intelligence and individual drive, a self-made man who rose above his humble origins. Perhaps his egotism would have offended people and prevented him becoming chairman of his university's department of anatomy. Maybe he would have joined suburban organizations with great enthusiasm and left them with equal vehemence when his ideas were thwarted.

But he was born in Iraq. In Arab and, to a significant degree, Kurdish society, group loyalty trumps everything else. The group can be the clan or the Ba'ath or your sect: Sunni or Shi'a. But to stand on your own is almost impossible. There my friend stood, with his family around him, stubborn and refusing to surrender his individual right to speak and write as he chose.

As his monologue continued, I periodically glanced at the sound level on my tape recorder and drifted off, wondering how I would react to living in a totalitarian system. Perhaps it is the game of a Jew born after the Holocaust in New York City. Since Solomon was building the Temple there has been no place on Earth where Jews have been safer, wealthier, or more influential. In this space of leisure in our terrifying history it is easy to ask: What would you have done in the Warsaw Ghetto? Would you have fled to the forest and joined the partisans? Would you have stayed and joined the underground and eventually died a glorious death in the uprising? Or would you have meekly gone to the Umschlagplatz when your name was called and taken the train to Treblinka, sucked into the collective psychology of defeat, comforting your family, seeing your impending death as inevitable?

As we grew closer, I found myself asking those questions again. . . . What would I have done, if I had three children and a fourth on the way? Would I have told the regime to fuck off quite as clearly as Ahmad had? Would my desire to stand as a free man, an individual, have overridden my fear of the personal consequences: prison, torture, possible death? Or would the conflicting desire to protect my family have made me meekly bow before the dictator's regime or, even worse, actively embrace it in the hope of getting a little more bread for my children or smooth their path to university or other forms of advancement.

Ahmad offered the example of resistance.

After he was "obliged to retire"—fired from the university— Ahmad dropped out of all intellectual activity. At that point in his life there were six children to feed; he had to find other work. He started a furniture-making business that did very well. He invested some of his profits in a billiard hall in Mosul's old town. He became wealthy. But the first Gulf War reawakened his political side, and he began to write again. He published the book of short stories that included the magical-realist political allegory called "Mr. Key." So off to prison he went again in 1996. He wasn't killed, for the simple reason that the Saddam regime loved money more than death. His family ransomed him for six million dinars—around forty thousand dollars at the time.

Ahmad fled to the Kurdish autonomous region. Afrah and the children followed a few months later. The family exchanged the bloody problems of Saddam's territory for the more existential problems of internal exile. There was no work for him in Erbil. More important, there was no respect for who he had been in Mosul. In 2002, as the war to overthrow Saddam was first being mentioned in the American press, Ahmad tried to flee Saddam's world. It meant leaving Kurdistan and going back through Iraq, but Ahmad didn't care about the danger. At a checkpoint four kilometers from the Jordanian border and safety, the truck he was traveling in was stopped. Ahmad's belongings were searched, and a little essay of his calling for Saddam to step down and save the Iraqi people was found. That was that. He was taken to Baghdad by the police, who detained him.

At just the moment Ahmad was telling this story, the rumble of a bombing run over in Iraqi regime territory came up through the ground and shook the plastic-shrouded picture window. Sami, Sindibad, and Ahmad all smiled at each other. "B-52s." They nodded. Soon. Soon it will be over.

The arrest should have been his death sentence. But as the international pressure built on Saddam in the autumn of 2002, the dictator gave a general amnesty to all prisoners inside Iraq's jails, political prisoners as well as violent criminals. An incredulous Ahmad was released. "What's going on? I didn't believe. When I get into the street, alone I gazed to the sun. I couldn't believe myself I see sun again."

He made his way back to Erbil. When he came through the

door, Afrah did not express surprise. Her belief in prayer is profound, and she had been praying for her husband since the day he left.

My friend had to admit that this last escape had inspired him to give at least some credence to religion. "I think sometimes . . . Maybe there . . . maybe there a God."

We sat quietly and stared for a few more minutes at the television. Then, without saying a word, we all stood up and stepped outside. I was jolted awake. The air smelled like a Paris perfume shop. I inhaled deeply. "What's that smell?"

Ahmad smiled and pointed to a couple of skinny trees in a corner of his little courtyard. "Orange and lemon blossoms."

We said good night, and Sami drove me back to the Dim Dim. In my room, I listened to the tape of our conversation to make sure the sound was perfect. The story of my friend's life was like a novel; told in his unique brand of English, every phrase had the power of poetic metaphor. As I listened, I felt something growing inside me—a solemn sense of obligation. It was something I had felt only once before, when I did a program on torture survivors. Ahmad had entrusted me with his life this evening, and I was obligated to tell his story to as many people as I could.

Chapter Five

"I Am Full of Proudness"

THE WAR, WHICH had started right on time, continued on a new, improved schedule, moving faster and faster toward its inevitable conclusion. Ahmad was now finding it difficult to believe the reality unfolding around him.

"In my life I never think this could happen," he said the day after our long interview.

"What?"

"America will come and overthrow Saddam."

A sunny Friday morning two weeks into the war found the cast of characters in the Dim Dim's lobby jumping around like a bunch of first graders on the last day of school. Drivers and translators were excitedly loading reporters and their kit into vehicles. Reporters were burning up minutes on their Thuraya satellite phones to spread the word to colleagues and to their news desks. In the night, the Iraqi Army had pulled back from the ridge above Kalak and was falling back toward Mosul. The day's work would be to see how far.

In fact, the Iraqi Army hadn't fallen back that great a distance. They were in new positions overlooking a bridge spanning the

Khazer, a small river flowing toward the Great Zab. We joined the parade of cars streaming through Kalak—where we had spent the first nights of the war—heading to the Khazer. A two-lane blacktop road curved up to the top of the ridgeline, the big speed bump on the western horizon that we had been staring at for almost two weeks. At the top, rolling pastures and a few deserted villages spread out from the road. The pesh merga had a checkpoint set up. The shoulder of the road had been turned into a parking lot. Hacks milled around trying to find out why we had been stopped. Then someone went running back toward his car, grabbed his driver from a group snatching a smoke, and took off. Like pigeons in Trafalgar Square, the whole flock of us whirled into action and followed the leader without a second thought. We went a couple of kilometers farther and stopped again. The road ahead dipped down off the ridge. The bridge over the Khazer was just out of sight somewhere down there.

Again the roadside was turned into a parking lot. Sami went a little farther forward than any other driver. He told us he would wait for us, and Ahmad and I jumped out to see some action. There was a holiday atmosphere. The pesh merga were in a very good frame of mind. Reporters roamed around in the fields that sloped up from the road, trying to find a good vantage point to the bridge. They were laughing, looking through field glasses, pointing at real or imagined traces of fighting in the distance. I thought of the affluent folks of Washington, D.C., riding out to Manassas, Virginia, in 1861 to enjoy a good day's battle around Bull Run. Ahmad was caught up in the mood.

"Can you see Mosul from here?" I asked.

"No, I can feel Mosul from here."

"You're smiling."

"I'm very happy."

Ahmad took me on recon. We went up a little berm on the

left-hand side of the road to get a good view of the Khazer and the country beyond. There was another little ridge just the other side of the stream; Ahmad explained that this would have to be where the Iraqi Army was dug in overlooking the bridge. "They will try for the next coming days to control these areas as long as they can, because behind that ridge there is a flat area until Mosul. They cannot hide themselves to make useful the geographical features on the ground."

We looked around through our field glasses. Up a little rise on the other side of the road I saw a couple of American journalists chatting with Special Forces troops. I nodded toward them and we started walking over. Then Ahmad changed the subject quite abruptly. "When I was in prison my family borrowed a great sum of money from their relatives. I have to work for a long time to return back this money. So it will be very difficult for me if I remain without a job again after a few days." Ahmad's war was coming to an end. The Saddam regime was teetering on the brink; his world was about to change irrevocably, but the mundane need to provide for his family had him preoccupied and apprehensive. Our deal was that we would stay together until the war was over and he went home to Mosul. The conflict seemed unlikely to go on for more than a week. I promised I would try to find him another job.

We scampered up to the other side of the road. The pasture grass was long and smelled of spring: wildflowers, honey, and a breath of onion. The American soldiers were standing around an old Land Rover that had been chopped and refitted, its backseat and cargo area opened up so it resembled a small flatbed truck. The soldiers hovered around a large radio set with maps open and were calling in coordinates of Iraqi positions somewhere up ahead. There were already four or five reporters hanging out with them when we arrived.

"What's the situation, fellas?" I called out as we approached the little group. "When are you going to take the bridge?"

The shortest of the soldiers clearly was in charge. He looked at us for a long beat. "Hey, you gave some guys a ride the other day, didn't you?"

It was one of the guys we had towed back to Erbil the previous week. A couple of days out in the field, no shave, and the wired look of sleeplessness had made him almost unrecognizable to me. We laughed and quickly shook hands while the Special Forces guy explained to the rest of his squad, "They squared me away the other day." Then he added, "If you guys just give us a couple of minutes we're going to reestablish a sight up here and then, uh, we'll give you a story."

I took out my tape recorder and turned it on as the soldier returned to the radio huddle. Then a screaming came across the sky for about a second, followed by an explosion about fifty yards away. Nervous laughter. There was a puff of smoke disintegrating in the sky a couple of kilometers to the northwest, presumably the mark of whatever artillery piece had just fired. The soldiers called in its approximate coordinates, then turned back to the gaggle of reporters hanging around.

"That was a pretty good one there, man," laughed one of the Green Berets.

"Yeah, it was," drawled another.

The pair started a double act, joking with this strange collection of noncombatants hanging around them on a battlefield.

"You gotta love that sound, *wreeahzhiwwummm*."

"It's best when you hear that sound, because if you didn't hear that sound . . . Guess what?"

"You'd be dead."

"When you hear that boom."

And, sure enough, from the ridge on the other side of the river came a boom.

"Like that . . . get down."

No need to tell us. We were already facedown in the sweet-smelling grass. The shell exploded just behind us on the road. The Iraqi battery had us sighted in. The soldiers told us to jump into one of their Land Rovers. We piled into the back of one, all except Ahmad, who was standing around like Ferdinand the Bull, looking at a few wildflowers at his feet. I shouted at him to get in the car. We fell back about two hundred yards and got out, and the Special Forces guys started to set up their radio again. We hadn't stopped for more than forty-five seconds when another shell came screaming by. We didn't hear this round until it was almost directly on us, maybe ten feet overhead. All of us immediately jumped back into the Rover and fell back another half mile or so through the pastures. As we bounced along, more rounds came in and landed near the road.

We came to a deep fold in the landscape where there was a small command center set up. Forty or fifty pesh merga were hanging around, either sprawled on the ground trying to rest or hovering around a truck on the back of which was an enormous samovar. Kurdish rules of hospitality were not suspended because of artillery fire. We were offered chai—very good chai, as it turned out.

Ahmad chuckled. "Always good chai at the front."

"What the hell were you thinking about back there?" I demanded.

"I not afraid," he replied. "I've been shot at like that before."

"Where?"

"At the front."

"But during the Iraq-Iran War, I thought you worked in a field hospital."

"Yes, but everybody had to visit the front for a week, at least once every six months. I visited the front five times. I saw there the real war and striking like that more than shells. What is called a collection of shells coming at the same time, at once?"

"Bombardment," I answered, surprised to be conducting a class in building word power with Ahmad in the middle of combat. He made a mental note of this new entry in his English vocabulary.

"I saw many of my colleagues wounded and injured this way. It is very normal for me to see such striking. I don't worry."

We finished our chai and walked over to the Special Forces. Our colleagues were gathered around already, taking notes. One of the fellows was explaining that they had no artillery to answer the Iraqis', nor did they need any. All they needed out on this ridgetop was a "radio, rifle, and an attitude."

The leader of the group got off the phone with his headquarters and came over. First things first. Ground rules: no names. "Can we identify what unit of Special Forces you are? Green Berets?" The leader nodded yes. "Rank? Captain?" The leader nodded again. As we had already heard one of his squad members call him Pat, he became Captain Pat of the Green Berets. He looked at the half-dozen reporters. "So, it's on you."

All the questions were the same: tell us what you're doing out here. Captain Pat summarized the story. Two nights previously, the Iraqi Army pulled back, and the Green Berets, working with the pesh merga, had filled in the area. But once they were on the ridge they encountered significant resistance. The Iraqi Army had launched several counterattacks, and the combined Green Beret and pesh merga unit had repelled them. Meanwhile, the Iraqis kept up a steady artillery barrage. The Green Berets thought it was a mobile howitzer, probably Soviet-made, launching 105 mm shells. Not the biggest artillery piece, but "when it impacts, it is still quite substantial. It makes an impression on you."

They had then spent the previous night hunkered down where we were now sitting, taking artillery rounds. We had hooked up with them as they were trying to find the gun. When they saw a flash of smoke after a round was fired, they would use a high-tech piece of equipment to gauge its position and call in air support. Every warplane in America's arsenal seemed to be in the sky for them: F-16s, B-52s, even B-1 stealth bombers. The jets flew in from the Mediterranean and up from the Persian Gulf. Some pilots were in the sky for almost twenty-four hours, taking calls from all over Iraq, flying in, dropping munitions on coordinates, and going on to the next target.

The plan for the Green Berets now was to push only as far as the Khazer bridge and "deconflict other assets in country." They were authorized to go forward "as much as feasibly possible." The soldiers all snorted at that contortion of the English language, as it was unlikely they could get much farther anyway. It was also difficult to gauge how much the Iraqi Army would resist, based on the fighting around the nearby villages. "They go really hard for a bit, then you take prisoners and they say they didn't want to fight to begin with . . . so it's kind of hard to figure." Then there was the question of numbers. The Green Berets in northern Iraq were organized and deployed as Operational Detachment Alpha teams, A-teams for short. The standard size of each A-team was twelve Green Berets and one Air Force tactical air controller. Each team worked with a larger group of pesh merga. But this A-team was slightly under strength. There were only ten Green Berets and about ninety-nine pesh merga trying to secure this wide-open area. To add a degree of difficulty to the task, the Green Berets had no translator. Captain Pat shrugged, as if this was just one more problem to deal with while the enemy is trying to kill you. "The first day out here, all hell was breaking loose. We communicated by basic hand commands. Just, you know, follow me"—he made the gesture—"and they do what you do." Despite the lack of direct communication, it had all worked out. "This is their backyard. They know the tactics and the terrain the best. They know this place like the back of their hands. They can tell two ridgelines away if a guy's pesh merga or Iraqi."

This was how the war was fought in the north. One Green Beret A-team, plus a group of pesh merga, plus all the firepower the United States could muster from the sky kept the Iraqi Army units in this specific area around Mosul sufficiently occupied that they could not be withdrawn to help defend Baghdad. It was a paradigm of Donald Rumsfeld's New Model Army at work. You don't need lots of soldiers; you don't need tons of artillery pieces and the supply chain to keep them loaded up. All you need is a few Special Forces soldiers with "radios, rifles, and attitudes," working with some local guerillas. And complete control of the sky.

Now fighter jets were swarming overhead. The Iraqi artillery fire had ceased. The Green Berets needed to hook up again with their pesh merga partners out along the ridge. All the journalists walked back down to the road. Their drivers had just pulled back from the area around the bridge when the artillery rounds had started raining down. The cars were waiting a quarter of a mile or so down the road going back in the direction of Erbil. Sami was not among them. Ahmad asked another one of the drivers where he was and learned he was still down at the bridge. We walked briskly back in that direction, and there he was, on the other side of the river. The bridge that inspired all this fighting wasn't even fifty yards long. We ran and jumped into his car. The Iraqi Army was still just beyond

Khazer, dug in on a little ridge. I asked Sami what the hell he was doing down there. Sami began rattling off a torrent of Kurdish—too much, too fast for a full translation, but the gist from Ahmad was "I told you I would protect you. I will never leave you. But please do not do this again. It is very dangerous. You must be more careful."

But Sami had been the man in danger. As we wheeled away, we caught sight of the day's only casualties; a Toyota flatbed truck about twenty yards from where Sami was parked had taken a direct hit. It obviously belonged to some gasoline smugglers, because the back had several large drums of fuel that had exploded on impact, incinerating the driver and his passenger. The passenger had managed to get out of the vehicle but had been caught in a secondary blast. His corpse was on the side of the road, a mummy of charred black except for his mouth, where the lips had burned away to reveal bright white teeth.

Within two days, the excitement around the Khazer bridge had faded. After Friday's engagement, the pesh stopped letting journalists up on the ridge to see the fighting. The overcast skies had returned, so it didn't seem likely there would be bombing runs going on anyway. We decided to investigate some of the villages along the Zab south of Kalak. These villages were safe havens for smugglers bringing oil and people from all over Saddam-regime territory. We thought we might hear some interesting information. The roads to these hamlets were easily the worst in Kurdistan, mere mud and rock tracks that at this point in the early spring had yet to solidify into hard dirt and dust. They were virtually impassable. In these villages, Ahmad informed me, the "village-ians" engaged in quite bizarre sexual practices during spring and harvest—a kind of wife swapping in which the people wore masks and designated women serviced many different men.

"Aren't they Muslim?" I asked.

"Of course" came his answer. "But long before Islam, these religions were here, from the beginning of time. There is no religion strong enough to stop these things. When the war is over, you will come back and I will teach you everything about them."

The lecture was interesting, but the chassis-shattering track was not. We turned around and struggled back toward Kalak and came across two brand-new Land Cruisers stopped in a muddy stretch of road. It was a crew from CNN considering the wisdom of going any farther. Correspondent Jane Arraf waved us down and asked if the road got any better in the direction we were coming from. "Absolutely not," I told her.

Just then, someone's Thuraya rang. Ahmad's war was also Thuraya's war. The satphone that fits in a breast pocket was the journalist's new high-tech weapon. In Bosnia, journalists schlepped suitcase-sized satphones around that required the skill of a Boy Scout with merit badges in compass reading and astronomy to find the place in the sky where the satellite allegedly was. Then you had to point a massive microwave dish in that general direction in order to get a signal, while remembering not to put your hand in front of the dish to make an adjustment, lest you get a nasty burn. But in a decade, microtechnology had shrunk everything in the suitcase down to almost cell-phone size and neutralized the health-and-safety problem. The Thuraya kept the press corps in Kurdistan linked to their editors in Europe, Asia, and North America and, more important for security's sake, linked to each other.

Someone handed Jane the Thuraya. She nodded and scribbled down some notes and then handed the phone to her security man. She turned to me and told me there had been a friendly-fire incident. Details were sketchy. Somewhere on the road to Kirkuk, near a crossroad at a place called Debaga, an

American jet had bombed a convoy of pesh merga and senior KDP officials. There were many dead. John Simpson's BBC crew had been part of the convoy and had suffered casualties. It was possible Simpson was dead. The CNN drivers pulled maps out of their Land Cruisers. Sami quickly pointed out where Debaga was. We jumped into the Trooper and, with CNN following behind, we all set off.

To get to the site of the incident we had to go back through Erbil. Crowds were lining the road around the city when we got there. In the previous week the city had filled up as families that had fled to the mountains before the U.S. invasion were returning to their homes. The mood of anticipatory elation had been like the good feeling in our car, magnified by a factor of half a million souls. The price of gas masks in the bazaar had dropped from around 180 dollars to 35. Locals laughed even as they were complaining about the lack of fighting. They wanted a chance for their pesh merga to get some payback against the Iraqi Army. But on this day, as we raced through Erbil toward Kirkuk, the smiles had been wiped off their faces. Thousands upon thousands of people lined the main road south to Kirkuk, watching the occasional Red Crescent ambulance race by toward Erbil's main hospital. The pesh merga checkpoints were chaos. Discipline had pretty much disappeared, as the fighters who were supposed to check people heading for the front joined their comrades to get a glimpse of the ambulances or to swarm around one of the eyewitnesses and pump them for information.

We forced our way through the checkpoints, marking the oddball selection of vehicles racing at top speed back toward the capital: troop-carrying trucks, taxis, and late-model Mercedeses carrying grim-faced officials. The highway cut through a small hill just before the Debaga crossroad. An angry group of pesh merga stopped us. We jumped out and left Sami to negotiate further passage with them while Ahmad and I ran to the top of the hill.

A real battle was in progress. Green Berets and pesh merga were taking on a squadron of Iraqi tanks out on the plain. A pair of F-14 Tomcats were darting around the sky. The air force wasn't waiting for good weather to go to work anymore. We heard the jets long before we saw one of them drop out of the cloud cover, lift its left wing, dip to the right, and release two precision-guided bombs. We saw the puffs of smoke out on the plain where they landed, about three seconds before we heard the explosions. The cloud and speed of the jets were the reason for the accident, the remains of which we could see just ahead of us.

The pesh merga, whose mood remained grim, let us through to get a better look. Ahmad wondered aloud what they were so upset about. "In every war," he said, "we have these accidents. We must expect them."

We walked through the smoking, still-hot wreckage. It was clear what had happened. By a crossroad, in a ditch, was an abandoned Iraqi tank. The convoy must have stopped to take a look. A kilometer or so farther along was another crossroad, with more tanks deployed in a field. It was this second crossroad that was the target, but the pilot had dropped out of the cloud and seen the first crossroad, a tank, and armed men swarming around it and had dropped the bomb. Most of the pesh merga were in the back of a truck that was apparently carrying munitions. These had detonated when the bomb went off and added to the carnage. Seventeen pesh merga were dead. KDP leader Massoud Barzani's brother had been grievously wounded in the head. There was one other fatality. Not John Simpson of the BBC, but his translator, a Kurdish man named Kamaran Muhammad. The incident had taken place no more than an hour earlier, but the bodies had already been removed. The roadside was still covered with splotches of blood and charred bits of flesh.

About two hundred yards farther down the road, a Green Beret A-team had set up operations in an abandoned Iraqi position looking out over the plain. The soldiers were focused entirely on the battle in front. They seemed utterly oblivious to the carnage just behind them. One soldier said, "We were smoking tanks out there, then heard this bang behind us. We sent our medics over. That was all we could do." Another soldier walked by and grunted, "This is war. Shit happens."

The battle had been going on for a while. The American position was filled with discarded casings for Javelin surface-to-surface antitank missiles. There was no need for field glasses here. The Iraqi tanks were visible just ahead. A patrol of pesh merga suddenly emerged from the landscape just below us and was taken over to an American officer with a map spread on the hood of a truck. One of the pesh merga began to point out locations on the map. The officer spoke something like pidgin to this scout, though it was hard to tell whether the pesh understood a word. I asked one of the Special Forces fellows, "Who started the fight?" "We did," he said with a satisfied smile. Up until now, U.S. troops and the pesh merga had been under orders simply to take ground the Iraqis abandoned, not to seize any. So this little battle represented an evolution in the fighting in the north.

I walked back to the wreckage and examined it more thoroughly. How anyone at all had survived seemed a miracle. By now the Thuraya-age bush telegraph had delivered a flock of journalists to the site along with a KDP spokesman. The reporters were so intent on determining what kind of jet had dropped which kind of bomb on the convoy that they didn't even hear an Iraqi mortar round land about fifty yards away. I did. A few minutes later an Iraqi tank round landed in front of the U.S. position. It seemed like a good idea to pull back.

We walked a few hundred meters away from the crowd. Sami's wife had made a picnic lunch for us, and we squatted on the road to eat. Going off the road, even onto the shoulder, seemed a bad idea. This area had not yet been checked for mines. We gnawed at baked chicken and watched the jets break out of the thick cloud cover. It was easier to see the planes against this background than when they seemed to streak out of the sun. The bombs could be seen quite clearly as they were being released and just as easily followed along their wobbling progress as they hurtled toward their targets.

A few days previously, Ahmad had asked what the English name Moorhouse meant. He had been reading an article by Geoffrey Moorhouse, a wonderful English journalist and travel writer. Ahmad understood the word *house,* obviously, but was confused by *moor.* Did it refer to a North African, as in Othello, the "Moor of Venice"? Was the journalist possibly of Arab descent? Without going into a lengthy discourse about Heath-cliff, Cathy, and *Wuthering Heights,* I had given him an explanation of what an English moor is. Standing a few hundred yards from the smoldering cars, the thick gray cloud above us and the hilly, treeless sheep pastures around and about us suddenly reminded me of English moorland. I explained to Ahmad that this landscape is what an English moor looks like. "Do moors make people sad?" he asked.

"They are places people go for solitude," I answered.

War stopped in the north for us after the friendly-fire incident. With no battles to watch, the days seemed longer than twenty-four hours as we waited for the inevitable fall of Saddam. We resumed the scramble for little bits of news. Iraqi Army deserters were being held near Dyana, in the mountains halfway back to Iran. We decided to drive there and see if we could interview them. Dyana the town was a dump, a scar in the middle of a wide, high valley surrounded by mountains. Just outside town a river cut a deep gorge that ran right through the peaks. It was more beautiful than one could bear, and this helped make up for the fact that when we found the prisoners' camp, some very tough pesh merga wouldn't let us near them. From a distance we watched the prisoners playing soccer; we could hear them laughing like young, single men in the suburbs playing a game at the local high school after work. They seemed to be having a very good time; death had passed them by, and soon they would go home.

The next day Ahmad had Sami take us on some back roads to a place a little north of the Khazer bridge, a stub of a mountain called Maqloub. There was an Iraqi Army listening post on the top that the pesh merga had seized in the previous days. We drove past some wreckage from recent fighting and started up the mountain on a switchback road. Ahmad told me Maqloub was where he had brought Afrah when they were courting. From the top there were panoramic views over the green plain of the Fertile Crescent. On the way down, we stopped at an Assyrian Christian monastery that had been carved out of the side of the mountain. St. Matthew's Monastery had been founded in the fourth century as a schism split the Christian world into Eastern and Western churches. Since then it had been a refuge for believers in Jesus. The number of monks had dwindled to a handful, but to this day, Assyrian Christians make an annual pilgrimage there. It was even reported that Saddam Hussein maintained living quarters in the monastery. It didn't seem impossible—if the dictator ever needed to hide, who would think to look for the new Saladin in a Christian sanctuary?

We continued to mark time. The next day we drove a circuit north to an area near Dohuk where Saddam had built a little city for Arabs transplanted from the south. It was abandoned, as were all the army fortifications halfway back to Mosul. There was time for one more of Ahmad's lessons on the religions of his homeland that trace their origins back through history to fire-worshipping and darkness. We stopped in Lalish to visit the Yezidi shrine. "Devil worshippers" he called the Yezidis. "They don't believe Satan is in hell." The Yezidis, he explained, pray facing the sun and believe that Lucifer was not cast out from heaven: rather he is an archangel and the creator of the material world we inhabit. He was forgiven by God for all his sins of pride. He did not tempt Adam and Eve in the Garden of Eden. The Yezidis seem to have developed a form of worship and ethnic identity from a little dollop of every religion that had passed through the region since the beginning of recorded history: Judaism, Zoroastrianism, Christianity, and Islam. There are about a million Yezidis worldwide, but their spiritual and ethnic origin is here.

We went to the shrine complex, or *khalwa*. It was swamped with refugees from the surrounding villages. In times of upheaval, common in this area, the Yezidi had learned through bloody experience that they would be attacked, whether by Kurds or Arabs. Laundry was dangling from every window in the multistory buildings surrounding the shrine, and a smell of too many unwashed bodies crammed together hung in the air. We were given chai and then invited to go into the shrine, a squat building topped by a huge dome in the form of a spherical cone. We removed our shoes and went from gray light back two and a half thousand years into darkness. Tallow candles barely illuminated the gloom as we stooped through low-arched doors to the center of the shrine. Faded peacock drawings could be seen on the walls. The peacock is the earthly representation of Lucifer for the Yezidis. There was no other adornment in the khalwa. We were as close as we could get to standing inside a temple that was exactly as it had been when the house of Abraham was being split by the man whose apostles believed he was the Messiah. The darkness and weight of millennia pressed down; the smell was grim, fifteen hundred years of tallow and bare feet. We left quickly.

"How do these religions survive?" I asked Ahmad as we began to make our way back to Erbil. He said the number of different groups was something unique to this part of Iraq.

"For example," he explained, "I am a Shabak. We are considered Kurds, but we are Shi'a, not Sunni. We are our own subgroup inside Kurds."

He had no explanation why this particular section of Iraq should hold so many different religious-ethnic groups. The conversation moved on to the nature of belief and the hold it has not just on individuals but also on groups of people. My friend was a rationalist. His Islam was part of his cultural inheritance. He looked with a mixture of pity and understanding on those who defined themselves only through their religious belief and observance. All the adherents of minority religions shared a history in his country, an endless cycle of violence caused by professing their religion, but persecution only deepened their faith, which brought on them more violence. Ahmad was adamant that all these strange religions needed the protection of whatever government replaced Saddam.

"This is why I say we cannot have Islamic state in Iraq. We must be respectful for all these religions. That is why only through an Iraqi national identity can the state exist."

The cloud began to lift as we worked our way back toward Erbil. I still had the scent of millennia of wax and unwashed feet from the Yezidi shrine about me. Ahmad and Sami were chatting in Kurdish. Sometimes they went on for minutes, oblivious of the foreigner in the backseat, which could be quite annoying.

"What are you guys talking about?" I demanded.

"Sami wants to know if you will help him and his family get out of Iraq if Saddam comes back."

"Is he joking?" I said with a casual laugh. "Tell him, yeah, sure, no problem."

"No, he is very serious," Ahmad said. "He cannot believe Saddam will go without a fight. Sami's afraid because he works with Americans he will be killed."

"Really?"

"Really."

Sami, who had waited for us by the Khazer bridge while very real shells came down all around him, was now afraid of something that seemed utterly improbable. Baghdad was on the verge of falling. The Iraqi Army in the north had never made an offensive move against the Kurds. Saddam was absolutely finished. But Sami's fear was not without basis. In 1996, as Saddam's army and the KDP headed for Sulaimaniyah, American NGO workers pulled out. At the UN's headquarters in the city I had watched Americans who were leaving town hugging weeping, fearful members of their staff who had to stay behind. To have had an American job is not a good thing at times like these. This is the way things work in war zones: we go; they stay. If the whole escapade falls apart, American journalists and relief workers get evacuated and can be swimming in a hotel pool, all expenses paid, by evening. Our translators and drivers return to their houses and wait in fear for reprisal against those who collaborated with the Great Satan.

I reached across into the front seat and put my hand on my

driver's shoulder. I looked at Ahmad. "Tell Sami he has nothing to fear." I paused so he could translate that sentence. "Saddam is finished, but if anything happens, I will make sure he is safe. And his family." When Ahmad finished translating I turned to Sami, who spoke some English, and said, "Okay?" It was an easy promise to make, since I knew I would never have to honor it. Sami brightened up. The mood in the Trooper changed. Sami promised that he would drive me to Baghdad. Ahmad chipped in: "We will eat fish on the banks of the Tigris, and we can decide if the fish is better in Mosul or Baghdad." "Then," Sami declared, "I will drive you to Basra. I know every road there from the war. We will be safe." I added: "Then, after Basra, we'll go to Kuwait and go to the beach for a swim." Ahmad translated. Sami laughed and made one more request. When I got back to London I had to send him a big photo of "Hajji" Bush. *Hajji* is the Muslim term of respect for those who make the pilgrimage to Mecca, and Sami always referred to George W. Bush as Hajji Bush. I promised to send him a poster when I got back.

It was late afternoon as we reached the outskirts of Erbil, and there were as much noise and traffic as if it were New Year's Eve. Every teenager in the town seemed to be cruising. They danced on the backs of their little Toyota flatbeds; arms dangled from the windows of school buses and pounded on the metal sides; motorbikes weaved in and out of traffic with two or three kids on each one. They were chanting something about Saddam. We came to a halt at a chaotic intersection, and Ahmad yelled out to some kids in a school bus: "What's going on?" The Americans have taken Baghdad, the kids answered. Saddam is finished. We crawled through the streets of Erbil while the noise grew. Many of these teenagers would have been among the children dragged to the mountains during the failed uprising of 1991. This was their liberation. The Monster was gone for sure.

In the evening we went back out to Kalak to see how far the Green Berets had pushed forward. We were stopped by a platoon of pesh merga and turned back. In the village of Kalak we stopped at a sweet shop where around fifty pesh merga were sipping tea, eating nuts, and watching TV. Over and over, Saddam's statue was being dragged down by the Marines in slow-motion replay. Every time it fell, the pesh cheered.

"Tonight, I must drink wine," Ahmad declared. Tonight was certainly a night to celebrate with something more than tea and nuts. My friend had an arrangement with his very devout wife. If he occasionally felt compelled to drink alcohol, that was okay, but he was not allowed to come home until the alcohol left his breath. When we got back to Erbil, I booked Ahmad a room in the Dim Dim, then took him to the dining room for supper and wine. We sat with some colleagues and ordered. The wine hit him fast and he began to gabble.

"When I get home this afternoon I watch the statue coming down. It took so long. I cannot believe this will happen. Shawkat and Rafat were watching with me. When the statue come down I leap up and start to dance. Then I run to the window and start to tear down the plastic sheets. I say, come on, boys, help me. They did not know what to do. I said, come on: cry, loudly cry. But they ran to their mother. Mommy, mommy, come quick. Daddy is going mad." He laughed and we poured him more wine.

"I am full of proudness."

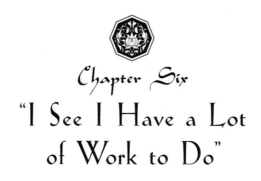

Chapter Six

"I See I Have a Lot of Work to Do"

IN THE END, there was never a battle for Mosul. With Baghdad captured and Kirkuk seized almost bloodlessly by the pesh merga, all it took was a couple of days of B-52 strikes, and Saddam's regime in Mosul simply evaporated in the middle of the night, leaving a city of a million and a half people in a state of anarchy. The news spread quickly to Erbil. It was safe for Ahmad to go home.

The day, April 11, was right for celebration. Spring had taken root. The sky was what you expect it to be every day if you've spent much time in the Middle East: cloudless and as blue as Persian turquoise. Ahmad and Sami turned up on time, the back of Sami's Trooper packed with their gear and that of Ahmad's oldest son. Sindibad, seized with a holiday mood, had shut down his tailoring business and was coming with us. We threw my bags on top and headed out. All of Erbil was seized with manic, holiday energy. The roads were crowded with folks planning a day out in liberated Iraq.

In the end, the Green Berets and pesh merga never took the Khazer bridge. Iraqi soldiers tried to blow it up as they ran away . . . but the charge didn't destroy the span, just collapsed part of it.

The bridge was quickly shored up and one lane was opened. By the time we got there, a massive traffic jam had up built around it. Every reporter in Erbil was in the melee, along with every smuggler, every refugee, and every wannabe looter. The pictures of looting beamed in on satellite TV from other parts of Iraq had inflamed imaginations in Erbil. Now Mosul was an open city without any functioning authority, and the Kurds were going to get their share. There were at least a thousand cars backed up along the road and up and down the hillsides where we had come under fire with Captain Pat and the Green Berets a week and a half earlier. After an hour of arguing amid vehicular violence, we pushed through and onto the bridge, tearing the bumper off an ancient Nissan flatbed as we did. We just kept going. The curses of the Nissan's driver followed us for a bit, but once we'd crossed the one-lane bridge, the road was clear, and Sami floored it.

The pesh merga were trying to establish some order and had set up checkpoints, but we barely stopped at them. I simply screamed out the window my attempt at the Arabic for American reporter—*Sahafi Americi*—and like Ali Baba saying "Open sesame" at the gates of the robbers' den, barriers parted, and we were waved on toward the city.

The word liberation has become debased and politicized by ideologues, but in its pure state liberation is a marvelous infection of the mind. In an instant it removes decades of disappointment from the soul. Ahmad was giddy with liberation. His life was flashing before him at seventy miles an hour. Every half mile we traveled there was some new memory to recall, but we were going so fast that before he could finish one story, we had passed someplace that inspired a different tale for him to tell. Sindibad, quiet, shy because of his poor English, was smiling a smile that threatened to burst his face.

The traffic began to thicken as we approached Mosul's out-skirts. The roadside was a surreal carnival. A blizzard of paper had settled along it, mile after mile, as if every file in every Mosul office had been thrown into the sky and settled into paper drifts. There were minutes of Ba'ath Party meetings, pur-chase orders from government agencies, even elementary school records: the bureaucratic detritus of a hideous dictator-ship. People were flowing in and out of ransacked government stores and supply depots. Kurds from Erbil and outlying vil-lages who had made it through the traffic jam at Khazer were piling their flatbed trucks with unlikely combinations of goods: blankets, bedding, three-blade ceiling fans, electrical junction boxes trailing wiring along the ground; wreckage and junk that later sat in Erbil's bazaars for months, waiting for a buyer to see some value in it. One boy of around twelve was pushing a giant tractor wheel twice as tall as himself down the roadside. Pesh merga had improvised towropes around Iraqi Army artillery pieces and were dragging them behind their trucks back toward Erbil. A couple of guys were driving a regime tank in the same direction. The big rig was belching smoke and clanking along at maybe three miles an hour.

The World Food Programme warehouse was being ran-sacked. A wheelbarrow went by, pushed by a couple of teenagers. Call it historical symmetry or historical irony, but it was packed high with sacks of rice from Vietnam. A fire had been set in the warehouse, but bags of rice smoke more than they burn, so thick smoke rose up from it without much flame.

As we got inside the city limits the noise level rose: a call and response among human shouts, car horns, and bullhorns, with gunshots providing an irregular rhythmic beat. We turned north off the main road and went through a warren of streets to the home of Ahmad's in-laws. In the narrow road a group of boys were playing while men stood around talking. Ahmad stepped out of the car, and you could see the men scatter up and down to spread the word. The regime really must have collapsed. Ahmad was back.

We stopped in front of his brother-in-law Ayad's house and were sucked into it by a gravitational field of welcome. At the center of this was Ahmad's mother-in-law, Sindibad's grandmother. If liberation for men is evinced by childish giddiness, then for women liberation is expressed in tears of relief. The grandmother hugged Sindibad for what seemed like an hour. An ocean of tears flooded down her face. She wailed a pitched note that balanced joy, fear, and warning to anyone who thought of taking her firstborn grandson away. She reached over Sindibad for Ahmad and wrapped her fingers into his. Then, without letting Sindibad go, she reached a hand out, pulled me over, and kissed my cheeks.

When it was time to go to work, to see the city, Sindibad's grandmother wouldn't let him come with us.

And first we had to drink tea. Ahmad and his wife's brothers spoke rapidly. Even now, with Ahmad among them, living proof that Saddam was finished, they were skeptical.

"They say Saddam is here."

"Where?"

"He was seen at a mosque three days ago."

"No way."

"I know, but this is the infection of dictatorism."

How could you offer these men, university professors most of them, proof that it was over? That it wasn't all another cunning trick by Saddam? They couldn't, for example, call someone else and get a second opinion. All the phone systems were down. The electricity was out, so they couldn't watch their city being sacked on al-Jazeera. And even though there was an American in the room, that wasn't enough to convince them to let go of their fears. In planning for the war, in waiting for the war, what no one understood on either the American side or the Iraqi side was how profoundly a quarter of a century of living under Saddam had affected people. The United States had destroyed Saddam's regime on the streets of Iraq. But in people's inner places—their hearts, minds, and souls—the dictator's rule still existed.

Friends were crowding the street, verifying for themselves that the return of Ahmad was real, not a rumor. Soon he was surrounded, and for a little while Ahmad forgot about me. In these weeks, as we had become friends, he was living in my world, speaking my language. Standing in this group of men, speaking Arabic, gesticulating animatedly—this was the first time I had observed him wholly inside his own culture. Surrounded by these men, he didn't seem as much of a dreamer. He was being listened to with a level of respect that added weight to his presence. My friend had told a lot of stories about who he had once been in Mosul, and sometimes the stories sounded slightly exaggerated. But watching him in the middle of this knot of fifteen or twenty men, I could see that he really was the grassroots activist he had always claimed to be.

We went on to the house of Ahmad's daughter Sana. At a certain point in life, parents give up trying to pretend they don't have favorite children. Among Ahmad's eight I could see who they were. Sana was one of them. Favored children don't always return a parent's affection measure for measure, but Sana did. When she heard her father's voice in the courtyard she began to ululate from deep inside her house. She greeted him at the door, a toddler on her hip. The boy took one look at the stranger hugging his mother and burst into tears. My friend introduced his grandson and namesake: "This is also Ahmad." The boy refused to get into the spirit of liberation and reunion.

He bawled inconsolably. According to his mother he had been nervous since the American bombing had begun in earnest several nights previously.

We drank the inevitable chai Sana offered and Ahmad debriefed his daughter on the true state of play in the city. Sana explained that anarchy had been building for days. There was no food, no water, and for the men, no work. Her family had been living off existing stores of rice and beans. There was gunfire throughout the day and night, but nobody could tell who was fighting whom.

We set off for the center of Mosul. The giddiness of liberation began to leak out of us in the car. The degradation of the city became more noticeable. In the months leading up to the war the most basic services had stopped. Sana said rubbish hadn't been collected for several months. It covered every empty lot, rotting in the warm spring sun. We could have been in Haiti rather than the country with the second-largest known oil reserves on the face of the planet. Schools were smoldering. Their yards were full of desks and chairs destroyed by looters who had no use for them. The bazaar, the heartbeat of any Arab city, was flatlining, completely shut down. With no shops open, thousands of people who had no interest in looting were wandering the streets and parks around the old walls of Nineveh in a daze.

For weeks Ahmad had chattered constantly about the beauty of Mosul. As we drove over the Tigris River Bridge into the Old City, I could see where Mosul had once been beautiful enough to deserve its nickname, the Pearl of the North. The Old City was a fantasy of Ali Baba architecture, with domes set against the sky. But the buildings were falling apart, the streets rutted with potholes. The most basic maintenance by the state had been neglected for decades. And our fish lunch would have to wait. The Tigris was in spring flood, and those who usually operated the dams upstream were not reporting for work. The terraces of the riverside fish restaurants were under eight feet of water.

On the west bank of the Tigris, the streets of the Old City were empty. Empty streets signal danger. Sami pointed the car toward the sound of gunshots. In Diwassa Square, the main public space of Mosul, stood the National Bank. It was being looted. The air around its grand front doors was filled with money confetti. The steps were covered in dinars. Despite a thin stream of smoke wafting out the doors, dozens of men were running inside to grab sacks full of the stuff, although Saddam's face on the bills had already rendered them useless.

The sense of danger was equal to anything we had experienced when we came under fire with Special Forces near the Khazer bridge. In every riot there is always a place where you know you will be safe. You look down a street and see police mustering and know that on the other side of those cops order and its first cousin, safety, exist. But in Diwassa Square there were no police. In the whole city there were no police. There were no American soldiers. There was simply no recognized authority to control the growing madness. At any moment, in any place, fighting could begin, and once it came toward you there was no place to escape to.

Some Kurdish pesh merga had taken it upon themselves to restore order. Most of the looters were Arabs and seemed disinclined to submit to Kurdish authority. The pesh merga were firing into the bank. The Arabs were firing back.

Sami pulled up about fifty yards away among a knot of spectators. A short, bald man in his forties was holding forth for the crowd on the meaning of democracy. He was unleashing a torrent of verbal abuse on America in general, and George Bush in particular. Ahmad shook his head in despair. "He says freedom means he can say any stupid thing. I must tell him this is not so." While the two began to argue, I grabbed my gear and headed toward the bank to record the gun battle. The firing was erratic. It seemed more like a Hollywood shoot-out, with Bonnie and Clyde inside the bank facing off against local law enforcement. Lots of wasted rounds of ammunition, nothing at all like the targeted, focused firing of life-and-death combat.

When I returned to the car, Ahmad was conducting a seminar/argument/political rally for the crowd. The subject apparently was the responsibilities of the citizen in a free society. The bald little man was still screaming his hatred of George Bush for doing nothing to stop the looting. Ahmad was losing his temper because the guy refused to acknowledge that it wasn't up to the Americans to stop Iraqis from looting. Iraqis themselves had to learn a bit of self-control if democracy was to work, he shouted; meanwhile, the guns continued to go off behind us. Ahmad was oblivious to the gunshots and the anger growing in the crowd. It wasn't the appropriate time for this dialogue. Sami looked at me, very concerned. We both pulled Ahmad out of the melee growing around him, jumped in the car, and drove back over the Tigris.

Now there was no joy left in the day. It was clear we couldn't stay in Mosul. The hotels had all been looted, and it would be an imposition on Sana or anyone else in Ahmad's family to stay with them. We started driving back to Sana's house in silence. Suddenly Ahmad shouted, "Look, look at that." He pointed at a smoldering wreck of a building.

"What is it?"

"It's the Security Management building."

"Security Management?"

"I was imprisoned here many times. Stop the car, Sami."

We ran across the road and looked at what was left of the building. It was three stories high. In half the building those stories had been pancaked down to the ground by what had clearly been a B-52 strike.

"I have been violated here by all kinds of violations."

"You mean tortured?"

"Yeah, tortured," Ahmad said. "And there were two floors underground. And I was always at the deepest one." Then he began to laugh.

Between the road and what would have been the entrance to the building was the inevitable massive picture of Saddam. It was one of the very few in the city that had not been vandalized. But with his security service's torture headquarters heavily smoking behind his portrait, there was a satisfying irony in looking at Saddam's smiling portrait. So the day went: elation at returning to his hometown, despair at the wanton destruction of that same town, elation again at seeing this terrible symbol of the regime a smoldering ruin.

At Sana's house we went up on the roof to count the columns of smoke from major fires around the town. There was no longer a fire brigade in Mosul, so they burned quite thoroughly. There were five pillars of fire, their smoke climbing straight up into the cloudless sky, then being sheared to the south by the breeze, forming a single thin pall over the city. We were upwind, and the roof was bathed in sharp spring sunlight. Ahmad pulled out a pack of cigarettes and offered me one. In an open lot behind Sana's home some teenage boys were playing soccer. In almost every situation of social disintegration, when you get away from the epicenter of violence you will find some small group of people, usually kids, doing something of the most utterly banal normalcy, like kicking a football around, completely oblivious to the fact that their entire world is violently changing. It's a grace note that resonates out of the most cacophonous chords. I stared at the game for a good long while, trying to let the emotional and physical intensity of the day drain away.

My mind went back to the scene at the bank. If Ahmad had kept arguing for another few minutes he would have been lynched. I felt guilty because maybe he had engaged that little bald guy on my account. If I hadn't been there, I wondered if the scene would have even happened. Reporters disturb the social ecology of the events they cover. Although we try to tiptoe around the edges of things and let them happen as if we weren't there, we always worry that our presence eggs on people whose societies are coming apart to even more extreme behavior. If you work in broadcast journalism, you know for a fact your presence does this. The minute a microphone and camera appear in a volatile situation—and we wouldn't spend time in an ordinary one—the effect is like throwing a bit of gasoline on a nicely burning log fire. And to report accurately, you have to think through how much of what you recorded occurred because you were there and how much would have happened anyway. If a riot happens in a city and there is no journalist there to record it, does it make a sound?

On that day in Mosul, if you were an American journalist you were also a participant in events. There was no choice in the matter. With no American military visible on the street, we became the de facto representatives of the conquering power. As in Rumsfeld's, Wolfowitz's, and Perle's fantasy, strangers kissed me on the cheek and washed me with tears of gratitude because I was an American; but within hours, in a terrible fore-shadowing of the neocon nightmare that postinvasion Iraq soon became, other strangers came up and berated me for the lawlessness engulfing their city. They demanded I tell President Bush what was going on. I tried to explain to one fellow outside the gates of the university that I was merely a journalist and didn't have that kind of contact with the president. He looked at me skeptically. I could tell my explanation didn't wash. Later I realized it was because in his world, journalists were functionaries of the state, half of them spies for the Ba'ath Party.

I asked Ahmad what on earth he had been arguing about down by the bank.

"I tried to make them clear what is the real meaning of democracy. Democracy is not just to talk as free as he can. I tried to make them understand how to protect their homeland, how to fight against dictatorism and prevent violation to human rights. I feel very sad. I didn't expect that my people is going to behave in such a strange manner. To rob everything from the former institutions just to express themselves that they are against Saddam. Well, if you are against Saddam, try to know how to protect these formal institutions, how to rebuild your homeland."

I should never have questioned my friend's motivation or assumed it was him defending me that put him in peril. There were more important things at stake that day than whether I got good tape. Ahmad went on for a while talking about the future. "I want to live as human being, not an animal." He paused for a moment. "I would like to travel." It had been decades since he had been abroad. He had visited Paris once for a weekend. He wanted to go back. But even as Ahmad spoke of this desire to see the world, he was pulled back by a sense of responsibility to his country. There were so many things he had to do to make his people understand the new era they were in: start a political party, open an institute to teach people how to live in a democratic society, to develop politicians "who are not ideologically domesticated."

"Ideologically domesticated?" I asked, confused by this choice bit of Ahmad-speak.

"Like communists or socialists or Ba'ath Party or nationalists, or Muslims," he explained. "All of them are domesticated ideologically. They are like animals repeating what their masters teach them . . . I now understand 'quite-ly' that I'm going need a long time to enlight those people. To make them at least understand some meanings—not all meanings—of democracy, modernism." He paused, thinking through the precise words he wanted to say. "They don't know how to negotiate between themselves. They don't know how to have a clear dialogue between themselves." He sighed audibly. "I hope I will be able to do something."

We picked up Sindibad and headed back to Erbil. As we left Mosul, men from the mosques were marching around with bullhorns, urging people to return their looted goods. The message was brotherly: bring the stolen stuff to the mosque and no questions will be asked. On the highway back to Erbil, vigilantes were stopping Kurdish trucks and forcibly removing the mattresses, refrigerators, filing cabinets, and useless bits of electrical wiring piled in the back. At the Khazer bridge, it was the morning in reverse. After about an hour, we got across and drove to the Dim Dim. The owner had kindly not rented out my room. He knew I'd be back. As I dragged my bags out of Sami's SUV, I tried to console my friends. "Tomorrow will be better."

It was, marginally. American soldiers were arriving in small numbers in Mosul. Little committees were forming around places like schools and hospitals to protect them. Amazingly, people had heeded the call from the mosques and lots of looted stuff had been brought to them. At one mosque across the street from the University of Mosul, three doctors had set up an impromptu clinic in a room full of medical equipment and drugs looted the previous day from the medical school and returned during the night. The courtyard was piled high with refrigerators and other stuff looted from dormitories.

A crowd followed us into the makeshift clinic. They pushed forward, trying to get their voices into the microphone. The one with the loudest voice was demanding the United States restore order by putting in place a new dictator. Ahmad translated: "As America brought and supported Saddam Hussein for twenty-four years, we want another one in a signed contraction to bring another dictator. But better than Saddam Hussein."

A small, bespectacled man tugged at my elbow. He told me he had been a diplomat assigned to the United Nations. His English was certainly good enough for that claim to seem plausible. I prefaced a question to him with "So, the war is over—" He interrupted. "Not yet."

Then he continued. "I know and I understand very well that there are no mass destructions weapons in Iraq. And Mr. Bush knows that very well. And you will understand that in the next days. They will find nothing. But they come here for political issues. We think maybe they come to help Israel in this region."

"But don't you think there is a benefit to you in the Saddam regime being destroyed?"

"No, there are benefits, I understand that. But the most benefits are to the Americans."

Afrah, and Ahmad's youngest child, Zainab, joined us for this second day of liberation. Zainab was six and her sister Sana's children were her age. They were more natural playmates than her adolescent brothers, so Zainab stayed in Mosul. But, as on the previous day, the reality in the city was too depressing, and the adults all returned to Erbil.

The morning after Saddam's statue fell Ahmad had said, "I have spent the happiest days of my life with you." It seemed a fairly typical example of exaggerated Arabic rhetoric, a way to express his joy at the dictator's downfall. "No,

I mean it precisely. I have spent the happiest days of my life with you."

"Ahmad, the happiest days of your life were the days your children were born," I said.

"You know what I mean."

I did. Now I wondered if he still felt these were the best days of his life.

As the days went by, disappointment settled across the family. Only little Zainab seemed to be okay. She stayed in Mosul with her nieces and nephews. Each day brought new reports of violence in the city. Throughout the period of "major combat operations" there was never a battle for Mosul, but in the first week after the regime collapsed, between thirty and fifty people were killed in fighting among Iraqis. For weeks Ahmad had been planning to move from Erbil back to Mosul as soon as the war was over. Now the war had ended, and instead all his Mosul family moved to the little six-room house in Erbil. His whole tribe was gathered inside his gates: eight children, six grandchildren, and two sons-in-law.

It was also time for me to go home. I could leave via Iran, but it seemed insane to travel east for two days in order to fly home to the west. Besides, I didn't want to rely on the not-so-tender mercies of Iranian border bureaucrats. The Turkish border was still closed. With the Bush administration, egged on by Ariel Sharon, rattling its verbal saber at the Syrian government, an exit via Syria didn't seem like a good idea for an American Jew. The U.S. Army was flying vast quantities of supplies from Germany to Harir. I thought I might thumb a lift back to Ramstein Air Base on an empty plane. Sami, Ahmad, and I drove over the two mountain ridges to Harir, where a very pleasant reserve officer told me he had no problem with the request but I needed to contact Centcom (U.S. Central Command), which I did. Centcom told me it wouldn't be possible for me to fly back on an empty plane because I was not an "embed."

The only way out was via Jordan, which meant traveling to Baghdad, and that meant waiting for the road to be safe. After the elation, fear had begun to creep into everyone. Fear was expressed as caution. It was best to drive to the city in a convoy. David Filipov and Anna Badkhen were ready to leave, and they decided to be part of the group. The old team was reassembled, but then Sami suddenly decided not to drive his car to Baghdad. He had heard that cars with Erbil license plates were being shot at or stolen in the capital. Then David's and Anna's driver panicked and refused to drive the route at all. There was a brief moment when it looked like we might be trapped for a few more days. But Sami said he knew of some taxi drivers who would take us, and he and Ahmad agreed to accompany us to Baghdad. Crisis averted. Sami went off and hired a group of ancient taxis for the trip. The cars had probably been looted from Kuwait in 1990, driven into the ground in Baghdad, and then sold to the Kurds when they were just this side of scrap. The taxis had Baghdad plates, and their drivers had already made the run a few times. They'd been shot at only once or twice, so the route was deemed safe. These pesh-merchants, men who face death for money, asked two hundred bucks apiece to do the trip.

Ahmad and Sami arrived at the Dim Dim before sunrise on April 18. I had been in Erbil one day less than a month. They loaded up the ancient taxis with our gear, found themselves room, and then we were off.

We left Erbil at dawn. There was sporadic fighting in the Arab villages along the southern end of the Baghdad route, and the hope was to get past these places before people started waking up. As the sun rose, the moon was just setting, and for one moment they shared the same angle in the sky, facing each other from east to west, a celestial honor guard saluting our departure. We rolled at breakneck speed between them. The taxis flashed across the dew-slicked, emerald-green plain that had been our war zone. It was like a film set just after production is finished: empty, but full of echoes of what had been enacted there.

There was the pesh merga camp at Dola Bakir, where we watched the distant action in the first days of the war. Empty. We slashed along the road past the fields through which we had walked to get a glimpse of Saddam's army. The fields were now dotted with the calling cards of a mine clearing team from the Mine Action Group: metal stakes topped by red triangles with a skull and crossbones painted on them, warning of explosive devices underfoot. We zoomed past massive, ruined barracks of the Iraqi Army. We had seen them from a ridge fifteen miles to the east while hanging around with Green Berets as they called in the air strikes that destroyed them. The roadside south of Kirkuk was lined with boots and uniforms. The Iraqi Army had literally walked out of its shoes and stripped off its clothes as it melted away. We passed from the green of Kurdistan into the desert. The change of landscape was almost immediate—there was perhaps a quarter-mile where grass and sand fought each other, and then the desert won.

We made Baghdad without incident in a bit more than four and a half hours. It was instructive to see the city. The war in the north had been a quiet affair. Not in Baghdad. We came in from the east side of the city, following the route the First Marines had taken. The main boulevard was lined with the detritus of a massive battle between Iraqi tanks and American attack helicopters. The tanks had been precisely and absolutely demolished; they were metal coffins for the crews that manned them.

The city was alive with a furious, incoherent energy. The

streets were filled with people, although most stores were closed. Traffic jams were building up despite the fact that there were no electricity, no water, and no place to work. We headed for the Palestine Hotel, where I was supposed to pick up a car to take me the rest of the way to Amman. Here, in downtown Baghdad, you could see what precision bombing really meant. Government buildings utterly destroyed by air strikes and residential neighborhoods just behind them untouched.

The scene at the Palestine Hotel, where the foreign press was headquartered, was one of panic. The Palestine Hotel is huge and sits in grounds of many acres. It seemed like every person who had been interviewed by a journalist in the last three months was trying to get in. There were thousands of Baghdadis waving pieces of paper and reporters' business cards, demanding to speak to a journalist. U.S. Marines were trying unsuccessfully to keep them out. They kept rolling out razor wire in a crazy quilt pattern in the forlorn hope of trying to establish a perimeter fence. It was clear they couldn't use force to shoo the Iraqis away. Yet each and every one of those people could have been wired up with a small bomb. There had already been a couple of suicide bombing attacks on American military personnel in the city, and this setup was an open invitation to anyone with a hankering to be a martyr. I felt sorry for the marines. They had not been trained for this kind of duty. You could read in their eyes as they scanned the crowd a mixture of cold professionalism and pure confusion. Despite the combat they had been through, they looked their age: young, very young.

I was supposed to share a ride to Amman with British journalist Patrick Cockburn, but we got separated in the mob. I looked for him for almost an hour. I returned to where Sami and Ahmad were guarding my bags. I asked if they had seen Patrick. Ahmad said, "Untie yourself from that man. Go now."

They found a guy with a Chevy Suburban looking to make the run to Jordan and began a heavy Middle Eastern negotiation with him. The driver's price started at eighteen hundred dollars and in less than a minute was down to seven hundred. They loaded my gear up, along with the lunch Sami's wife had packed for us. There was no time and no place to enjoy it. Nor was there time to hold hands and speak the long speeches in our hearts. The panic around the hotel was palpable, and Ahmad and Sami both calculated the possibilities for a bomber in this mad mix. We all needed to be past danger before dark. We kissed cheeks three times and then I was gone, although not immediately, for Amman. My driver, being a good middle-class young man, had to go home and tell his mother that he was going to Jordan for a couple of days so she wouldn't worry.

I arrived in a blizzard and departed in spring. I came through the mountains and left through the desert. In the month I was in Iraq, a whole nation was changed. When I returned to my home in London, nothing was different. The debate about the war was the same as before: vitriolic and ill-informed on all sides.

I had changed as well. Part of me remained in Iraq. I thought frequently of Ahmad, who had guided me to the heart of his country in the time of what we thought was its liberation. "You are my most intimate friend," Ahmad whispered as he kissed me good-bye upon the cheek. *Intimate* means "close," I reminded myself. Then he reiterated, "I have spent the happiest days of my life with you."

This time I didn't argue with him. With the tear-brimming optimism of people who survive history, we assumed that for the rest of our lives there would be regular trips to Mosul, to visit, to remember, to eat fish from the Tigris.

I pledged to return in the autumn. "That's good," my friend said. "Autumn in Mosul is beautiful."

Ahmad's Life

Chapter Seven

"It Doesn't Matter to God Whether You Are a Kurd or an Arab"

MOSUL IS WHITE like a pearl. The Pearl of the North is what Iraqis call it. White domes swirl above the banks of the Tigris. The river is wide and fast-flowing in spring, narrow and slow-moving as a tired snake in summer. Ahmad Shawkat first opened his eyes on this world in the 1950s and was dazzled by its brightness and beauty. In those days, before Mosul was overwhelmed with cars and pollution, the little boy looked at the city and saw it as the setting for the children's stories he heard. The characters of *The Thousand and One Nights* lived here. Ali Baba walked in the narrow streets of the old city. Among the ancient buildings overlooking the Tigris, there was a great mansion with a balcony. That was where Sinbad the Sailor lived. Walking with his mother to the bazaar, Ahmad squinted at the sun glinting off the domes and imagined himself flying over the city on a magic carpet.

In the 1950s no place in Iraq was like Mosul. The city had been a provincial capital under the Ottoman Empire, a trading and manufacturing center for the whole region even beyond Iraq's borders. The vestiges of its importance could be found in the architecture of some of the grander houses in the city, but the imperial past endured most in the minds of Mosul's citizens. Baghdad was bigger and it might be the nation's capital, they would say, but Mosul was where the talent of the country was born and nurtured. In its Ottoman heyday, the diverse groups that populated the plain and the Kurdish mountains had been drawn to the city and managed to live together. Ahmad's neighborhood, Faisaliyah, was the center of the mosaic that is Iraqi society. His playmates were Kurds, Arabs, and Turkmen; Sunni and Shi'a Muslims; Chaldean and Assyrian Christians; and Yezidis. He heard whispers of another group, recently departed: the Jews.

These were Mosul's gifts to Ahmad: a setting to fill his imagination and so many different kinds of people to try and understand. From childhood he never stopped loving the city for this. Mosul was also a stage for modern Iraq's political dramas, which began to erupt during his boyhood. He would spend most of his life acting in them.

Iraq was born in the aftermath of World War I, as the victorious Allies carved up the Ottoman Empire, creating the nations of the modern Middle East. Britain assigned itself control of the Ottoman provinces in Mesopotamia, and from this area around the Tigris and Euphrates rivers they founded Iraq. During the period of their mandate over the country, the British created an Iraqi government modeled on their own. A constitutional monarchy was established. Because Iraq was a new nation, there was no hereditary monarch to put on the throne, so elections for the post of king were held. In a stage-managed plebiscite—the British didn't want any nasty surprises—the monarch elected was Faisal I, whose relationship with T. E. Lawrence is dramatized in the film *Lawrence of Arabia*. Subsequently a government with a parliament and prime minister was elected. But Iraq was not independent; it was a part of the British Empire, and real power lay with the British high commissioner.

The British Mandate period lasted roughly from 1920 through 1932. During this time the British put in place the foundations of a modern state. An Iraqi Army was created and a military college established to train a professional officer corps; a modern education system was created and run by Arab educators. Through these institutions—and one other—the British would maintain influence when their mandate ended. That other source of influence was the Iraqi Petroleum Company. The British-owned IPC had exclusive rights to exploit the new nation's most significant natural resource, oil.

When the British Mandate ended in 1932, Iraq was left to develop more or less on its own, although British influence remained through its control of the oil industry and at a personal level. Many of Iraq's first leaders had been handpicked by the colonial rulers and owed their positions to them. During the 1930s political trends emerged that continue to shape Iraq today: Arab nationalism; anti-Western Islamic clericalism; military, rather than civilian democratic, rule. Methods for taking power developed that would be used into the 1950s and 1960s. The new nation's largest ethnic minority, the Kurds, aggressively asserted a desire for political autonomy. Sometimes this desire was violently suppressed by the Arab majority.

There was no democratic tradition for reconciling political differences, so governments changed via coups and counter-coups. The monarch's symbolic power dwindled when Faisal died and his son, Ghazi, proved a weak leader. With an ineffectual monarchy, political factions looked abroad to the great powers to bolster their positions. In the 1930s this meant establishing connections with the Allies or with the Axis powers.

Those who chose the Axis—primarily Arab nationalists and Islamists—found their power crushed as the British military swept back into Iraq at the start of World War II to suppress a revolt of nationalist army officers.

During World War II the British reoccupied Iraq. When the war was over, British influence over the state was reasserted. Oil production, centered in the north of the country around Kirkuk, increased, and royalties from the British-owned IPC began to enrich Iraq. Roads were improved, connecting north and south. Schools were built, and literacy increased. Slowly the population of Iraq began to migrate. In what has now become a familiar pattern in the developing world, Iraqis began to leave their peasant villages and relocate to the cities.

Up in the old Ottoman province of Nineveh, a Kurdish couple, Shawkat Alyas and his wife, Shokria Hasan, were among those taking that journey from peasant village life to a middle-class city home. Shawkat came from the village of Darawish, twenty or so kilometers northeast of the provincial capital, Mosul. In the late 1940s he had moved to the city and started a business wholesaling sheep at Mosul's weekly meat market. Between-times he ran a butcher shop. Shawkat and Shokria entered the middle class, and their family grew. In 1951 their fifth child—a fourth son—was born. They named him Ahmad.

Iraq in the 1950s was sleepwalking into the postcolonial era. It was a nation and a society slowly being reshaped by political movements gathering pace outside its borders and by population movements within them. By the time Ahmad was old enough to read and imagine, the constitutional monarchy was reaching the end of its useful existence. Change was in the air, but what kind of change was unclear. Iraqis could look west to

Egypt and just east to Iran to get a sense of which way the political winds were blowing in the Middle East.

In Egypt, a group of Arab nationalist army officers led by Gamal Abdel Nasser overthrew the monarchy and seized power in 1952. That same year, in Iran, the popularly elected leader, Muhammad Mossadeq, nationalized his country's oil industry. In 1953 he was overthrown in a CIA-backed coup. Both events offered lessons to politically astute observers in Iraq. If Iraq was going to join other Arab nations on the march to modernity, army officers would have to take matters into their own hands. From Iran came the lesson that taking control of your greatest natural resource required cunning, because the West would not easily relinquish its ownership of oil.

Iraq's political dramas were provincial and derivative by comparison. A young king, Faisal II, had taken the throne in 1939, but until 1953 the country was actually governed by the king's regent, his uncle Abdullah, and Prime Minister Nuri Said. Both had longtime connections with the British and kept Iraq firmly pointed toward the West. But it was a choice that ran against the tide of history. Arab nationalism was gaining strength as an ideal. The creation of Israel, the "Zionist entity," as it was called even then by its Arab critics, provided a unifying cause for Arabs throughout the Middle East. Israel was perceived as a creation of the Western powers, a last expression of colonial rule.

Gamal Abdel Nasser's popularity broke down national barriers: he was a leader who appealed to Arabs in all countries. Nasser had consolidated his power in Egypt and was trying to build a pan-Arab state, a union of all the Arab countries, which he would lead. Nasser believed the Arabs were one nation, divided by Europeans into many different countries so they could control the Middle East. The creation of a United Arab Republic would give the Arab people power to shape their own destiny in the postcolonial era. It was a powerful message. Nasser stood apart from the West and the Soviet Union. Along with India's Jawaharlal Nehru, he became a leader of the "nonaligned" movement, asserting Egypt's right to be aligned with neither power bloc. This made him a hero across the Arab world and it also made him a figure of fear in Cold War Washington, where the ruling dictum was "That which I cannot control makes me weak."

U.S. Secretary of State John Foster Dulles was building a pro-Western defense alliance in Muslim countries across the Middle East and South Asia. In 1954 Turkey and Pakistan signed a mutual defense agreement, negotiations with Iran were under way, and Iraq was invited to join the alliance as well. Nasser spoke out publicly against any Arab countries signing up with this pro-Western alliance, saying this went against the "nonaligned" principles that best served the wider Arab nation. Nevertheless, Iraq joined its non-Arab Muslim neighbors Turkey, Iran, and Pakistan in a mutual defense alliance headquartered in Baghdad.

The "Baghdad Pact" alliance came together in 1955. Nuri Said had put his country firmly in the Western camp at the very moment that Arab nationalists, resentful of the colonial powers, had an inspirational leader for the first time. Nasser spoke out against the Baghdad Pact. His words resonated among ordinary Iraqis. The following year, the Egyptian leader nationalized the Suez Canal, precipitating war with Britain, France, and Israel. The fact that Iraq was unable to come to the aid of a fellow Arab nation because of the government's tilt to the West inflamed Iraqi public opinion. Nasser was seen as a hero for nationalizing the Suez Canal, and the Iraqi people angrily wondered why their own great resource—oil—wasn't similarly nationalized. In the army, small groups of officers organized cells to discuss pan-Arab politics and plotted to seize power. On July 14, 1958, they did just that. The royal family was summarily executed. Nuri Said was caught trying to escape the country dressed as a woman. He was shot and buried. Later, a mob dug up his corpse and dragged it through the streets of Baghdad.

The coup didn't bring Iraq to a halt. People still had to work; they still had to feed themselves. In Mosul, Shawkat Alyas continued to sell sheep and watch his family grow. Since Ahmad's birth in 1951, Shokria had given him two more sons, Mahmood and Abdulfaraj. The father saw that his youngest children were benefiting from the changes in Iraq. The modernizing trends, particularly in education, were especially helpful to Ahmad. His teachers told Shawkat that his son was exceptional. The father already knew that. The boy's mind was on fire with curiosity. He was constantly asking questions. When Shawkat couldn't explain something, Ahmad found the answer for himself in a book or by asking another adult. Shawkat wanted to encourage his son to know more about the world beyond Mosul. He bought a radio for his family, a rare thing in the neighborhood. Playing with the dial, Ahmad found the BBC World Service. Already fluent in Kurdish and Arabic, he began to teach himself English.

Ahmad loved explaining things to his friends, and they loved to listen. His youngest brother, Abdulfaraj, idolized him and was his best pupil. Whatever Ahmad learned, he told Faraj. He heard the word *muslin* on the BBC. It was confusing to his ear because it sounded like *Muslim*, but the person on the radio was talking about clothing. He looked it up. "Muslin comes from the name of our city, Mosul," he told Faraj. "It was first made here and sent all over the world. And so people called it muslin. Do you see how important our city is?"

From the time the state was founded, politics in Iraq has been about simply seizing and exercising power. Throughout the country's modern history there have been many political movements with well-defined ideologies—Communism, Pan-Arabism, Islamism, to name a few—but the real dogma motivating Iraqi politics is the leaders' personal drive for power. Ideology is something to be written on banners and chanted by crowds; ideology provides a convenient label for outsiders to put on Iraqi politicians. Even today, saying this person is a nationalist, that person is an Islamist, makes it easy for foreign diplomats to categorize Iraq's politicians. But it is misleading, because ideology means little—power is everything.

The 1958 coup that overthrew the monarchy was led by two army officers—Abdul Karim Qasim and Abdul Salam Arif—who shared a desire for power but had no clear ideological plan for what to do once they had it. In the immediate aftermath of the July 14 coup they had set up a government comprised of Iraq's main political parties, with representatives from the nation's largest ethnic and sectarian groups: Shi'a, Sunni, and Kurds. It was easy to agree on uncoupling Iraq from its Western entanglements, like the Baghdad Pact. But the larger question of linking Iraq into the pan-Arab program was not resolved. Nasser had begun to build his dream of a pan-Arab state earlier in 1958, when Egypt and Syria had formed the United Arab Republic. Arif wished to join Nasser's grand project. Qasim was more of an Iraqi nationalist and did not want to join a union in which, he was convinced, Iraq would be a junior partner and his own power diminished.

The men plotted against one another, and Qasim won the power struggle. He had Arif arrested. His former colleague, now rival, was sentenced to life in prison. But even that didn't end the argument about Pan-Arabism. The dispute would be violently acted out in Mosul.

As the months went by, Qasim increasingly relied on left-wing parties to bolster his authority, particularly the Iraqi Communist Party. Within the army there were many disgruntled pan-Arabists who felt betrayed by Qasim's alliance with a group whose ideology they regarded as coming from outside the Arab world. In March 1959, a quarter of a million communists and their sympathizers gathered in Mosul for a rally. Skirmishing broke out between the leftists and the Arab nationalist sympathizers, who also had allies in local tribal leaders who feared the communists wanted to confiscate their land and usurp their traditional power. With so many supporters of Qasim in one place, pan-Arab officers who had been planning to strike against him decided to make their move and proclaimed a revolt. Qasim bombed the Mosul army barracks, and the uprising quickly failed. But the bloodshed in Mosul didn't stop. Anarchy ruled. Bloody riots sparked into life, then faded. Communists lynched nationalists. Christian and Muslim neighbors turned on each other.

In the middle of the chaos, Shawkat Alyas became gravely ill. His wife, Shokria, took him to the city's main hospital on the other side of the Tigris from Faisaliyah. Once there, he collapsed. Doctors told her Shawkat would need to stay with them for some time.

Shokria went to visit her husband every day. Sometimes she took her youngest son, Faraj. One day, at the height of the rioting, mother and son came to the old iron bridge over the Tigris and were stopped by the police. There was something going on by the bridge and it was dangerous for a woman and young child to cross. Shokria tried to explain to one of the policemen that her husband was very sick, maybe dying, over in the hospital. She had to see him. The policeman told her to come back later.

Shokria took Faraj to a teahouse and after a while returned to the bridge. Faraj saw a man hanging from a telephone pole nearby. When he got home Faraj excitedly told his big brother, Ahmad, what he had seen.

"Ahmad, Ahmad," the little boy said. "They took all his clothes off. He just had one shoe left on." The older brother asked what else he had seen. "There was another dead man, he was also naked, but they had set him on fire."

Ahmad explained to Faraj what had happened in their neighborhood while his brother and mother had been trying to get to the hospital. A mob of communists had descended on the house of a family friend named Thannon. They dragged Thannon's father out of the house. One of the communists threw a noose around the father's neck and they were hanging him right by the front gate. Thannon's mother began to scream.

"I never heard such noise," Ahmad said. "She screamed so loud, the leader of the mob suddenly told his men to stop and they cut him down."

"Then what happened?"

"He was almost dead. But now I think he is okay."

For weeks the stories of murder during the rioting swirled around the schoolyard. Boys boasted about the atrocities they had seen and who had been bravest in looking at them. The rioting consumed itself as people ran out of energy to continue. The dead were mourned and then forgotten by all but their closest relatives. The city returned to normal.

Shawkat died soon after the rioting ended. Besides the usual bewilderment that a child feels when a parent dies, Ahmad felt something else: dread. There were whispers in the house that had nothing to do with mourning. Men came to the door and had angry arguments with his oldest brother, Muhammad. His mother seemed to be weeping two kinds of tears: tears of sadness for his father and tears of panic. When Ahmad was a little older he finally understood what was going on: his father had run up debts; the men who came to the house were demanding payment. But there was no money, and Muhammad was without work. His brother argued with the debt collectors, but they insisted on payment. The family had to sell their house to pay off the creditors. For the rest of his life Ahmad lived with the fear that he would lose everything and have no money.

The network of connections that could help care for Shawkat's widow and children was back in his home village of Darawish, so Shokria took her children to her husband's village.

It was June and the last remnants of spring were burning off the plain when Ahmad and his brothers arrived in Darawish. The mud track they traveled up was already cracking apart in the early summer heat. As the dust settled around the car that had brought them, Ahmad looked at his new world. It was not pearl white. It was the color of dried mud. He stood in the middle of an open common area, like a plaza, only there were no shops as in the urban world he knew. The plaza was surrounded by compounds of single-story mud-brick houses hidden behind long walls. The walls were washed in a mud plaster. Animals wandered everywhere: sheep, cattle, chickens, ducks, and geese. In one corner of the open space was the village well. The well had been dug by Ahmad's grandfather, Alyas, and was called by his name. As new children in the village, Ahmad and his brothers basked a little in the reflected glory of being the grandchildren of Alyas. When they heard a woman order a child to bring water from Alyas's Well, it made them feel like they truly belonged to Darawish.

Ahmad and his brothers fell into the peasant life. They did farmyard chores: moving animals from pasture to pasture, putting tools in order so that the next day's work could begin on time. In his spare time, Ahmad explored the area around Darawish. There was an old Assyrian Christian tomb with a roof like a spherical cone. He could hide from his brothers behind it. About a half-kilometer from his family's compound was a little hill from the top of which he could see back to the road that led to Mosul and get a clear view of the plain in all directions. The northern horizon was guarded by a small mountain, Mount Maqloub. It stuck up from the plain, catching the wind from all directions; it was the first hint of the mountains beyond in Kurdistan.

Ahmad's desire for education now turned to learning the practical skills of his peasant relatives. He spent hours watching his uncle Ismail make furniture. Ismail was a craftsman. The boy paid close attention to the way his uncle worked the wood. Ahmad kept asking him questions about why he did things a certain way. The young man gave Ahmad little lectures on woodworking, then showed him the shortcuts that a lazy furniture maker might take and the ways a true craftsman worked wood. He taught the boy inlaying techniques to adorn the furniture. Ahmad learned how to hide the joins to make the line of the furniture beautiful. After a short while, Ismail started giving Ahmad bits of wood to make toy furniture. The uncle saw that his nephew had been watching him closely. Soon Ahmad was allowed to measure and cut material for Ismail. Carpentry became a skill that would serve him his whole life.

He spent hours watching his uncle work and frequently ran late for his own chores. Then Muhammad would come down on him hard. Muhammad, almost twenty, was trying to replace his father but simply couldn't command the respect of his little brothers. Ahmad and Faraj were a unit, smarter and already better educated than the others. Ahmad wouldn't be ruled by his oldest brother. He wouldn't be ruled by anyone. He did what he wanted, when he wanted. If he wasn't working with wood, he was reading and writing. The little hill outside the village became his study. In good weather he walked to the top, sprawled in the sunshine, and devoured new books.

No chores got done when Ahmad went up the hill. His next older brother, Khalil, picked up the slack at first. Then one afternoon he went to the kitchen where his mother was chopping vegetables for dinner and complained about how lazy his little brother was. Shokria put down her knife, looked at Khalil, and said, "He's not lazy." She gestured to him to sit and told him a story. "When I was pregnant with Ahmad, I had a dream. He would be a very great man. I had this dream many times." She looked at the boy and asked, "Do you understand?" Khalil nodded. "And it is like the dream says. You see how smart he is. How much he reads. This is the prophesy of the dream. He is preparing himself. You must help him in his work. I am certain Allah has chosen him to be a messenger. Do you understand?" Khalil nodded again.

The family remained in Darawish for more than a year. Then Muhammad found a job back in Mosul, and they returned to the city. In the schoolyard Ahmad told stories about the village. They were his calling card. Stories about animals and old-fashioned village customs helped him make new friends in the city. Sometimes he just made up stories about village life to keep the other boys' attention. He kept up his habit of disappearing after school. Instead of walking through the pastures and up to the summits of little hills, lost in his thoughts, he walked along the partially excavated walls of ancient Nineveh on the east bank of the Tigris, across from Mosul's Old City. Though a few of the gates had been completely excavated by European archeologists in the nineteenth century, most of the ancient city's walls were no more than long, grassy mounds.

On top of the walls Ahmad felt he was floating between the twin poles of his existence: the city and the village. He looked across the Tigris to the Old City of Mosul and northeast toward Mount Maqloub. He took history books with him and sat on the walls reading and daydreaming. He read everything he could about the ancient times. He felt the pride of being descended from the first civilized people. The history of the region and the names of the ancient kings of Assyria and Sumer were committed to memory. At night he would tell Faraj, his little brother and best pupil, "Nineveh—this is where civilization began."

Ahmad read and absorbed ideas far beyond his years. His schoolwork was excellent, and in 1963 he skipped a grade and entered high school a year early. He was just twelve, the youngest and smallest person in his class, but he immediately started spending time with the older, smarter boys in the school. At first he was treated as their mascot. But Ahmad had read as much as any of them and he didn't back down verbally in arguments. Soon he was just one of the group. Ahmad's older friends were already involved in politics and Ahmad was drawn into their world.

It was inevitable that he would become fascinated by politics. Partly it was the times. The sixties were not just a phenomenon of the West. What the civil rights movement was to young Americans, the national liberation movement was to young Iraqis. Both movements—with their promise to redress long-standing injustices—appealed to young people. Ahmad's political interest also came out of witnessing the events of 1959. Though only eight years old, he had been thrilled and fascinated by the chaotic power unleashed by the political upheaval in Mosul that year. Having experienced the dislocation of falling from the urban middle class into peasant life, he had a keen sense of economic injustice. Listening to the BBC, he had learned about more settled democracies and he understood that by comparison his society was unformed. There was something still molten about Iraq. It was a society in the forge, waiting to be hammered into shape. Ahmad and his friends felt if they worked hard they could be the ones to wield the hammer and create a new society.

A coup was coming. They could feel it. Iraqis had developed a sixth sense about this. All governments grow tired and lose touch with the people. When this happens in democratic societies, administrations or parties limp to the polls and are voted out. In Iraq, exhausted rulers stayed in power until removed in a coup. The Qasim government was showing signs of terminal exhaustion. The man who had engineered the overthrow of the monarchy five years earlier had failed to widen his power base. In the last spasm of chaos in 1959, a group of officers belonging to a pan-Arab party called the Ba'ath had tried to assassinate him. They failed. One of the conspirators was named Saddam Hussein.

After the attempt on his life, Qasim narrowed the decision-making circle he relied on. He modernized Iraq in many ways: redistributing land to peasants; improving women's rights by guaranteeing, among other things, more equal inheritance rights; and taking the first solid steps toward wresting control of Iraq's oil fields away from the British. But he acted in a peremptory fashion, imposing policy without preparing the public for it. His high-handedness did not gain him the popularity he might have expected. His policy failures, on the other hand, hurt him with public opinion more than they might have had they been decided in a democratic fashion. One of the built-in benefits of democratically elected leaders governing with a cabinet is that when things go wrong—as they frequently do—it is possible to spread the blame around. When a strongman makes the decisions on his own, all the blame falls on him when policies don't work. If he doesn't have a ruthless security apparatus to keep the critics in line, his position is at risk.

Qasim built no bridges to pan-Arab parties after the failed assassination attempt. He might have tried to co-opt them. But he didn't. That was a mistake. Since the 1959 rioting in Mosul, Pan-Arabism had become the dominant political trend for most Iraqis. Qasim had continued to rely on the Iraqi Communist Party for support. He tilted Iraq's foreign policy toward the Soviet Union at just the time when the majority of his people were against any outside interference in Arab affairs.

Ahmad and his friends were certain it would be only a matter of time before Qasim was overthrown. And when he was, Iraq could join the other Arab nations in the United Arab Republic that would be led by their hero, Egyptian president Gamal Abdel Nasser, the pride of the Arabs.

Nasser's face gazed out from posters in the street and news programs on television. His face was everywhere: movie-star handsome, the face of a pharaoh, and a reminder to the world that the first civilization had been Arab. Nasser called from the radio and the television for one nation, the Arab nation, all brothers, to unite and reassert that greatness. Ahmad was sure this was the man who could unite the Arab masses and lead them to a progressive future. They would no longer be in thrall to the old colonial mentality of the British and French and the new colonial mentality of the Americans. Unaligned with either the West or the Soviet Union, the Arab masses would lead the global fight against imperialism.

In Nasser's face Ahmad and his friends saw Iraq's destiny: the Arab nation would be a great force in the world again. In a pan-Arab nation, modern ideas of democratic socialism and justice would liberate peasants from being in thrall to the landlords. After his time in Darawish, Ahmad knew better than any of his friends how hard peasant life was. People who scratched out their living in primitive villages must have their lives made easier, he thought. The profit from oil shouldn't go to British companies. It should go into modernization projects for peasant villages. Make the peasants' long days of toil easier by paving their roads and bringing electricity to them, he told his Nasser-supporting friends. Their natural intelligence needs to be liberated so their talents can enrich society.

And people should have the right to vote for their leaders. A pan-Arab democratic-socialist state would end the easily corrupted rule of military strongmen like Qasim who seized power via coups d'état and then sold their influence on the international market to the highest bidder. The masses would decide who was to rule them.

Ahmad's little circle of friends wrote pamphlets and made posters extolling the Nasser vision of Pan-Arabism. Ahmad spent hours after school posting them around Mosul. It never seemed odd to him that he was a Kurd working for a pan-Arab state. Mosul was a melting pot, and he thought of himself as an Iraqi, and if Iraq could be made a stronger, more just society by being part of a United Arab Republic, then he was a pan-Arabist.

The coup came on February 8, 1963, the fourteenth day of Ramadan. It was swift and decisive. Forty-eight hours after the revolt began, Qasim was executed. The coup was organized by the Arab Ba'ath Socialist Party—pan-Arabists, but not supporters of Nasser. The name *Arab Socialist Ba'ath Party* conjured up Arab nationalism; a redistributive, centrally controlled economy; and a rhetorical claim that implied a new beginning: *Ba'ath* means "renaissance" in Arabic.

Ahmad and his friends followed every twist and turn of the coup as word traveled from Baghdad via news media and rumors in the bazaar. The one thing they were clear about was that the Ba'athists were not the right people to lead the pan-Arab movement. The Ba'ath was a very small party at that point, with no real popular base. The party's appeal to ordinary Iraqis rested on its willingness to deal with perceived enemies of the Arabs in Iraq—like the communists and Kurds—in a brutal way. In Mosul, in the weeks after the coup, many communists had been assassinated, and fighting with the Kurds had resumed. Ahmad and his Nasserite friends feared this was the way the country would be governed, with all dissenting political views crushed by violence.

But in 1963 the Ba'ath had only a program for seizing power; there was no program for what to do once it was in control. The coup leaders turned to Qasim's old rival, Abdul Salam Arif, and made him president of Iraq. Arif was not a member of the party and was meant to be a figurehead while the Ba'ath leadership exercised the real power. But even the Ba'ath leadership was divided; they had taken control of the country but were split between civilian and military factions. The two groups spent the months after the coup vying for power. As arguments raged across a whole range of issues—union with Egypt, an accommodation with Iraq's Kurds—they lost their grip on the country. On November 14, 1963, another group of army officers led a coup that swept the Ba'ath Party away and consolidated control of Iraq under President Arif. The Iraqi president brought Nasserites into his circle of advisers and moved Iraq's economy toward Nasser's vision of Arab socialism. Arif even flew to Cairo to meet his Egyptian counterpart to begin exploring the possibility of recreating the United Arab Republic. The first UAR with Egypt and Syria had fallen apart in 1961. Arif's vision was for Egypt and Iraq to join together.

The nation settled into a comparatively calm period. Ahmad was doing well in school and in his self-education. A steady stream of mail from abroad found its way to his home in Mosul. He subscribed to English-language magazines, and in the back of some of these periodicals were classified ads placed by young people hoping to correspond with teenagers in other parts of the world. Ahmad had pen pals ranging from Portugal to India. These conversations by mail were not much different from the kind of international chats being conducted at Internet cafés in Iraq and around the world today, except they took weeks to carry on, not seconds. Invariably, there was a stage in these pen pal relationships when Ahmad's correspondent would express a desire to meet and would invite him for a visit someday. Ahmad began to dream of travel, of exploring the world outside Iraq.

Each summer Ahmad returned to Darawish to help his uncle Ismail make furniture. He always packed books and notebooks for these return visits. The little hill outside the village was still his favorite place to read, and now he started writing poetry. He gave his imagination over to the heartbroken romantic verse that bookish adolescents often write. He spent hours on his hill, writing and staring at Mount Maqloub on the northern horizon, watching the rocky outcrop change color as the sun progressed through the sky each day. There was a gash in the mountainside two-thirds of the way to the summit, white at midday and honey-colored at sunset. He asked his uncle what it was. "The

Christian place," he answered. Ahmad was intrigued. One summer morning he got up early and set off through the fields determined to visit the Christian place. It was a long walk to Maqloub but not a difficult climb. There was a military road switching back from side to side all the way up the mountain. He simply followed it until he came to Mar Matte, or St. Matthew's Monastery.

He walked through the gates and sat on a low wall to catch his breath and let the sweat cool him down. From up here he thought he might be able to see Darawish, but he could not. He could hardly hear himself think, though the monastery was quiet. His pulse was pounding in his head and there was a gusting breeze that didn't seem to blow down on the plain. When his heart stopped pounding, he began to explore the monastery. The once-magnificent buildings were in a state of disrepair. The crumbling weight of their history had given the complex a kind of architectural unity, even though there were centuries dividing the various buildings' construction.

Ahmad walked through a courtyard and up a flight of stairs, along a gallery, then through a heavy door into the main chapel. As he stood at the back, looking up at the chapel's vaulted ceiling, a monk walked in and greeted him in Arabic. Brother Paul asked the young man if he needed anything. Ahmad explained he lived in a village down on the plain and had seen the monastery from a distance and wanted to visit. Brother Paul offered to show him around the complex.

The monastery was one of the oldest in the world, Brother Paul explained as they walked around. It had been founded in A.D. 363 by Matthew, a Christian fleeing persecution near his hometown of Diyarbakir in what is today the Kurdish part of eastern Turkey. Matthew joined other Christians living in caves on Maqloub. He was a very holy man and performed a miraculous cure of the local king's daughter, and in gratitude the king had allowed Matthew to build a monastic community around the caves.

Ahmad was fascinated. "Matthew was from Diyarbakir. . . . Was he a Kurd before there were Kurds?"

"Perhaps. Does it matter if he was a Kurd or a Turk or an Arab?" the monk replied.

"No."

"No," Brother Paul agreed. "It doesn't matter to God whether you are a Kurd or an Arab or a Muslim or a Christian."

Toward the end of the first millennium, as many as four thousand monks lived in the monastery, Brother Paul explained. Mar Matte became one of the most famous monastic communities in the world. Ahmad didn't doubt the number four thousand, for hewing the massive buildings out of the mountainside would have taken many laborers many years. The monk continued his history lesson. When the Mongols began their raids on Iraq in the fourteenth century, the community fell into decline, and when Tamerlane finally destroyed what was left of Iraq's bright, medieval society, the monastery's community was scattered. During the centuries of Ottoman rule, new buildings were occasionally added, but the fame of the place had faded.

Ahmad sat and talked with Brother Paul for hours. He wanted to know the difference between Assyrian and Chaldean Christians. Brother Paul's answer was complex, and Ahmad got lost trying to follow the complicated feuding of the Church in its first few centuries of existence that led to the schism between Catholic and Orthodox Christians.

"Is it like the Shi'a and Sunni split in Islam?" Ahmad asked.

"Yes, although perhaps less bloody."

Ahmad was suddenly struck by an ironic fact. Saladin, the great Kurdish warrior who drove the Crusaders out of Jerusalem, was born in Tikrit, not all that far from the monastery. While he was reclaiming the holy places for Islam, in his own home Christianity was flourishing at Mar Matte. Ahmad asked Brother Paul how this could have been. The monk simply told him that that was the precious beauty of this place, of his home. In most places religious difference is a cause of war, Paul said. But in this part of the world God placed tolerance in peoples' hearts.

It was time for Ahmad to leave; he had a long walk back to Darawish. He thanked Brother Paul for showing him around. The monk told him he was welcome back any time. Over the years Ahmad would visit the monastery regularly.

The comparative political calm in Iraq ended in 1966. Force majeure rather than a coup brought about the change. President Arif was killed in a helicopter crash. His brother Abdul Rahman Arif was made president, but this Arif was not the politician his brother had been. The army increasingly made policy. The long negotiations with Nasser to join a United Arab Republic came to nothing. That familiar feeling of imminent political upheaval returned.

Ahmad's older Nasserite friends had all started university. Ahmad was left alone in high school waiting for his turn to enter the grown-up world of college. He saw his older friends occasionally. They would meet in teahouses and sit around analyzing the latest political news, working out a line to take on each event. They would write their analyses in an article. Ahmad was no longer the little kid who just posted their essays on walls and telephone poles around the city. His ability with words meant he was now asked to write these essays as well. He also posted weekly "newspapers" in Arabic and English on his high school's walls.

Perhaps because of his visit to the monastery, he fell in love with a Christian girl in his neighborhood. The romance broke off when her family moved away, but it gave Ahmad more sweet despair to turn into poetry. At high school he had become a leader, the kid who was smartest in his class and also a regular guy. Stories swirled around about him, often told by his youngest brother Faraj, tales that made him a young legend in his neighborhood. Ahmad, in his little brother's stories, was brave and a little crazy.

Faraj would tell schoolmates about the time Ahmad was playing soccer after school with a group of boys. Farhan, the son of Abdullah Sharafani, a Kurdish warlord, wanted to play. But there were eleven on each side already. So Ahmad told him there was no room for him. Besides, this kid's father was fighting with the government against the Kurds, and to Ahmad that just wasn't right. Farhan then went to the smallest kid on the field and told him he should make room for him. The little kid didn't want to quit. Ahmad went over to Farhan and told him to leave the boy alone. Farhan asked, "Do you know who my father is?" Ahmad said yes, then slapped him in the face and told him to get out. Farhan did, but a few minutes later came back with his bodyguards. Ahmad managed to outrun them and hide.

Later that evening Faraj asked, "Ahmad, why did you do that?"

"He had no right. . . . Just because his father is famous? He is no better than that small boy. He should have waited his turn."

At a certain point, usually in a college-bound person's junior year, high school becomes tedious. The realization hits that there is much further to go in education and you would just as soon get on with it. When Ahmad reached that point, the only thing he didn't know for certain was what to study at the University of Mosul. He knew clearly that his destiny was to be a writer, and he was drawn to the study of literature. It was also obvious that he did not come from a wealthy family, or one with extensive connections. He needed to study something that would gain him employment, and a degree in literature simply would not do that. His teachers steered him toward the sciences. They told him his country needed to make up the gap in scientific knowledge with the West if Iraq was to achieve its place of leadership in the world. The idea appealed to Ahmad. He was also aware that oil revenue was being used by the government to build this modern society, and there would be a job for someone who graduated with a good degree in science. Ahmad made the decision to study biology at the University of Mosul and settled back into the torpor of high school life, writing his political essays on the situation in the Arab world, falling in and out of love with girls, waiting impatiently for the liberation of college.

War with Israel was coming. The Arab nations wanted it and so did the Israelis, it seemed to Ahmad. All that was needed was the right sequence of provocations, and Nasser would reclaim all of Palestine for the Arabs and drive the colonialists back to Europe. In the spring of 1967 the sequence was initiated when Syria, governed by its own branch of the Ba'ath Party, stepped up its attacks on northern Israeli towns near their border. The skirmishing started on the ground and then moved into the sky. Israeli and Syrian jets engaged each other. Although Syria and Egypt had not been able to sustain Nasser's dream of union, they maintained a mutual defense agreement. The escalation in military skirmishing led the Syrian government to call on Nasser for aid. The Egyptian president moved one hundred thousand troops into the Sinai Peninsula, up to Israel's border. He then demanded that UN military observers leave the area, which they did. Finally, on May 22, Nasser closed the Strait of Tiran on the Red Sea, effectively blockading Israel from the south.

Each step on the road to war was greeted with excitement by Ahmad and his friends in Mosul. They spent afternoons after school debating the future. After the Zionists were defeated, they agreed, Nasser would undoubtedly be acclaimed by all as the true leader of the Arab world. So far Pan-Arabism had failed, in their view, because too many local Arab leaders were unwilling to cede authority to the Egyptian, even though their own people's lives would be better in a pan-Arab state. But the popularity Nasser was bound to gain from defeating the Israelis would change that dynamic. The Ba'ath would be in retreat. The Arab nation could consolidate under the more thoughtful democratic-socialist program of Nasserism. The big question locally was: Where would Arif place Iraq's troops when the war began? Would they be in the vanguard? They were convinced a glorious role in the great victory would provide tangible benefits to Iraq in the postwar period. In all their discussions the possibility that the Arabs might lose the war never came up.

On June 5, 1967, war began. The first day was dreadful for the Arab cause. In a preemptive strike, the Israeli Air Force destroyed the Egyptian Air Force before it could even get into the sky. By the second day, Iraqi radio reported that the onslaught had been stemmed and the tide was turning. The Egyptian Army was rolling toward Tel Aviv, it claimed. Ahmad tuned to the BBC for confirmation. Instead he learned two painful truths: the war was going disastrously, and the Arabs' leaders would always lie to their people.

Six days after the war started, it was over. The Israelis had seized the Sinai Peninsula. They had taken all of Jerusalem, including the holy places. Palestine had been overrun to the west bank of the Jordan River. Around the Arab world people were dazed and enraged by the defeat. Their leaders had lied to them about the power of their armies. As the war went on, they had lied to them about its terrible progress. The people's rage was suffocated by the humiliation of how easily the Israelis had triumphed.

Ahmad was filled with bitter disappointment. He wondered why America and its Western allies had not used their influence to intervene and prevent conflict or to rein in Zionist aggression once it started. Why did America and Britain always aid the Jews? he wondered. The young man loved the English language and knew American culture and British culture intimately. He had acquired his understanding of what a just, modern, democratic society could be from listening to the BBC and reading English-language political journals, but he simply could not understand how the Americans and British could follow such unjust policies in the Middle East.

But as angry and disappointed as he was with the United States and Britain, it was nothing compared to the sense of shame at his own government's failure to respond in the Arabs' hour of need. Ahmad was not alone. Throughout Iraq, shame and disappointment burned in every part of society. Iraqi troops had played virtually no part in the fighting. Perhaps if they had been committed in large numbers to the front, Iraqis felt, the war's outcome might have been different. The familiar feeling of an imminent coup filled the streets, fields, and barracks. When it came, it would be the last coup for a very long time.

Chapter Eight

"You Are Feeling More Free Than the Freedom We Have"

NINETEEN SIXTY-EIGHT WAS a year of hope crushed by violence. All over the world, it was a time of epic political change. In America and Europe, political events had much in common with the way politics was practiced in Iraq. Murders shaped the political landscape in the United States. On April 4, Martin Luther King, Jr., was gunned down in Memphis, and two months later Robert Kennedy was assassinated in Los Angeles. Two months after that, the Democratic National Convention spawned a police riot. Throughout the month of May, France teetered on the brink of a revolution that had begun as a general strike among students in the universities and then spread to workers in factories and came within a whisper of overthrowing the government of Charles de Gaulle. In Prague, a brief flowering of socialism untethered from the degrading tyranny of Stalinism was crushed by Soviet tanks.

In the middle of all these events, news of yet another violent change of government in Iraq hardly got coverage in the Western media. On July 17, 1968, the Ba'ath Party overthrew the government of Abdul Rahman Arif. It was the third time in a decade the Ba'ath had attempted to seize power in Iraq. This time their success would be complete.

Ba'athism stands at the intersection of mutual incomprehension between the Arab world and the West; the place where fundamental ways of interpreting experience and organizing society oppose each other and cannot be reconciled.

Ba'athism is a political philosophy that perfectly suits a world in which power is everything and ideology is no more than rhetoric to serve the powerful. It also provides a political theory for those Arabs who want to say to the West: "We are not like you."

The origins of the Arab Ba'ath Socialist Party can be traced back to Syria in the early years of World War II, a period of lingering transition from the French colonial rule of that country to its independence. The Ba'ath grew out of the theorizing and organizing of two men, Michel 'Aflaq, an Arab Christian, and Salah al-Din al-Bitar, an Arab Muslim. Both were students at the Sorbonne in Paris in the late 1920s, and there they were exposed to all the ideas floating around in the fetid air of interwar Europe: Fascism, Marxism, nationalism, and social-scientific theories of race and nation, blood and soil. 'Aflaq and Bitar also observed the decadent nihilism of young Europeans seeking to obliterate memories of World War I in the pursuit of sensual pleasure.

The pair returned to Syria in the early 1930s and spent the decade teaching school and theorizing their way to a distinctly Arab political program that would take not just their country but all Arab countries out of the colonial era. The Ba'ath, or Renaissance, Party was founded in 1943. At its core is a set of principles written by Michel 'Aflaq. 'Aflaq is the mind and soul of the Ba'ath; his theoretical writings are the movement's sacred texts, as important to understanding what is happening in the Middle East today as the writings of Lenin were to understanding the Soviet Union.

'Aflaq developed a poetic notion of pan-Arab nationalism that constantly defines itself against the nationalism of Europe. In Paris, during the time he studied there, European ideas of nationalism were framed in social-scientific or pure scientific language—the Nazis' racial theories were always couched in this way. But to Michel 'Aflaq, that was wrong. "Nationalism is not a science," he wrote. "It is a living remembrance."

'Aflaq's pronouncements were romantic, mystical, and self-consciously religious. The Arab "mission," the Arab "spirit," the Arab "ideal" are his themes. In the first Ba'ath manifesto, published in 1943, 'Aflaq wrote: "There is no alternative, there-fore, but to disregard and elevate oneself above realistic stan-dards and to absorb the eternal standards of the historical mission"; and "Eternity is not the passage of the present into the future, it is the implantation of the future in the present."

The Ba'ath Party is a paradigm of reactionary politics. It was set up in reaction to existing parties and political movements. For example, the Communist parties were the largest and best-organized opposition forces in Iraq and Syria in the postcolo-nial period, yet a basic principle of 'Aflaq's Pan-Arabism was that Communism, because of its European origins, was an alien ideology, in part because it came from the theories of Karl Marx and his "spiteful Jewish spirit." Another core principle was that the true Arab nationalist could not incorporate Western ways of thinking—humanism, rationalism—in the process of modernizing the Arab world. They, too, were alien. Emotional commitment and faith in an idea was the Arab way to progress.

As for political leadership in building the new Arab society, 'Aflaq had no use for democratic niceties. "The Leader, in times of weakness of the Idea [of the nation] and its constriction, is not one to appeal to a majority or consensus. . . . He is the master of the singular Idea from which he separates and casts aside all those who contradict it." This endorsement of dictatorship would have dire consequences for both Syria and Iraq when the Ba'ath finally came to power.

The ideas of the Ba'ath took hold slowly. There were probably no more than a few hundred members when the Syrian group held its first party congress in 1947. Despite 'Aflaq's critical writings about alien Western concepts such as humanism and communism, the party adopted socialism as its economic ideal and invented an organizational structure similar to the Soviet Communist Party. 'Aflaq was appointed the Hamid, the supreme arbiter of doctrinal questions and practical party matters.

The Ba'ath in Syria initially appealed to students and younger academics, and it was via Syrian students studying at Baghdad University that its ideas spread over the border to Iraq. The Ba'ath offered a place to belong for people who, for reasons of class or religion, could not join the Iraqi Communist Party. As in Syria, its first members were academics and the urban intelligentsia attracted by 'Aflaq's notions of Arab spirit. In 1958, at the time the Iraqi monarchy was swept away, the Ba'ath was a small group. It was, more than anything, a political brand name and nascent party structure waiting to be taken over by a strong man. In Iraq, strong men were to be found in the army.

After Abdul Karim Qasim overthrew King Faisal II, he froze out the pan-Arabist army officers who had helped him seize power. One of them, Ahmad Hassan al-Bakr, began looking for a pan-Arab group to be his base for overthrowing Iraq's new dictator. He settled on the Ba'ath as a vehicle for his ambitions. In

1959 a group of Ba'athists tried to assassinate Qasim and failed. In 1963 the Ba'ath, led by Bakr, staged a full-scale coup and succeeded in murdering Qasim and seizing power, but the party could hold on to it only briefly. It was still a rather small group of people and, more important, there was a split between its civilian base and its military leadership. While the Ba'athists argued doctrine among themselves, a group of army officers staged a coup against them, and the Ba'ath lost control of the country.

The Ba'ath Party leadership did not sulk upon losing power. It reorganized. The party's structures and decision-making procedures were changed and made more streamlined, ruthless, and pragmatic. Despite Michel 'Aflaq's endless rhetoric about the Arab masses, the Ba'ath was not a mass movement— it did not have hundreds of thousands or even tens of thousands of members. Bakr understood that the Ba'ath had to rely on groups and individuals outside the party to regain power. He also knew he had to be ruthless toward those allies once the Ba'ath controlled the country. By now 'Aflaq was living in Iraq, and he suggested to Bakr just the man to carry out these ruthless tasks: Bakr's cousin Saddam Hussein.

As the months passed after the Israeli victory in the Six-Day War, shame and rage deepened throughout the Arab world. For Ahmad and his friends in Mosul, it was no different. But the blame for the disaster did not fall on Nasser. The Egyptian president wore the defeat on his face—he looked awful in the newsreels—yet when he offered to resign, the Egyptian masses demanded that he stay in office. So he did. To Mosul's young Nasserites, this was a mark of the man's nobility. Out of loyalty to his people, Nasser was willing to stay in office despite his obvious pain. His followers among the students in Mosul felt they must reciprocate that loyalty. They focused their anger on their country's ruler, Abdul Rahman Arif. In this they were not alone. Iraqi troops had played virtually no role in the war and many Iraqis felt ashamed by this. Their anger was directed at Arif.

A stronger ruler might have shrugged off the loss of public opinion, but Arif was a weak man; and by 1968 plotting to remove him from power began. Two members of his inner circle, Abdul Razzaq al-Nayif, deputy director of military intelligence, and Ibrahim al-Daud, head of the Republican Guard, linked up with Bakr and Hussein and decided to remove Arif. The coup was staged on July 17. The Ba'ath, a political party with at most a few thousand members, took over Iraq, a country with a population at the time of eight and a half million.

When Ahmad began his studies at the University of Mosul two months after the July 17 coup, there was no thought of shifting his pan-Arab allegiance to the Ba'ath. At first the university's Nasserites took a "wait and see" position. The previous decade had seen four changes of regime, three by military coups; and there had been more military coup attempts that had not been successful. There was no reason at first to think that the Ba'ath regime would survive any longer than the previous governments. How many people were in the party, anyway? they asked each other. A few thousand around the country at most. There were more Nasserite sympathizers in Mosul than that, and hundreds of thousands more communists. Besides, the Ba'ath had seized power before and not been able to hold on to it. So they watched and waited.

But this time things really were different. The purges of non-Ba'athists in the postcoup government happened almost immediately. To begin with, Bakr's coconspirators in the coup, Nayif and Daud, were purged a mere two weeks later and driven into exile. Real power to decide policy was vested in the new five-man Revolutionary Command Council; all were Ba'ath Party members or strong supporters of the party. Three of the five—including Ahmad Hassan al-Bakr and Saddam Hussein—were from the small city of Tikrit and were connected to each other by either blood or marriage. Although the number of Ba'ath members was small, by fiat of the RCC all major government positions were held by members of the party. An omnipresent state security apparatus was immediately put in place. There were several different secret police organizations, but in the end they all became known by the name Mukhabarat.

There were two other events that allowed a few thousand people to bring an entire nation under its control. In November 1968, the former foreign minister, Nasir al-Hani, was murdered. Next, a group of senior businessmen in Baghdad, mostly Jews, were accused of spying for Israel. They were tried in secret and then publicly hanged. Their bodies were left on the scaffold while crowds of Iraqis filed by to look at them. The message was clear. This was not a weak regime; to oppose it meant the prospect of arrest, exile, torture, or death.

Ahmad's first months at the university went by in a blur. There was an urgency to student life in the fall of 1968, in Iraq as well as the United States. Learning and politics were not separate pursuits—they were one and the same thing. The long days stretched from classrooms to political meetings to study sessions and back to political meetings. Ahmad quickly established himself in the classroom as an excellent student and in the university's Nasserite network as an indefatigable organizer. He'd always had enormous energy; now the thrill of working underground in what he thought was a real national liberation movement gave him even more drive. He organized clandestine meetings where the twists and turns of Ba'ath policies were dissected and the network's response to these policies was decided. If the group decided to publish its views, Ahmad was the man assigned to write the editorial. He could quickly turn out an essay analyzing the specific ways in which the latest actions of the Bakr regime were betraying the pan-Arab ideal. One of his friends told him he needed to sign his essays with a nom de guerre. Ahmad chose al-Fatih, "the leader."

For a while Ahmad and his friends held their clandestine meetings without too much danger. The Ba'ath government did not have a particularly effective secret police apparatus at first. The "Republic of Fear" was not built in a day. By the start of Ahmad's second year at university, however, things had begun to change. The Ba'ath began to recruit the faculty. An older professor who had been a vocal supporter of Nasser's vision of Arab socialism for many years published an article in the university newspaper declaring he would not join. Then he disappeared. Rumors about his fate bounced through Ahmad's network, each rumor more fearful than the last. The professor turned up in Beirut some months later. Exile is better than death, Ahmad thought. Others began to disappear, but they were not so lucky; some were sent to prison, others were executed.

All politics is not just local, it is also personal. Ahmad and his friends looked at the kind of people joining the Ba'ath in Mosul. They were neither well educated nor "well cultured." People with education and a bit of political knowledge were involved with the Iraqi Communist Party or in Nasserite networks. But the Ba'ath's support came from the strata of society that had no hope of improving their positions unless they could latch onto the new power. More and more of these new party members were turning up at the university and in professional institutions. They were all, one way or another, providing information to the Mukhabarat about people at the university who were not loyal to the regime.

Student politicians began to be arrested with greater frequency. With each arrest, Ahmad's own network became more and more cautious. In the first months after the Ba'ath coup, the group organized their get-togethers with discretion. Now these meetings had to be organized in conditions of full-blown secrecy. Rumors of impending arrests blew through the network, and occasionally they proved accurate. By now, eighteen months after seizing power, the Ba'ath recruiters had brought many students into the party. Some were old friends of Ahmad's and they could be relied on to pass on bits of information gleaned from party comrades involved in security matters. One of them told Ahmad that he had seen his name on a list of people to be arrested.

That evening Faraj came home from school to find his big brother shoveling papers into the *thanoor*—the cone-shaped oven in which their mother baked the family's bread.

"What are you doing?" Faraj asked.

"I need to burn all these papers. The Mukhabarat have my name on a list."

"Are you sure?"

"Yes. Now bring me everything you have hidden as well. If they come searching in this house, they can't find anything."

The brothers burned everything in the house linking them to their underground network. It didn't make any difference. A few days later Faraj was dragged out of his high school's playground and taken away to prison. The beatings began immediately. The interrogation was crude; all the Mukhabarat wanted to know was who else was in this Nasserite group. Faraj had no names to give up—the few he knew, they had already. Faraj quickly figured out that he had been arrested to frighten Ahmad. It was the

Ba'ath regime's way of saying to his big brother: Your actions will have consequences for your family.

A small comfort to Faraj in this frightening situation was that he was not alone in the jail. Two of his school friends were in the same cell, and all of them were receiving the same treatment; not having to endure it alone made it bearable. At least, it was a comfort until a couple of the Mukhabarat came into the cell and grabbed one of his friends, Mothana Kasmoola, and began to beat him. The blows were hard, and his friend couldn't help crying and pleading with them to stop. Faraj tried to look away but one of the Mukhabarat grabbed him by the hair and forced him to watch. Mothana's crying seemed to incense the security police. They kicked him to the ground, then hauled him to his feet, and one of the guards punched him with all his strength on the cheek. A crack like a small pistol shot filled the room as the boy's cheekbone broke. He lost consciousness. The guards let his body fall to the floor and began kicking him again. His body went across the floor limp and heavy as a sack of flour until it came to rest against the cell wall. One of the guards aimed a kick at the unconscious boy's head, which slammed against the concrete wall. That was probably the blow that killed Mothana.

A week later Faraj was released. Then they came for Ahmad. The Mukhabarat kept him in prison for a month. The beatings were severe, but Ahmad gave up no names. In the hours when he was alone, he remembered things he had read written by Michel 'Aflaq. Ahmad and his friends had studied the founder of Ba'athism's writings in the hope of trying to understand their political enemies better. In defining his world against all things Western, 'Aflaq had railed against humanism. Ahmad thought of himself as a humanist, but he also thought of himself as an Arab nationalist, a Kurd, a poet, and a scientist.

Ahmad was just nineteen and contained multitudes in his imagination. He believed the most divergent political and artistic points of view could be synthesized in himself. Studying biology had taught him how complex organic life was, and he applied those lessons to his social existence. When his comrades' rhetoric became overly simplistic, Ahmad would remind them that men are complex physical and social animals and the societies they make are equally complex. The followers of 'Aflaq hated complexity.

'Aflaq wrote that Ba'athists must "engender fierce hatred until death towards those persons who represent a contrary idea. . . . The antagonistic idea does not exist by itself; it is embodied in persons who must perish, so that it too may perish." Ahmad sat in his cell between beatings, thinking: *They want to kill me, to kill all the ideas that I represent.* Fear, anger, resignation filled him up. Ahmad knew then exactly how his life would turn out—one way or another the Ba'ath would kill him. The death might be swift: a bullet in the head; or painful: tortured until his heart gave out; or slow: living in exile. But the Ba'ath, if they stayed in power, would get him. The insight was a burden and a release. Ahmad knew then that he had no choice; so long as the Ba'ath were in power, his death could come at any time, so he would do whatever he wanted to do, write whatever he wanted to write, and, he hoped, leave "contrary ideas" planted all over Iraqi soil. *'Aflaq is wrong. They can kill me but they can't kill the idea,* he told himself, waiting for the Mukhabarat.

The Ba'ath had been in power for almost three years and were growing stronger. Ahmad's comrades who had confidently predicted that this Ba'ath government, like the 1963 Ba'ath government, would fall apart under its own egotistical ineptitude were proved wrong. Slowly but surely the regime was strangling the political life out of the country. The university campuses were being turned into recruiting centers for the one-party state the Ba'ath's deputy leader, Saddam Hussein, was building. A new strategy for dealing with the regime had to be designed, one that required direct confrontation. Word went out surreptitiously among the Nasserite groups at all Iraq's university campuses that a conference was to be held in Baghdad to decide how to organize nationwide demonstrations against the Ba'ath. The various universities held elections for delegates to the conference. Ahmad was one of those elected to attend from Mosul. The list was sent to the conference's organizers in Baghdad and a letter came back questioning Ahmad's name. Isn't he a Kurd? the letter asked. This is an Arab movement. He can't be a delegate.

The leadership of the network summoned Ahmad. They showed him the letter. He read it and looked at his comrades.

"So what? I was elected in a free vote. These guys in Baghdad can't disregard that."

One of his comrades apologized. "Look, I know, but we need to send a strong delegation to Baghdad. If you go, there will be arguments about your presence rather than the things that we need to really spend time talking about. Don't take it personally, we will be fighting for what you would fight for: a general strike."

"But there is a principal here. I was elected in a quite free and fair election. You should write back and remind them of this. If they can't respect a decision arrived at in this way, how can they call themselves democrats?"

One of the other comrades said, "I'm sorry, we have to follow these instructions. Party discipline is as important to a revolutionary movement as the result of a vote."

"Your disciplines are too strict and limited if you think that."

The local network chief intervened. "I'm sorry, Ahmad, but this is an Arab movement. We value all your work and want you to continue, but you can't be a delegate."

Ahmad became enraged. "I thought we fought for democracy and socialism. Not racial supremacy." He stormed to the door, opened it, and turned around. "Fuck you. I'll set up my own democratic party."

A few days later he was walking down the street at lunchtime on his way to a little shawarma stand when a car pulled up beside him. He looked over and saw it was Mukhabarat. He kept walking.

"Hello, Ahmad," said the cop in the passenger seat.

"What?" Ahmad said, and kept walking.

"Ahmad, come with us."

"Why? What have I done?"

"Come with us."

Ahmad thought quickly about whether to indulge in a bit of bravado and keep ignoring them, maybe even run for it, or to just give up and go with them. Maybe it would shorten his visit to prison. He stopped walking and got in the back of the car. When he got to jail they took him to a cell and gave him a good beating, then left him alone for two days. He thought, so much for the theory that cooperating will make these thugs less brutish.

They finally came and took him to an interrogation cell. The interrogator asked questions about the members of the Nasserite network. Ahmad said, "I don't know what you're talking about."

He anticipated the blow, a full slap across the face. "We know you are the leader. What are their names?" the interrogator asked.

Ahmad laughed bitterly. "I'm not the leader of anything."

The interrogator continued to demand names. Despite the slaps and punches, Ahmad said nothing.

"I don't know why you are so loyal to them," the interrogator said. "Who do you think denounced you to us?"

He was hurt by this news more than by the beating. Ahmad worked hard to suppress the desire to tell them every single name in the network. But he could not cooperate with these people. The betrayal by his former comrades was small in comparison to the self-betrayal that naming names and cooperating with this thug represented. He remained silent and took his beating. Several more days went by, then he was summoned to an office. A political officer of the Ba'ath was seated there. The officer told Ahmad that authorization for his release had come through, but first he had to sign an oath renouncing membership of any political party except the Ba'ath.

Ahmad rubbed his cheek where there was a slight swelling from his beatings. Something written by Michel 'Aflaq popped into his head. He looked at the political officer and repeated it. " 'When we are cruel to others, we know that our cruelty is in order to bring them back to their true selves, of which they are ignorant.' "

The Ba'athist looked puzzled and a little angry. "What do you mean?"

"Nothing," Ahmad said. It hardly came as a surprise that this monitor of Ba'ath Party political purity couldn't recognize the words of the founder of the Ba'ath's political program. Ahmad reached for the paper and signed it. His signature on the pledge meant nothing. He had every intention of continuing to work for the overthrow of the regime; signing this oath simply gave him the opportunity to get out of jail and get restarted.

"You belong to us now," said the Ba'ath party comrade, smiling.

Ahmad was instructed to attend Ba'ath recruitment lectures

at the university. He sat through two and, uncharacteristically, hardly said a word. Then he stopped going. Faraj came home from school late one afternoon and found Ahmad there. The young man knew his brother was supposed to be at a party meeting. He asked Ahmad why he was at home. His brother mumbled something about not wanting to listen to Ba'ath lies anymore.

"Look, brother," Faraj said, "for a few weeks more you should go to these meetings. No one actually believes anything they hear in them. Your friends know what you think. If you don't go, they will arrest you again."

"So what?"

"Go to a few more meetings—they won't bother you after that."

"I am a free man; no one owns me, no one tells me what to think or what I can do."

Faraj didn't like to argue with his brother but he felt Ahmad was being unrealistic. He said gently, "You are feeling more free than the freedom we have."

Ahmad thought about this. *Faraj is right,* he told himself. *I do act as if I had the freedom of an American or a Briton even though I am a Kurd living in an Arab country governed by a dictatorship.*

Faraj broke his train of thought. "You've been like this since our father died. Why?"

"I would have been like this anyway. It is my nature."

"So you think it is a genetic matter?"

Ahmad suddenly felt oppressed by these questions. He snapped at his younger brother, "I can't explain these things to you. Don't ask me about them again."

Faraj respected his older brother's wishes and never spoke to him again about why he acted "more free than the freedom we have."

The final years of university went by quickly. Ahmad floated among small groups of politically disaffected students; some called themselves socialists, others communists. He wrote occasional pamphlets but never signed them. Most of the time he concentrated on maintaining his high academic standing; he had been promised a lecturer's job at the medical college in Mosul if he kept up his good class work.

Geopolitical reality had hit the Ba'ath government. In the years since 1968, when Bakr and his comrades had seized power, Iraq had had to make decisions on where its international interests lay. It had come to power, in the wake of the Six-Day War, with an aggressively anti-Western stance. America supported its two most detested neighbors, Iran and Israel. The regime therefore was reliant on the Soviet Union for arms. The pro-Soviet tilt of the regime meant doors were opened for exchange programs to countries in the Soviet bloc.

At a writer's conference in Baghdad, Ahmad met a young woman from Poland. They flirted while she was in Iraq and began a passionate affair by mail when she returned to Warsaw. In 1972, when Ahmad finished his exams, he flew to Warsaw. It may be hard for a Westerner to think of Poland as exotic, but for Ahmad it was. The place deranged his senses in the same way traveling to a tropical island may unhinge a northern European. Everything he saw, smelled, and touched was different: blond hair, beer, the cold. In Warsaw he was an oddity, but also something of a celebrity among his girlfriend's circle. He spoke no Polish, so they communicated in English. During the day his girlfriend went to work at the Ministry of Culture, and Ahmad stayed in her flat and read. She had English translations of

French existentialists. He read everything. At night they went to the theater; it was the heyday of playwrights like Eugène Ionesco and Samuel Beckett and the Polish director Jerzy Grotowski. Ahmad learned about avant-garde theatrical movements like the theatre of the absurd and Antonin Artaud's theater of cruelty. The phrase "theater of cruelty" did not strike him as overly aesthetic—it seemed a proper scientific label to put on the Ba'ath regime.

For a few months it was fun, then the strain of conducting a relationship in an offshore tongue began to wear. Ahmad's money began to run low, and his girlfriend made it clear that perhaps it was time for him to go home. He agreed. In any case, his appointment as a lecturer in anatomy at the medical college of Mosul had come through. It was time to return to his personal theater of cruelty, but before leaving Europe there was one thing he had to do.

Ahmad took the train to Paris. He had almost no money left, but he couldn't be this close to the city and not see it with his own eyes. Everything he had been reading in Warsaw seemed to have emanated from Paris. Ahmad, like young writers everywhere, wanted to breathe its air in the hope of ingesting some of whatever was inspiring Beckett and Sartre, if only for one day. He spent more time on the train to Paris from Warsaw than he did walking the city's streets.

In his single day in Paris, he had time to visit the Shakespeare and Company bookshop. His eyes raced over the titles; he picked out volumes, flipped through the pages, and put them back. He found a used paperback of *The Portable Faulkner.* Faulkner was one of those names out there in the student ether whose work was regarded as important, so Ahmad took the book to a corner of the shop and sat on a stool and leafed through the table of contents. His curiosity was piqued by the title of one story, "A Rose for Emily." He turned to it and got lost in Faulkner's world. Hours went by as he sat on his stool, oblivious to the pretty girls browsing through the shelves and the glares of the bookstore's crotchety owner. When he had exhausted himself with Faulkner, he put the book neatly back where he had found it. There was just enough time to have a glass of wine at a small bar on the rue St. Jacques, around the corner from the bookstore. Then he had to get to the train station and get back to Warsaw.

He had not been there long enough for the reality of Paris to have cut through his idealized image of the city. He still saw it refracted through his dreams and the words of others writers. For the rest of his life, he held on to the dream image and the desire to go back and see the place more clearly. Many years later, on the day Saddam's regime finally collapsed in Mosul, he would tell a friend that he had never stopped dreaming of going back to Paris, and now, finally, he would be able to go.

Ahmad Shawkat in Mechko's teahouse.

Roaa al-Zrary, Ahmad's daughter.

My driver, Sami Abdul Qader.

A statue of Kurdish poet and historian Ibn al-Mustawfi gazes over Erbil's bazaar from the height of the Citadel.

Anna Badkhen and some pesh merga enjoy the spring sun while waiting for action that never came to Dola Bakir.

Ahmad and his sons Rafat, Shawkat, and Sindibad sitting in their furnitureless living room in Erbil.

Ahmad's oldest child, Sindibad, is a talented tailor and embroiderer. He supported the family with this work after they were forced to move to Erbil.

The Green Berets at Debaga Pass. A hundred yards behind them was the still smoldering wreckage left after an American jet accidentally bombed a column of pesh merga and the BBC's John Simpson's crew.

Left: What was left of the convoy mistakenly attacked by an American jet at Debaga.
Right: The remains of the truck in which most of the friendly fire victims were travelling.
The press pack is standing to the right, so intent on getting details that they didn't hear the
incoming mortar rounds.

Our driver Sami and a couple of pesh merga standing on an abandoned Iraqi tank at Debaga.

Ahmad scans the cloudy skies for American warplanes at the site of the friendly fire incident.

The Kurdish mountains near Dyana, their beauty is almost too much to bear.

Looted goods stacked high in the courtyard of a mosque across the street from the University of Mosul the day after the regime collapsed. In the first days after Mosul "fell," committees from the mosque were the only source of order in the city.

Ahmad greets his daughter Sana on the day he returned to Mosul. The child on her shoulder is his grandson and namesake Ahmad.

A villager walks into the fields in Darawish.

Left: Ahmad outside the ruins of the Security Management building. He had been imprisoned in the basement and tortured there in 1996. **Right:** The grave of Ahmad Shawkat. The tombstone reads: "God's promises are true."

Chapter Nine
"Life Without Problems
Is Not Interesting."

AHMAD RETURNED TO Mosul and in the winter of 1973 began lecturing in anatomy and histopathology at the medical college. Standing in the lecture theater looking out at his students, he felt a surge of strength. Here in the classroom, he truly became al-Fatih. You don't have to be a politician to exercise power, he told himself. You can build cadres dedicated to political change by engaging young minds in a lecture on science and then inviting your students for tea to talk about something else, like literature.

Nineteen seventy-three was a critical year for the Ba'ath regime. A well-planned coup against Ahmad Hassan al-Bakr by Nazim Kzar, head of the state's security apparatus, came within hours of succeeding. This gave Saddam Hussein a reason to purge the party's top ranks and put even more of his kinsmen from Tikrit in sensitive positions. The process of nationalizing the oil industry was completed. Henceforth, all revenues from the sale of Iraqi oil would go directly to the state, and the government would control how foreign companies gained the right to drill for the stuff. Finally, the Arabs discovered their ultimate weapon in the never-ending war against Israel and its Western allies: the price of oil. Following the Yom Kippur War, the price of oil quadrupled almost overnight. Iraq was poised to become a rich nation. In 1972, the year before nationalization, Iraq's treasury received $575 million dollars in oil revenue; by 1980 that figure would rise to $27 billion. Prosperity can buy even the most dictatorial regime the goodwill of its people.

There was time for work and time for art. Ahmad and his friends met regularly at a café in Mosul's Old City to talk about music and literature. They sipped chai, smoked, and talked and talked. The Writer's Café was a regular scene for Mosul's bohemians, with scheduled lectures and poetry readings. Here, too, Ahmad was al-Fatih. His time in Europe gave him cachet, and his broad reading of foreign literature meant he always had some new reference to throw into the conversation. His talks were always well attended. Sometimes he invited his medical students to the Writer's Café lectures.

Ahmad often gave talks on modernist poetry. He loved its abstractions. "What it says is not what it means. What it means is not how it is said. How perfect for our society. We never say what we mean. Allusion in our speech carries the same weight as literalism in English. For the English, metaphor is poetic adornment. For us, metaphor is literalism. Therefore, we live in a state where we must constantly interpret meaning.

"And in our present situation, modernism is perfect for what our society is today. Do we speak directly? Do we speak with the clarity of science? No. That's why I love these texts."

He worked at translating the writers he had come to know in Warsaw—absurdist masters like Ionesco and Beckett—from English into Arabic. The originals were in French, so they were already once removed from the inspiration of the author, but

Ahmad was amazed at how easily he was able to convey both the basic words and their ambiguities into Arabic.

He read as much Faulkner as he could. Initially he found that reading the author was like solving a puzzle; the first challenge was to figure out who was telling the story. But soon he realized that the writer was actually telling the story through many different voices and writing through their stream of consciousness. The whole idea thrilled him. Stream of consciousness wasn't just a literary technique—it was the way his mind worked. In an ordinary hour of the day, his stream of consciousness was filled with an extraordinary concatenation of memories and thoughts triggered by passing a place where he had seen a political murder, or by lecturing on the pure certitudes of anatomical science, or by walking along the unexcavated walls of Nineveh where civilization began. His streams of consciousness went all the way back to the beginning of history. James Joyce had his Dublin mythology. Standing on the walls of Nineveh, Ahmad gazed out on millennia. Nineveh is a real place, not a mythological one, he told himself. Try and encompass that in your mind.

Across the street from his mother's house in Mosul lived an Arab family, the family of a man named Abdulrazak. He had a beautiful daughter named Afrah. She had been Ahmad's neighbor for a long time, but it was only recently that he had noticed her. Afrah had physically crossed over from adolescence into young womanhood. "When did that happen?" he asked himself. But once he had taken notice of this new young woman on his block, he began to see more and more details about her appearance. She had beautiful eyes, deep and dark. Occasionally, he heard her gossiping and laughing with friends in the narrow road outside his window. She was not silly like other girls of fifteen. And he liked the sound of her laugh. It wasn't a schoolgirl giggle. He became more and more aware of her comings and goings. She was in high school, so it wasn't hard to figure out what time of day she would leave and when she would return. Ahmad managed to just be hanging around in the street when she came back from school and struck up conversations. She really was very mature for her age, he told himself. After a couple of these not quite by chance meetings, he asked her if she would like to attend one of his talks at the Writer's Café.

She said yes immediately, thrilled to be invited into a grown-up world. She became a regular at his talks at the teahouse and the impromptu ones he held in his house across the street from hers. It was exciting for Afrah, hanging around with university students and young lecturers, listening to ideas that seemed daring and rebellious. Ahmad spoke about poetry with a passion that no other teacher could muster. He noticed her looking at him as he spoke. When he asked questions she always tried to answer. There was no guile in her, just a sweet exhilaration at being in the café listening to these exotic ideas. She also felt free enough to tease him a little bit whenever the sound of his own voice carried him away. This made the others in the group giggle and it made Ahmad laugh as well.

Ahmad began to feel love creeping up on him again. He knew the symptoms well. He diagnosed himself: How often do you think about this young woman? Do you hear her laugh when she isn't around? Does your work become uninteresting when you haven't seen her for a few days? When you see her talking to one of the boys in the class, do you suffer panic? All the answers in this psychological history confirmed the diagnosis: he was falling in love. Now that he recognized the fact, he needed to find out whether she recognized it. He invited a small group of students to his house for a talk. When it was over, he indicated to Afrah she should stay behind. It might have been scandalous, a pretty fifteen-year-old spending time unchaperoned with a twenty-three-year-old teacher, but Afrah's home was just across the street, and it seemed perfectly natural for them to exchange a word or two before she went to her father's house.

"I have many things I want to say to you," he said. "Do you want to hear them?"

"Yes," she said. "I have things I want to say to you also."

"We need to speak alone," he said. "How can we arrange to meet?"

She asked him to wait a few days and she would work out a plan. She figured out a way to sneak off the school bus just after the pickup point. The next morning Afrah left the bus exactly where she was supposed to. When she stepped down, he walked out from behind some cars. It was all very clandestine. She laughed and skipped over to him. He took her hand and began to stroll toward the school. Ahmad was in a serious mood that morning. She noted it and asked him why.

"I have a lecture this morning," he explained. "I'm thinking of that and other things."

"What other things?"

He did not know how to explain at first. This was unusual for him, Afrah thought. Words usually tumbled out of him as from a waterfall.

"Is it something secret?" she asked.

He looked at her for a long moment. "Yes."

"You can tell me, no one will know."

"It will be dangerous for you," he replied.

That might have been the most seductive thing Ahmad ever said. Afrah looked at him earnestly. "You can tell me everything. If this is about politics, I will tell no one."

Ahmad stopped walking and looked into her eyes. He thought about bringing her into his world. She was still so young. Than he asked himself: *Why am I hesitating? I'm standing here in the street with her. Why? I want to take her into my life, so she has to know all of these things. I cannot make her my wife and then tell her, "Oh, I am a member of an underground movement." She needs to understand who I am.*

He looked at her again and saw Afrah not as a pretty girl but as a serious woman whom he could trust not to reveal secrets. He relaxed a little and resumed walking. She followed along and he began to tell her about his other life, the world where poetry led to politics.

Most mornings they met this way. Not all were as serious as the first morning. Sometimes in the afternoon Afrah would meet him at the teahouse or at one of his literary study groups.

In the warm weather he took her to Mount Maqloub. They walked up the mountain and looked out at the emerald-green plain, leaning into the fierce breeze that always blows around the summit. At Easter he took her to St. Matthew's Monastery. They watched the Christians from the local villages make their way into the church, and sat outside listening to the liturgical music.

"It is so different from the muezzin and reciting the Quran," Afrah said.

"Yes, but they are like us. They are the same people but we make them different because they come here, because they are Christians. We live in this place, we are in some cases the same genetic group, but still we persecute them."

"We?"

"No, not you or me, but so many times Kurds or Arabs attack them. They invoke Islam as a reason. For so long this has happened, yet they still cling to their faith. I wish I knew why. I cannot believe in God so much, to suffer persecution."

"What would you die for?" Afrah asked.

"For you." Ahmad smiled and took her hand. She laughed and pulled it away.

"No, I want to know. What would you die for?"

This was why he was in love with this young woman. She asked good questions. He was silent for a long time thinking of an answer. He did not want to be glib or pompous.

"I would die for justice. I would die to speak the truth."

She said nothing. He grew nervous. "Maybe you don't want to be with me now."

She remained silent, thinking. He couldn't bear the quiet, so words began to tumble from him without much thought. "I am not someone who should have a family. . . . I mean these words. I will not be quiet. I feel sometimes like a wild stallion in a corral. I kick at the fence and will break through it or injure myself and they will come and put me down. I cannot stop myself. You don't want this life. I will make trouble for you. I—"

"Stop talking," she interrupted. "Don't tell me what I want. I want you."

Now came the time for negotiation of marriage. The custom dictated that Ahmad's mother should visit Afrah's family to make the initial inquiry about marriage. Then Ahmad's father should make a second inquiry, although, since his father was dead, it would have to be his oldest brother. Then, when all was agreed among the parents, a party announcing the engagement would be held. Ahmad decided to skip all the customs and go directly to Afrah's father himself. He told Faraj what he planned to do. Faraj suggested he might want to consider following the old ways in this matter. Ahmad was dismissive. "What is the point of the old ways in a modern society? I have a good job. I earn a good living. I love her very much."

Ahmad went directly to Abdulrazak to ask for his daughter's

hand in marriage. The response was predictable—Afrah's father refused. It wasn't just that Ahmad's disregard of the proper rituals was rude. In his view, Ahmad came from no family. What had his father been? A peasant who sold sheep in the bazaar. He was not even an Arab but a Kurd.

Ahmad felt the rejection as keenly as any poet. He became depressed. He contemplated suicide. At night he wrote poems bathed in love. He reread them in the morning, saw they were coated in pathetic sentiment, and burned them. If he had had money he would have gone away again. But he didn't. He had to work, and in the hours when he wasn't preparing his lectures he wrote his first book, a study of ancient Mesopotamian pottery. This was a subject that had interested him since he first dug pot-sherds out of the walls of ancient Nineveh when he was a boy. These activities provided a counterbalance to his disappointment.

And he could still see Afrah. She urged him to wait and try asking again. He waited for a while, then asked her father for her hand again. The rejection was absolute. Again depression visited. Afrah began to lobby friends of her parents and her older brothers to argue Ahmad's case. She loved him and wanted him for her husband.

One of Ahmad's friends, Ghazi, took pity on her. "Do you know what you're letting yourself in for?" he asked. "Ahmad is my dear friend, but I'm telling you he is drawn to trouble. He is good to be with now while you are young and want excitement . . . but to have a family? Do you think he will change? He won't. He will exhaust you."

Afrah told him, "Life without problems is not interesting."

Another friend, Omar, said to her, "The Ba'ath regime already has his name written down many times. Your name will go on that list and then your father's name. And when you have children their names will go on the list too."

Afrah replied, "Do you think the Ba'ath regime is forever? Only Allah is forever. Ahmad works to remove the Ba'ath."

A year went by and slowly cracks appeared in Abdulrazak's resistance. Finally, the persistent lobbying wore Afrah's father down. He gave his permission. The wedding was Western in style. The bride looked beautiful in her dress; her head was uncovered, for she had not yet turned to Islam as a way of life. Ahmad rented a tuxedo. His wife told him he looked like a movie star in it. He spent the day imagining he was in a romantic film in which the hero overcomes many trials and prejudices to win the heart of his true love and begin a happy life. In fact, things were very good for him. He had a prestigious job and a beautiful wife. He was writing stories. His country was modernizing, and the money from oil was being put to good use. Education was improving. When enough people had a good education, they would see the Ba'ath for what they were, and rise up against them.

The newlyweds could not keep their hands off each other. At lunchtime Ahmad would come home, and when the meal was finished they would have a siesta. Ahmad would go into the kitchen and dip a finger into the honey jar on the way to the bedroom—some older friends had told him it would make him potent—and make love to his wife. Afrah became pregnant quickly.

"It's a son, I am sure," she told him. "What shall we name him?"

"Nothing from religion," Ahmad said firmly. "His name must come from literature."

"Are you sure? Shouldn't our first son be named in honor of the prophet or one of the early sages?"

"No, no, no. My father named three of his sons after the

prophet, including me. That's enough for any family. Let me think."

They returned to the subject during the months Afrah was pregnant. They went through names of their favorite poets. Then Ahmad decided to give his son a name not in honor of a writer but directly from literature.

"We will call him Sindibad, like the character Sinbad in *The Thousand and One Nights.* He will be clever. He will be rich. He will have a life full of adventure. This is what a father wants for his son."

Sindibad was born in 1976. In Arab culture, after a first son is born, friends and family honor the parents by affectionately calling them Abu, meaning "father," or Um, meaning "mother." Ahmad and Afrah became Abu Sindibad and Um Sindibad to their family and close friends.

It was a good time to start a family, perhaps the best time in modern Iraq's history. The quadrupling of oil prices after the 1973 war had made the country wealthy. Ahmad worked for the largest employer in the country: the state. His job at the medical school was prestigious, his salary and perks were generous. But Ba'ath power was congealing all around the society. The university was infiltrated with loyal Ba'athists who kept an eye on the faculty. Ahmad was forced to take indoctrination lectures and register his name with the party.

In the meantime he wrote articles critical of the regime and had them published in Arab political journals from Damascus to Cairo. The regime didn't seem to notice. It was possible to sit back and laugh at the ineptitude—although not too loudly—of their Stalinism with an Arab face.

Shortly after Sindibad was born, Ahmad wrote a monograph called *Childhood and Adolescence.* Then he turned his hand to fiction and wrote a volume of stories titled *The Snow and the Sparrows.* In order for it to be published it had to be passed by the Ba'ath regime's censor, so he dropped the manuscript off at the Ministry of Culture, and then, a week later, he was summoned to meet with the Ba'ath Party representative on the medical faculty. He explained the book would not be published because Ahmad was a scientist and his job in building the state was to teach science, not write stories. Then the Ba'athist started talking about Ahmad's lectures at the Writer's Café.

"Why do you need to teach these things? You teach anatomy."

"I do this in my free time. Why should I not be allowed to do this?" he asked.

"Your students are medical students. They don't need to know these ideas. Don't do it anymore."

The threat was implicit. A few days later Omar invited Ahmad for coffee. Ahmad's friend told him there was a strong chance he would be arrested when the term was over. Omar had heard the rumor from someone who was close to the local Ba'ath leadership in Mosul. Ahmad thanked his friend for the warning and went home. He told Afrah the story.

"I think I should leave the country after the school year is over."

"Where will you go?"

"Egypt. I will find work there as a journalist. . . . They've published some of my articles."

He went to Darawish to visit his older brother Khalil. Ever since their mother, Shokria, told Khalil about her dream while pregnant with Ahmad, his older brother had helped him out financially. Ahmad told Khalil he needed to travel to get his book published and to make some contacts at Arab publishing houses. Khalil gave his little brother some money to take the trip.

He arrived in Cairo, the Nasserite homeland, in 1978, more

than a decade late. The crushing defeat by Israel in 1967 had undone the Egyptian leader's mystical hold over the masses. Nasser had died in 1973 a broken man. Now the Egyptians were moving toward God, and Pan-Arabism was being replaced by pan-Islamism in their hearts. In their view, the leader of the nation, Anwar al-Sadat, was betraying the Arab cause by making peace with Israel.

Ahmad tried to love Cairo. He found a job at a magazine and he went to the writers' cafés and bars and stayed up very late talking literature and politics. But exile was painful. What he longed for while trapped in the increasingly strong tentacles of the Ba'ath state was a chance simply to speak his mind and write what he wanted to write. What he didn't realize until he got to Cairo was that many of his attitudes were suspect not just to Ba'athists but to Arabs generally. He knew he was regarded as a nonconformist in the context of Iraq, but he was surprised to find himself being looked at in the same way in the intellectual capital of the Arab world. *I am a rationalist,* he thought, *yet my Egyptian colleagues consider me an odd person because my style in thinking and writing is different to theirs. What do they expect? I cultured myself on Western things, Western novels, stories, and criticism. So what?*

The last shred of his belief in a workable form of Pan-Arabism disappeared in Cairo. He encountered snobbery among educated Egyptians who thought they were superior to other Arabs. Ahmad had seen in Nasser's face the look of the pharaohs and once felt deeply connected to that civilization. Yet in Cairo he was not made to feel that it was a civilization he shared. A feeling had been gnawing at him since he'd been forbidden from advancing in the Nasserite network; now it was confirmed: the dream of the United Arab Republic could never work. The rhetoric could never match the reality. Egyptians were different from Syrians who were different from Iraqis. Pan-Arabism was simply a slogan the rulers sold to their people to maintain their hold over them. The colonial rulers may have been correct when they drew up their maps of the Middle East after World War I. They invented borders for Iraq, but the Iraqi people already existed.

In Cairo, where he mingled with Arabs from all over the Middle East, he had time to think about how different Iraqis were from Syrians or Lebanese. In his view Iraqis were simpler, less sophisticated than the others. The sectarian and cultural mix of his country was more complex than in other Arab countries. This complexity was reflected in a level of toleration that didn't exist in more homogeneous Arab states. Teaching his countrymen about their Iraqi identity and leading them toward a simple kind of nationalism was the only way forward for his country. The Ba'ath needed to be removed, not just because they were corrupt and antidemocratic but because Pan-Arabism was a lie and Ahmad's country could only progress toward justice and equality for all by forging an Iraqi identity.

As the months went by, Ahmad grew homesick, not so much for the Ba'ath Party's Iraq as for Mosul. He had had a dream when he arrived in Cairo of building a career there and leaving Iraq forever. The plan had been to get a good job and send for his family. But the dream was false. He knew he needed to go home. While he was away Afrah had had another baby, a daughter, named Rasak, and he had yet to see her. Sindibad was almost three; it was time to begin teaching him the alphabet. Ahmad wrote letters to friends with influence at the university. They lobbied on his behalf. One thing they all agreed about was that Ahmad was a gifted teacher. His presence was missed. Ahmad was told he could have his old post back. So he returned to Mosul.

Chapter Ten

"This Is How They Strangle Us"

RETURNING TO MOSUL was sweet. Ahmad drew breath, played with his children, spent evenings with his brother Faraj quietly discussing politics. But this was Iraq, and the time for these small pleasures was brief. On July 16, 1979, Saddam Hussein became president of Iraq.

During his quarter-century reign, Saddam compared himself to many glorious leaders of Mesopotamia's past—from the ancient tyrants of Sumer to Saladin—but in the way he insinuated himself into control of a mass political party, initiated a reign of terror by purging senior colleagues, and turned the party into a personal cult, the historical figure he most resembled was Joseph Stalin.

The dictator started his rule as he meant to conduct it, with a show of terror. On July 22 he attended a special meeting of the Ba'ath Party's regional congress in Baghdad. A member of the Revolutionary Command Council, Muhyi al-Din Abd al-Husain, was brought to face the assembled comrades, and confessed to leading a plot against the new president. He read a list of names of his coconspirators, most from the senior ranks of the party. Those who were in the hall were arrested on the spot.

The whole scene was televised. Twenty-two of the alleged conspirators were later executed.

As always in Iraq, a violent change of ruler did not bring the country to a halt. This was the way governments had always changed, and the scale of the catastrophe that Saddam represented wasn't clear at first. Except for those in the inner circles of the Ba'ath who were flying too close to Saddam's sun, very little about the country immediately changed.

The university term began on schedule in the autumn. Ahmad resumed lecturing on anatomy and histopathology at the medical school. The oil industry continued to enrich the nation, particularly the middle class. His teaching salary allowed him to take Afrah to the goldsmith and buy her bracelets; she wore the family's nest egg under her clothes. Ahmad remained politically engaged. He wrote some articles about the regime that were published in Syrian and Saudi Arabian political journals. But there were no reprisals. For all their brutality, the Ba'ath comrades in Mosul were not very well organized. Yet. Their minds seemed to be focused on the changes in their party being wrought by Saddam. New personalities were rising; the average party member needed to pay more attention to who was up and who was down than to some university lecturer who liked to write the occasional article in a foreign periodical criticizing the regime.

Ahmad's main interaction with the Ba'ath concerned his little brother Faraj. Now an engineer, Faraj had been accepted to a postgraduate course at Wayne State University in Detroit. The Saddam regime, in its Stalinist way, was concerned about a brain drain and made it almost impossible for young academics to leave the country. In order to get an exit visa from the government, Faraj needed someone to be his surety, in effect to be a hostage. Ahmad agreed to be Faraj's stand-in. If his brother stayed in America, Ahmad would be punished.

There was another seismic political change affecting Iraq in 1979. In February, a revolution in Iran had established a theocratic Shi'ite state led by Ayatollah Khomeini. In November, students in Tehran seized the U.S. Embassy, taking sixty-six Americans hostage. Even as he purged his party, Saddam looked across his eastern border at events in Iran and saw an opportunity. All the great powers were frightened by the idea of a militant Islamic government in charge of an oil-producing nation situated strategically on the main shipping route for the world's petroleum. As the West had armed the shah, its leaders were more than aware of the Iranian military's capabilities should this religious regime choose to exploit its strategic position and disrupt the flow of oil. The hostage crisis isolated Iran's new ruler. To Saddam, the time seemed right to start a conflict that would consolidate his power in Iraq and establish his own credentials as the preeminent leader of the Arabs.

Saddam was not alone in seeing war as a way to consolidate power. The Khomeini regime was not averse to conflict as a means of establishing its authority either. Dictators have long known there's nothing like a little war to create a sense of patriotism and help a revolutionary regime quiet political opponents. Many middle-class Iranians had backed the overthrow of the shah, whose regime they considered corrupt, but they did not embrace Khomeini's extreme Islamism. For the ayatollah, the prospect of a fight on behalf of the Shi'a against the Arab Sunnis looked like a good way to bring Iran into line behind his revolution. There may even have been something personal in wanting to fight Saddam. Khomeini had been a political exile in Iraq for many years, but Saddam threw him out in 1978.

For Saddam a casus belli was required. Since the creation of Iraq there had been tension with Iran over a range of border issues, and among these problems a pretext for war was always available to a dictator. Saddam focused on the Shatt al Arab waterway in the south, which separates the two countries. The deep channel is Iraq's sole gateway to the Persian Gulf. The invisible boundary line between the two countries on the waterway had been a constant source of contention and negotiation. As recently as 1975 a new treaty had been signed delineating the border on the Shatt. Now Saddam demanded more negotiations.

Both regimes encouraged dissidents inside their opponents' countries. Khomeini allowed Kurdish fighters living in exile in Iran to return to Iraq. Saddam supported Arab rebels living in the Iranian border province of Khuzistan.

The march toward full-scale conflict took almost a year. Sniping and niggling marked the way. An attempt on Iraqi deputy prime minister Tariq Aziz's life in April 1980, allegedly by the Iranians, led to the expulsion of Iranian Shi'a from southern Iraq's holy Shi'ite cities. By August there were military skirmishes along the border. On September 4, Iran shelled two southern Iraqi cities. Two weeks later, Saddam announced that the 1975 treaty was null and void and the Shatt belonged entirely to Iraq. The Khomeini regime bombed cities on the Iraqi side of the Shatt. This gave Saddam the pretext he needed to invade Iran on September 22, 1980.

Both dictators may have been vain, megalomaniacal, and cruel, but they understood one thing very clearly about their people. No matter how despotic their rulers were, the people of Iran and Iraq would respond with intense patriotic resistance to any foreign invasion. In a two-week blitz the Iraqi Army rolled over the

Shatt onto Iranian soil, seizing a long, narrow strip of territory. The army captured the city of Khorramshahr and was in the outskirts of Abadan, Iran's main port on the Shatt, when the offensive ground to a halt. Iranian resistance was fierce. Over the next two years, the Iranian Army slowly clawed back the ground taken by the Iraqis. In the summer of 1982, Saddam announced that the Iraqi Army would withdraw to its prewar borders and he offered to negotiate a new treaty. Khomeini, sensing weakness in his opponent, now attacked into Iraq. His forces drove toward Basra in the south and across the central border from Kermanshah. But Khomeini and his army found out exactly what Saddam and his army had learned—the enemy fights with determination on its home soil and there is no quick path to victory. The two armies settled into a war of attrition.

The whole of Iraqi society was on a war footing. Men up to the age of forty-five were liable for conscription. There were no deferments for men with families. Ahmad, thirty-one years old and the father of three children, with a fourth on the way, received his call-up in 1982. He was assigned to a medical battalion. But before going to the battalion hospital he had to go to the front. All medical personnel had to do time on the front lines as ordinary infantrymen.

It was World War I without the mud. Trench works stretched as far as the eye could see. By this point in the war the scale of carnage was known to everyone in Iraq. Soldiers marched to their positions knowing the odds were against their marching back. As Ahmad's unit headed toward their position they passed an artillery battery. A couple of the artillerymen pointed, laughed, and mockingly waved bye-bye. Another soldier mimed drawing a knife across his throat. "You won't be back," he called out.

The bombardments from both sides were constant, the ways to die were many: shrapnel from incoming artillery; hand-to-hand combat with the suicide waves of Khomeini loyalists; or, if the wind shifted at the wrong moment, blowback of poison gas fired by your own side. Ahmad survived his week at the front and went to a military hospital, where he was put in charge of its pharmacy. The mass carnage he had witnessed at the front now passed before his eyes, one broken body at a time, in the hospital. After six months in the hospital, he had another rotation at the front.

Shortly after Ahmad returned to the hospital, the Ba'ath Party comrade in his unit summoned all medical personnel. By now Saddam had managed to insinuate the party into every level of every institution in Iraqi society. From these positions, comrades were able to monitor loyalty in ordinary citizens and report back to the state's security apparatus. Being summoned by a party hack to meetings had become a common experience. The medical team assembled in a court-yard and looked at one another, shrugged, and rolled their eyes. The Ba'athist explained that the nation needed money. The war had interrupted oil production, and in order to purchase more weapons to fight on to victory, Saddam was calling on every loyal son of Iraq to hand over his family's gold jewelry. The meeting was dismissed. By now Iraq's people had learned to control their public faces, so there were no groans, no signs of dissent. Later in the day Ahmad called over the one or two friends in the hospital whom he absolutely trusted and asked them what they were going to do.

One of them said, "What can we do? Saddam doesn't know how much gold my wife has. We can give them a few pieces and they will leave us alone."

Ahmad urged his friend to refuse any cooperation. "We are

fighting for him, risking our lives. That is enough. Let's stand together on this."

This was not an issue ripe for solidarity, and none of his friends would join him in dissent on this point. Ahmad went alone to the party comrade and told the Ba'athist he refused and told him why he would not consent to the state's appropriation of his property. The comrade looked at him and said, "That is your choice."

The next day he was taken to the military prison in Kirkuk. He had resigned himself to a beating, a few slaps, and assumed he would then be sent back to his unit. Instead he was taken into a bare room with a hook in the middle of the ceiling, hung upside down by the ankles, and whipped with frayed electrical cables. Irons were heated—his terror building as he smelled them warming up—then they were put on his back and buttocks. He could not believe the sounds that came out of him. He split into two people. One Ahmad floated above the scene, the other was all too much a part of it. When he passed out, he was revived with cold water and a doctor checked him to see if he could take more. If he could, the process began all over again. After a week of brutal abuse the interrogation started. There was nothing he could tell them that they did not already know. They had searched his locker and found copies of articles he had sent abroad for publication. The articles detailed the carnage he had seen at the front and criticized the regime's tactics in the war. He could only acknowledge writing the articles.

The torturers weren't satisfied. They strapped him into an electrical chair. It was an ingenious contraption in which the arms, seat, and back of the chair were on hinges or rods and could push inward on whoever was sitting in it. The effect was to crush a person from all sides, pressing the victim inward until his viscera were about to explode and there was not a breath of air left in the lungs. They interrogated Ahmad while he was seated in this crushing chair. He had barely enough breath to answer. His torturer was a big man who looked him right in the eyes and kept repeating, "I can't hear you, I can't hear you," until Ahmad lost consciousness.

Two things help a person survive torture and cope with its aftermath: anger and a steadfast commitment to a political cause. Anger drives the body's will to live. Being committed to a political cause provides an explanation for the unimaginable cruelty being inflicted on oneself. Those who don't survive torture and its aftermath are frequently those who have no involvement in politics and have been arrested by mistake or as part of a campaign of terror. Ahmad lived through the torture sessions because he had enough anger inside him for an entire revolutionary army and his political sensibility was acute. He knew very well the risk of standing up to the regime, and was prepared to give his life to overthrow it—although he never thought that the gateway to death could be filled with so much pain.

Wasta is an Arabic word that means something close to "influence." *Wasta* is a person's juice with the authorities, the degree to which important men help you along. Faraj had returned to Mosul after two years in the United States and he was using what *wasta* he had to get his brother out of prison. He found out whom to bribe and how much was expected. He raised money from Afrah's family and some friends and put the money in the right hands.

Arrest and torture had many purposes for Saddam. They were used to liquidate enemies slowly, thus strengthening the regime; they were used to instill fear; and they were used to extort money. Ahmad's torture and its outcome were driven by those last two reasons. A person who is tortured, allowed to live, then released back into the community gives living testimony to the power of the state. Returning a dismembered corpse, hastily interred, creates fear only for those who choose to remember the victim. Most people quickly forget the dead. A torture victim walking broken through the street is a much more powerful tool for maintaining order through fear. The fact that Ahmad's family had money made him worth sparing. There would be further opportunities to arrest him and extort another ransom from his people.

The torture stopped, although Ahmad languished in the Kirkuk prison for a while longer. His body healed. One day his torturer came to his cell. "We seem to have made a mistake. You can go now. Bye-bye." Ahmad was returned to his medical unit and served out the remainder of his call-up. He shrugged off questions about what had happened during his six months in Kirkuk's military prison. Most of the time he acted as if nothing terrible had happened to him, but every once in a while, for no reason at all, his mind seemed to leave his body. For the rest of his life he would have these "quite-ly" sad moments of detachment.

The war had been going on for four years and was mired in stalemate when Ahmad's military service ended and he returned to the university. The classroom brought him peace. The stint in jail and the sights of the front were suppressed from his memory. He enjoyed meeting his new students. Their relationship was different than in his earlier teaching stints. Then, Ahmad and his students were almost the same age. Now he was much older, if not numerically—his years at the front and in prison had aged him. When he began teaching, his students were like his brothers and sisters, now they were almost like his children. To get to know them better, he began organizing literary get-togethers at the Writers Café in Mosul's Old City once again.

Ahmad thought long and hard about what to teach in those unofficial lectures. The students were young and full of adolescent passion, so he read them love poetry. In the words of lovelorn poets he found a key for talking to them about the balance between the individual and his connections to the rest of society. Suffering for love is a universal experience, but a person in the throes of adolescent passion cannot be consoled by that fact. A person suffering for love thinks he or she is the only person on earth in such agony. But Ahmad believed the spirit to gain the beloved against all odds was the same as the spirit to struggle for a just society. This was the message he wanted to give his students. It was something for them to take back to the hospitals in Ramadi, Baghdad, or Basra, where they would make their careers. They would be little bright points of enlightenment embedded deep in the society. When the regime weakened, as all previous regimes had, these enlightenment points would provide the leadership for a better nation.

The students who attended the talks looked at him in a way that healed him further. Ahmad knew himself well enough to know that sometimes he said things for the sheer pleasure of hearing his own voice. But when he saw the look on his students' faces, he reined in his own egotism. Everything he said had a purpose. These talks were a special curriculum in culture. The Ba'ath was killing off the one gift of the colonial period: an education system that created "well-cultured" people. It was a little more than a decade since he had begun teaching, but these young people were already showing signs of terrible deprivation in comparison to the first students he taught. The regime had cut them off from the world. These kids did not know world cinema or the literature of other countries. At the one time of their lives when they should be learning about the brotherhood of man by reading books or watching films from other cultures, they were ignorant. Ahmad focused on filling in this vacuum. He told them the stories he had read in English, using the stories to point out what they had in common with people outside Iraq. There were universal values that linked them to other human beings. "We have so much in common in how we feel and suffer," he told them. The way the students looked back at him as he spoke told Ahmad they understood everything he was trying to tell them.

The war had become never-ending. The dead piled up in the thousands, but neither victory nor defeat seemed near. More warm bodies were needed. The faculty was summoned and told by the highest-ranking Ba'ath comrade at the school that a special unit from the University of Mosul was being organized to go to the front. All male teachers were being called on to volunteer.

Rage roared through Ahmad. *They've had enough of my blood,* he thought, *I won't sign up.* But he had learned his lesson and said nothing. His face was impassive. He simply ignored the summons. Over the next week or two, colleagues who were enthusiastic party members asked him if he had volunteered yet. Ahmad mumbled excuses. He sought out his old friend Ghazi and asked him what he was doing. Ghazi said, "Look, join. I've joined. They won't send you to the front. This whole business is so the head of the university can go to the Revolutionary Council and show them how loyal the faculty is. He just wants to prove to them he's in control of his employees. They don't want us to fight anymore. We're too old for that shit now. It's nothing. It's so they can remind themselves that they control you. But you know and I know they don't. That's what matters."

Ahmad found himself resisting the very idea. "You cannot give in to them on this. This war is a disaster. If we stop giving them bodies to send to the front, it will end."

But Ahmad's friend was adamant. "Look, you have children, you have a career. It's nothing. Join up. We all hate them. God will know your heart. He will know you are not one of them."

"I cannot," Ahmad said. "They are fascists. I'm not a fascist. They are destroying our country with this endless fucking war. How can I help them with that? If we stand together, we can force them to negotiate and push them back."

"No, my dear friend, we cannot."

Ahmad looked at Ghazi and thought, *How sad. He's been beaten.* Then a more terrible idea went through his head: *Why is he so insistent about me joining? Is he an informer now? Maybe he's being put under pressure to get me to sign and will get in trouble if I don't.* It was best to end this conversation. Ahmad told his friend that he would not join. They kissed each other on the cheek and went their separate ways. That night he told Afrah about the conversation.

"This is how they strangle us," he said. "My friend grew old there before my eyes. Suddenly afraid of losing everything he has, as if he has anything of value while we live under the rule of this monster."

The next day, when he went to the university, Ahmad didn't think anything of the conversation. There were others in his circle who were not so tired and afraid. They would join him in resisting this demand. But he was wrong. *Solidarity* is a wonderful word, a romantic word, but who can stand together when one by one the state and its informants pick off even the most idealistic? Ahmad thought he would find solidarity. Instead he found silence. All his university colleagues advised him to give in and sign up. He told the Ba'ath party representative he would not join. The man shrugged his shoulders and waved him out of his office.

Ahmad knew his time at the medical school was running

out. Before he could be dismissed he found a job at an agricultural college south of the city.

"Do you want to come or to stay in Mosul?" he asked Afrah. She told him, "I chose this life. I will stay with you."

So they packed up the children and moved. The Ba'ath pursued him even there. "You will join the university battalion and go back to the war," he was told. Ahmad refused. A few days later he was summoned to the chief administrator's office at the agricultural college.

"This came for you," the chief said, and handed him a letter.

It was from the Revolutionary Council, the Ba'ath's politburo. It informed Ahmad that he was officially retired from teaching. He was thirty-five years old.

His first reaction was anger. He had been put on earth to teach. In the classroom he fulfilled his dream to be al-Fatih, the leader. Maybe they could stop him from teaching in the university. But a university isn't the only place to reach pupils. Ahmad brought the family back to Mosul. He contacted some of his favorite students and told them he planned to have a literary discussion at the Writer's Café the next afternoon. He asked them to spread the word. Only a few showed up. Ahmad could not disguise his disappointment. He could not pull himself together to talk about poetry to three people. He sat quietly drinking chai, fighting back tears. One of the students tried to console him. "There wasn't enough time to organize this. Let's try again next week. More people will come." That cheered Ahmad up. "Okay, same time next week," he told him. But the following week no one, not a single person, came. His points of enlightenment, his cadres of modern democratic thinkers, had been taken away from him. He had been defeated. The regime had been able to frighten them more than he had been able to inspire them.

Depression crushed down on Ahmad. He stayed in bed for days. A wave of tears pushed on the back of his eyes, always on the verge of breaking but never actually flowing. This was the regime's worst torture, deeper than any pain he had suffered before. His entire identity was bound up in his teaching. It was the platform from which he waged a single-handed underground campaign against the Ba'ath. In the classroom and at the Writer's Café he was a free man. Teaching was who he was. Now that teaching had been taken away, he lost all sense of himself. Afrah and the children moved quietly around the house. Yet every sound they made echoed like artillery fire in his head. Weeks went by and still his tears never came. He became ancient lying motionless in bed.

One morning, a month or so after Ahmad had gone to bed, his five-year-old daughter, Sana, brought him something to drink. He heard her coming. For a change, the noise was not painful. He noted the fact with surprise. The sound of her padding across the floor and opening the door was sweet. She gave him the water and said, "I love you, Baba. Feel better." He took the glass and kissed her forehead. She turned and left the room. As he heard her quietly pad away and call out to her mother, Ahmad finally began to weep. The ocean of pain dammed up behind his eyes poured out. Remorse now washed up and out of him. He had put his family in terrible danger from the regime; now he was endangering them by not earning a living. The dread he had known when his father died and he had fallen out of the middle class returned. He would not bring his family to the same pass. *This has to stop, this has to stop,* he told himself. He got out of bed, washed, and dressed. Then he went to the storage area of the house and went through some boxes until he came across his old woodworking tools. They hadn't been used for a while. Ahmad had an idea for how he would support his family. He would become a carpenter. He made a list of equipment he had and what he was going to need. Then he told Afrah he was going to the bazaar.

In the bazaar he bought a few more things, then went around to suppliers to find out what wood and other raw materials cost. A friend who owned a shop offered him some space in the back for a workshop. The rent was cheap. Ahmad returned to his wife, explained what he had in mind, and she, the family banker, went into their savings and gave him money to get started. Ahmad went to work. If Ahmad's depression was rage turned inward, what was happening in Ahmad's life now was rage channeled into work. The regime wanted to take away his livelihood. They didn't know how many ways he had to take care of his family. He made sketches of a range of furniture. Then he built two cabinets inlaid with delicate Italianate designs. The craftwork was excellent. He put them outside his friend's shop and within the morning one was sold and there was an offer on the second. But Ahmad decided not to sell it; he would leave it outside the workshop as a calling card. Soon he had regular orders for cabinets, armoires, and tables. Most of the time work took the place of sadness, but at night, tired from the day's labor, he would be overcome. One morning Afrah rose for the dawn prayer. When she finished she returned to the bedroom and found him weeping again. "I am so sorry," he said between sobs. "All I do is make your life hard. Forgive me." She held him. She told him she had nothing to forgive him for. She loved him. This life was her choice. She urged him to go to the mosque and talk to Allah. In prayer he would find mercy and strength. "You will see, Abu Sindibad," she said. "Allah is the source of forgiveness."

At noon that day, Ahmad closed up his little workshop and went to the mosque. He pressed his forehead to the ground with the same fervor he brought to his teaching. Just as Afrah had said, he felt mercy rise up from his stomach. In standing before Allah, humble as a slave, in prostrating himself before the master of the universe, something left him: guilt, remorse. He returned to his shop renewed. He was a trained scientist, so he decided to have a little experiment with himself: an experiment with "God's blessings." He returned to the mosque for the mid-afternoon prayer. The feeling of his burden being lightened returned. He bought a copy of some religious writings and other meditative tracts in a bookshop to read when he got home.

The next morning, when Afrah awoke to pray, Ahmad joined her. She said nothing. She had not always been devout herself and understood there are many pathways to God in this life. Each person will find his own way, she had always reminded herself. She did think it was typical of her husband when, after a few weeks, he stopped shaving and grew a beard. He was not a man for half-measures. She loved him for this passion and his newfound devotion. But there was another reason for his beard.

It did not take long for Ahmad to be noticed in the mosque. He attended noon and evening prayers every day. The fellow-ship inside a mosque's walls is sincere. Strangers talk to each other with ease. After a week a fellow came up and asked him whether he was new in the area. Ahmad answered no, then explained that he lived and worked nearby but had recently found his way back to Islam.

"Welcome back, brother. We missed you," said his new acquaintance.

Ahmad and his new friend exchanged small talk about God, Iraq, and the regime. Through this friend he was drawn into a circle of regular worshippers who were also members of the Muslim Brotherhood. He spent time after prayers talking with them. He took his experiment with God's blessings from intense, personal devotion into the realms of politics—a brief experiment, as it turned out. The first phase involved a fiery critique of the regime from a religious standpoint. Ahmad happily discovered the many scriptural injunctions against the kind of despotism represented by Saddam. The second phase, the Brotherhood's program, was something he had great trouble with. He was a progressive, and their program harked back all the way to the earliest days of Islam. The role of women in their ideal society particularly galled him. Ahmad was educating his daughters in a modern way and hoped they would build careers. When he mentioned to his new political friends that it was possible to establish an Islamic state that accepted these modern improvements in the role of women, he was amazed by their vehement arguments against the idea. The experiment ended when he realized that there was no flexibility in their thinking. The Muslim Brotherhood's rhetoric *was* their entire program: return Iraq and the Muslim nation to the days of the first caliphs. Ahmad had gone too far down the path of modernity and science to ever embrace it. He withdrew from their company, shaved his beard, and retreated from Islam.

There was no party left to join. There was nothing to do but wait, he told himself. The dictator was ruining the country. It would only be a matter of time before the army rose up in revolt, as it had throughout the modern history of Iraq. If the army didn't revolt, someone in Saddam's inner circle would put a bullet in the tyrant's head. They are all thieves, and thieves always fall out among themselves sooner or later. Now was the time to make money and provide for his family.

He bought a small plot of land in a neighborhood of university professors and physicians and designed a house. The typical modern house in Mosul is a brutalist concrete box—all hard angles, with the second floor overhanging the first to create areas of shade at ground level. There is usually a room on the second floor that juts over the entryway, supported by a narrow column. Ahmad decided to add a curve or two to his house. He designed the room over the entryway as a three-quarter circle. This would be his and Afrah's bedroom. The windows were set all around the arc of the circle. He told Afrah that this would be their dream space. From the moment the sun came up until the moment it set, light would flow around their room. Although his carpentry business was doing well, Ahmad didn't have enough money to hire a full crew of builders. He took out some how-to books from the library, and with skills remembered from the days in Darawish working with his uncle, he started building the house with his own hands. Sindibad, barely ten years old, was his main helper.

He had always had intense energy, but now he drove himself to a level of manic activity. His furniture business was doing so well that he had to employ a couple of cabinetmakers to meet the growing demand for his furniture. In his spare time he continued to work on his house. The regime had taken his life's work and thought it left him a cripple, but every hour he worked in his shop, every tile he laid in his house, was an act of defiance against Saddam. The regime's watchmen in the neighborhood did not understand this. They reported back to the Mukhabarat that a troublemaker had apparently learned his lesson. This cooled the Mukhabarat's interest in him.

Friends from the Writer's Café days who had avoided him for a while began to come around the shop during the day to chat about nothing in particular. He was invited to a poetry reading at the house of Junayd al-Fakrhi and became a regular member of the informal salon that hung out there.

The salon of Junayd al-Fakrhi was the center of Mosul's

artistic and intellectual community. It was a sanctuary for people who had been educated to serve a society that had disappeared in front of their eyes. It was a place to wait for the end of the regime. Junayd came from an old-moneyed family and lived in an enormous mansion overlooking the Tigris. The house had been built in Ottoman times, and to enter its gates was to leave the hell of late-twentieth-century Iraq and return to a time when the Pearl of the North had been an imperial center of grace and culture. The two-story house was built around an enormous courtyard. A large tree in the center of the courtyard provided shade, and smaller potted plants gave off a sweet odor when they were watered in the evening just before the group gathered. A gallery ran around the second floor so guests could promenade above the courtyard and look down into it. There was also an open balcony that looked onto the river. On the second floor just off the gallery was a massive library. It was a magnificent room with a bit of modern cachet: film director William Friedkin had shot some of the opening scenes of *The Exorcist* there. Ahmad loved to wander through the library, looking at the old leather-bound books on the shelves. Only someone who had known the economic catastrophe of Ahmad's childhood—the fall from middle-class to peasant status in the stilling of his father's heartbeat—could really appreciate the sweet security of this kind of settled wealth.

Junayd was a generous host. He still basked in a bit of celebrity from the time the Americans had come to film the *The Exorcist* in his home. Some evenings at Junayd's mansion there were performances of traditional Arab music, other nights there were classical performances. Guests read poetry, their own or classical Arab verse. There was always good food, and wine for those who drank. After performances there were discussions that lasted into the small hours of the morning. Servants brought out water pipes, and visitors broke up into small groups to smoke and chat. They indulged in dilettantish picking apart of this or that work of art. They also made careful small talk about the regime, everyone aware of the red lines they should not cross in discussing Saddam. One evening Junayd asked, "Who is the greatest Arab artist?"

Names were suggested and rejected. Ahmad said, "Saddam is the greatest Arab artist."

The salon giggled at the joke.

"I'm serious," Ahmad said earnestly. "His origins are crude. But his sense of cruelty is exquisite. It is truly artistic. Saddam cripples a few bodies and infects a thousand minds. You have to admire his skill. And if you want to argue that cruelty itself is not artistic, it at least inspires art."

Then he recited a passage from the *Epic of Gilgamesh*. "The oldest poem in the world," Ahmad reminded his listeners, "written not far from where we sit, almost five thousand years ago."

> *The City is his possession, he struts*
> *through it, arrogant, his head raised high,*
> *trampling its citizens like a wild bull.*
> *He is king, he does whatever he wants,*
> *takes the son from his father and crushes him,*
> *takes the girl from her mother and uses her,*
> *the warrior's daughter, the young man's bride,*
> *he uses her and no one dares to oppose him.*
> *But the people of Uruk cried out to heaven,*
> *and their lamentation was heard, the gods*
> *are not unfeeling, their hearts were touched.*

He did not have to explain the relevance of this passage. Everyone who listened knew Gilgamesh was Saddam and felt the bitter irony that words written so many millennia past could so accurately describe their dictator's behavior. Saddam was rampant. All around them was the charnel house of the tyrant's Iraq. Fresh sacrifices were made to him every day on the battlefield and in the torture chambers. More bitter still, though, was the knowledge that the "gods" did not hear their cry. The contemporary gods, the great powers—America, the Soviet Union, France, Britain—whored after Saddam as if he were the world's most beautiful courtesan rather than one of its most brutal dictators. The West and the Soviets continued to sell him every kind of weapon; gave him economic credits, turned a blind eye to his regime's corruption. If they would just stop, Ahmad thought, then the regime would collapse.

Years went by. Ahmad finished his fine house and drew in upon himself. The country's slow decline into physical decrepitude as Saddam looted its wealth carried on. The war with Iran dragged on until 1988. The Anfal campaign against the Kurds commenced, its atrocities culminating when five thousand Kurds were gassed to death at Halabja. Nothing roused Ahmad to action. The warm evenings in Junayd's courtyard listening to music and poetry became the center of his existence. His carpentry business continued to thrive. He invested money in another business, a billiard hall and teahouse in Mosul's Old Town. He needed the income. There were more children. After four daughters in a row, Afrah gave him two sons.

When Saddam invaded Kuwait in the summer of 1990, Ahmad breathed a sigh of relief. "This is it," he told the group at Junayd's. "He's gone too far this time." He watched events with quiet confidence, taking pleasure as the Americans moved a vast army into the region, smiling at the utter predictability of Saddam's rejection of all opportunities to negotiate a withdrawal. The war was swift. As a veteran of the eight-year conflict with Iran, it seemed to him more a pinprick than a war. The American president called on the Iraqi people to rise up against Saddam. The uprisings started almost as soon as the American rout ended. "I told you this would happen," he reminded his friends. "It will all be over soon for Saddam."

But it wasn't over soon. The Americans stayed in Kuwait. In the south, the Shi'ite uprising was crushed, and then the Kurds were slaughtered in the north. The first President Bush did nothing despite his initial incitement of the rebellions. The final peace agreement left Saddam in power and the people of Iraq to endure a new disaster: UN sanctions. Trade stopped. The tattered economy fell apart.

These events finally goaded Ahmad back into political activity. In early 1992 he started contacting old friends from the Nasser days who had not fled the country, like Isam Mahmood, who was now a general in the Iraqi Army. His brother Faraj knew some people as well. The brothers' friends came to Mosul from as far as Ramadi and Baghdad. The gathering was informal. The participants exchanged information about the economic conditions in their respective parts of the country; who was rising in the Ba'ath, who was losing his position. They agreed to form a political party, although "network" would be the more accurate description. They called their group the Democratic Liberator Party. There was no program, no plan for immediate action. The only activity was identifying potential members. Waiting was the only option. Saddam could only grow weaker. The army, Isam assured them, would rise up soon.

In the Iraqi tradition, groups of army officers plotted against Saddam. But Saddam's security apparatus had an unparalleled ability to sniff out plotters. All assassination attempts failed. The Democratic Liberator Party's underground network never had the opportunity to step out of the shadows. Ahmad filled in the hours writing short stories. By 1995 he had written enough to bring out a small volume of them called *And Thus*... Before a printer would publish the book, Ahmad needed to get a state censor's approval. He took the manuscript to the censor and got the requisite permission. But on the way to the printer he added the story "Mr. Key"—an allegory about contemporary Iraq in which Saddam appears as a donkey—into the pile of papers. It was a risky thing to do, but he was certain Ba'ath Party members were so illiterate they would never even bother to read the volume. He paid the printer to run off a thousand copies, and had them delivered to a bookseller in the Old City bazaar. A few weeks later, as he was walking home from his billiard hall, the Mukhabarat drove up beside him and took him away to the Security Management building.

He knew what was coming. They took him to a room with a hook in the ceiling and suspended him from it. They whipped him with electrical cords. They took him down and tied him to a chair, then attached electrodes to his genitals and gave him shocks until he lost consciousness. They dragged him to the building's subbasement and locked him in solitary confinement. Nothing about the routine varied. They brought him back for more beatings, then put him in the chair and crushed the breath out of him. When they had finished torturing him for fun, the interrogation began. "Are you the author of this story?"

"Yes, I admit this freely."

"Who told you to write this story?"

"Nobody tells me to write anything. I write this freely for myself."

His interrogators seemed incapable of understanding that. No one writes for himself; there must be an order to write from someone else, from an organization. All his interrogations foundered on this point. The torturers served a totalitarian regime. They couldn't understand the existence of a single, individual intelligence inventing a story on its own. At one point Ahmad told them, "These are the same answers I gave you yesterday and the day before. Please, you don't have to hurt me more. I faithfully tell you I write this by myself. I don't deny it. Please stop."

Eventually they did stop. They simply locked him in the subbasement of the Security Management building. For a week, Ahmad waited for them to return. He slept and cried. He kicked at the rats crawling around him. Sometimes false courage crept into his brain and he mocked them in his mind. "They were so stupid, they didn't even ask about the Democratic Liberator Party." More time went by. "When they will come to kill me?" he wondered. Then he got the game. They were waiting for a ransom. They love money more than they love death.

He was in solitary for almost six months. His brother-in-law Iyad made contact with the Mukhabarat and negotiated a ransom price. There was one final indignity before he left the Mukhabarat's custody. They took him to the bookstall in the bazaar and built a pyre of the entire print run. While shoppers gathered round, they forced him to set the pyre alight and watch it burn. One of the Mukhabarat officers found a few more copies in the back of the shop. They made Ahmad throw the last few copies in one by one.

Chapter Eleven
"Apologize to Saddam"

AHMAD'S BODY STEADILY recovered from torture. It healed itself
bit by bit, each day a little better. His mind dealt with the experience out of sequence. Some days he was fine, anxious to get
to work. Then days of black despair would follow. There was
no anticipating what each day would bring. Sometimes it
looked as if he would fall away forever into the waste pit of
depression. Afrah held on to him. Soon she was pregnant again.

When he was mentally and physically fit to work, there was no
job for him. His furniture business and pool hall had been confiscated. Acquaintances who in the past might have been able to
give him work avoided him. People gave names under torture, or
they became spies to save their necks. He was not trusted. He was
toxic even to know. Ahmad realized that, for him, Mosul was finished. He had to get out. Not just because there was no work but
because the Mukhabarat would inevitably come for him again.
They had their money. They could come back to make him a
corpse any day, so there was very little time to lose. In July he told
Afrah he was going to the Kurdish safe area over the Zab, but he
did not tell her where. "I will send for you as soon as possible," he
told her, then escaped to Erbil by back roads.

His absence was soon noticed. The Mukhabarat came for Afrah, who by then was four months' pregnant with Zainab. They kept her in the cells for several days, constantly demanding to know the whereabouts of her husband. They verbally abused her and threatened her children. Afrah could tell them nothing because she really had no idea where Ahmad was. Finally, they released her.

While his wife was being interrogated, Ahmad was somewhere between Iraq and what he hoped would be freedom. As soon as he had crossed the Zab to the relative safety of Kurdistan, Ahmad had hired a people smuggler in Kurdistan to get him to the West. They had walked over the border and through the mountains into Turkey. Once inside Turkey, they were met by a truck. The driver hid Ahmad in the back. For two days the truck rolled across the southern underbelly of Turkey until it reached the Mediterranean port of Bodrum. Passport inspection there was lax and Ahmad was able to board a ferry heading west. He took a series of ferries, island-hopping across the Aegean, and made it to Athens' port of Piraeus. He presented himself to the Greek authorities, asked for asylum, and languished briefly in a detention center while the Greeks considered his case. Asylum was denied, and he was repatriated to Iraq. The only break the Greeks gave him was that they sent him back to northern Iraq, to Kurdistan.

He ended up in Sulaimaniyah, in eastern Kurdistan, hard by the mountainous border with Iran. It was the wrong time for a stranger to turn up in that city. Tension was building between the two main Kurdish parties, the Kurdistan Democratic Party and the Patriotic Union of Kurdistan. This tension was about to burst into the fighting that would see the KDP invite Saddam to send the Iraqi Army over the cease-fire line to help them battle the PUK, which was headquartered in Sulaimaniyah. Ahmad was detained and interrogated by PUK security forces. "Who are you? Where are you from?" they demanded. He gave straight answers because he had nothing to hide. He explained he was a refugee, a Kurd from Mosul who had tried to escape to the West but had been sent back by the Greek government. The PUK security police did not accept his answers at face value. Someone from Mosul does not just turn up in Sulaimaniyah just as fighting is about to break out. Assuming Ahmad must be a spy for Saddam, they threw him in jail.

The fighting came and went. The KDP and PUK patched up their differences, but Ahmad remained in prison. The Red Cross maintained an office in Sulaimaniyah; Ahmad managed to petition the organization's representative to look into his situation, and the NGO eventually obtained his release in the autumn.

A few weeks after Ahmad was released, Afrah was sitting at home in Mosul when a young man knocked on the door. He was a Kurdish deserter from Saddam's army. He had been fighting as a pesh merga in the north and was risking his life to visit his family in Mosul. He brought a message from Ahmad, who was now in Erbil: "Please, come see me."

It was not impossible for people from Mosul to visit Erbil. The Kurdish area—protected from Saddam's predations by American, British, and French warplanes—had become semiautonomous, with its own regional government, but it was still part of Iraq. People and commerce went back and forth every day. Afrah took Sindibad and crossed over into the Kurdish safe area. Ahmad showed her around the city. The couple discussed how they could get the family out of Mosul. It had become very dangerous for everyone. Sindibad, who was studying engineering at the university's technical institute, had had a visit from the Mukhabarat. They were asking questions not just about his father but also about his uncle Faraj, who had been teaching at the institute. Faraj and his oldest son had fled the country, and the security police were demanding to know where they were.

Sindibad decided to stay in Erbil. Afrah decided to go back to Mosul and wait until Ahmad had made arrangements for a place to live. After a few months Sindibad sent a message telling her to come. Afrah went to see her oldest daughters, Rasak and Sana; both were married and had started families of their own. She kissed them good-bye and said she would send word when they settled. She took Roaa and Rasha to her father's house. They would stay with him until the school year was finished. She got a small amount of money from her older brother Iyad and kissed her mother and brother farewell, then gathered the youngest children and set out for Erbil.

When the school year ended, it was Roaa's and Rasha's turn to flee. They put on peasant clothes given to them in Darawish to hide their middle-class status. Then, accompanied by Sana's husband, a truck driver, the girls were driven by taxi to the Kalak bridge and joined the queue of cars waiting to cross from regime territory into the Kurdish safe area. The checkpoint at Kalak, the last in regime territory, was commanded by the notorious Abdul Awash. He was a legendarily cruel man, famous for the creative ways he found to abuse Kurds crossing the Zab to visit their families. He had grown rich, so the stories went, shaking people down for bribes. Kurds going to visit relatives could never be sure that their car wouldn't be selected to be stripped down to the rivets as Abdul Awash looked for cash, gold, or jewels to keep for himself. Roaa had brought more cash for the family with her and was hiding it under her peasant clothes. She was afraid that their disguises would not work. Roaa, just thirteen, was trembling by the time they got to the bridge. Petrified fear turned out to be useful in getting past the checkpoint. The two girls really did look like frightened peasants barely capable of comprehending the checkpoint games of Abdul Awash. After a cursory search of their meager belongings, they were waved through and crossed the Zab to look for their father.

Ahmad's family were exiles in their own land, immigrants in Iraq who could not even speak the local language, Kurdish. They knew only Arabic.

For a while they lived in a hostel while Ahmad searched for a house to buy. Then the family settled into a small place in an older part of Erbil. It was simple and functional. There were no rounded bedroom windows through which light streamed in, marking the sun's arcing daily progress from east to west. To make the place feel like home, Ahmad and the boys planted a few lemon and orange saplings. Fruit in the future, sweet smells in the spring.

The adjustment for Ahmad's family was difficult. Because they spoke no Kurdish, the children went from being among the brightest in their class to among the least able. They left all their friends in Mosul and could not speak the words to make new ones in Erbil. For Afrah, the house was barren. Their possessions in Mosul had been confiscated, not that they could have brought them over the Zab in any case. Money was tight, and it was not possible to buy even a sofa or two for the living room. All they could afford were some throw pillows.

Ahmad seethed with bitterness. He had been someone in Mosul; who was he here? He expected help from the local authorities and at least a little sympathy and respect for what he had suffered at Saddam's hands. Instead, he found himself still under suspicion. Saddam had plenty of agents working in the Kurdish safe area; so until Ahmad could prove that he was not a spy for the dictator, he was going to be isolated. He needed to find a job that would bring him in contact with others who would be able to vouch for him and remove the stain of suspicion. The Kurds had a governmental structure in their autonomous region and Ahmad visited many offices looking for work. But Kurdish officials were as masterly as the Ba'ath at putting off decisions, drawing out any bureaucratic process until a person practically begged for a favor.

Ahmad did not help himself by his attitude. He had the arrogance of a big-city cosmopolitan encountering the provincials. He had been a lecturer at a prestigious medical school; there was no medical school in Kurdistan. Mosul's beauty may have been fading as Saddam ran Iraq into the ground, but Ahmad's city was still clean and white. Erbil, it had to be said, was a dump. The fighting the previous autumn had left an already poor city in even worse condition.

He found the politics and political games childish. Everything he heard proclaimed Kurdish nationalism. The only ethnic nationalism Ahmad had ever embraced had been Pan-Arabism, and he'd had that belief tortured out of him. He had decided the only way forward for his country was through an Iraqi identity, one that embraced all the ethnicities and sects of the nation. But he quickly found that saying such things alienated people in Erbil, most of whom found their way into the national liberation movement through family ties or political party. No matter how many disasters that movement led them into, they stayed loyal to their party.

If you took torture and mass murder out of the equation, Ahmad concluded, the Kurdish safe area was no different from the other side of the Zab in Saddam regime territory. There, unless you came from an old, wealthy family, you had to be part of the Ba'ath to advance. Here, in dirty, impoverished Kurdistan, you also needed to belong to a party to get anything accomplished. There were two main parties to choose from, the KDP and the PUK. Once a person had chosen his allegiance— or had it chosen for him at birth—he still had to carefully negotiate the shifting tides between the two. An alliance one month between the KDP and PUK could turn into civil war the next.

From time to time, particularly since Saddam's Anfal campaign against them at the end of the Iran-Iraq War, the Kurdish situation bursts onto the world media's consciousness. The poison-gas massacre at Halabja and the failed revolt after the first Gulf War provided the pictures of human suffering that command airtime. However, the complexities of Kurdish politics causes interest to disappear once the bodies have been counted. But it really isn't a difficult story to follow.

Modern Kurdish nationalism has its origins in the same historical event that gave birth to Iraq: the carve-up of the Ottoman Empire after World War I. The 1920 Treaty of Sèvres was the legal document that divided up what was left of the empire. In that treaty, the Kurds had been promised their own state, in much the same way as the 1917 Balfour Declaration promised Jews a homeland in Palestine. But over the next two years, at subsequent conferences to fill in the details of the Sèvres treaty, the Allies argued among themselves on the precise details of the maps and how else they might divide the Ottoman spoils. While French and British diplomats wrangled, Mustafa Kemal Ataturk led a revolution that overthrew the last Ottoman sultan and founded the modern state of Turkey. A new treaty, the Treaty of Lausanne, superseded the Treaty of Sèvres. It recognized the territorial integrity of Turkey well into the eastern part of the country, the area that might have become the center of the Kurdish state.

Ataturk's commitment to creating a secular, democratic nation, with mosque and state firmly separated by the new constitution, appealed to the Western powers. This new fact on the ground—a secular, unified Turkish Republic—overrode any commitment made to the Kurds, even though the Kurds made up almost a quarter of Turkey's population. When Ataturk took the next step in forging a modern Turkish state—abolishing the notion of Kurdish ethnicity by banning the Kurdish language and all Kurdish customs—late in 1923, the Western powers did nothing. A secular Turkey firmly in the Western camp was too important to risk by honoring previous pledges of creating a Kurdish homeland. The Kurds were condemned to becoming the most numerous ethnic group in the world without a state to call their own. Their indigenous land was thereafter divided among Syria, Turkey, Iraq, Iran, Armenia, and Azerbaijan.

In most of those countries the Kurds are relatively powerless. Iraq is different. Today the Kurds make up around twenty percent of the population, around four million people. The Arab majority is riven by the sectarian difference between Shi'a and Sunni. But the Kurds are overwhelmingly Sunni. So there are webs of connection and interaction with the majority that don't exist for the Kurds in more homogeneous nations like Syria or Turkey. In cities like Mosul, many Kurds were assimilated and drawn to work in national institutions such as the army and in political parties. But in the north, where the population is almost exclusively Kurdish, the dream of a state of their own has never diminished. Sometimes this dream is no more than an aspiration. At other times it is so tangible that the Kurds have risen up in revolt to demand it.

There is one critical factor that makes the Iraqi state fight to keep its Kurds: oil. The Kurds have long made a territorial claim on Kirkuk, the oil-producing center of the north, although the city itself probably has more ethnic Turks— Turkmen—living there than Kurds. The surrounding country-side, where oil seethes near the surface and in some places simply bubbles out of the ground, has always been Kurdish territory. But no government would let such riches disappear without a fight.

Kurds have fought the central government for autonomy in Iraq since the 1930s. The leader of the guerilla army was Mullah Mustafa Barzani, a tribal leader from the mountain village of Barzan. Over four decades, he rebelled against and made accommodations with various Baghdad governments. His clan-based organization took over leadership of the KDP, a leftish grouping of city-dwelling Kurds, in the 1940s. Late in that decade Barzani's fortunes ebbed, and he fled the country. He spent more than a decade in exile in the Soviet Union, not because he agreed with Soviet ideology but because the Soviets were willing to have him. He returned to Iraq after the over-throw of the monarchy in 1958, and the alternating pattern of accommodation and rebellion resumed. But while he was out of the country, Kurdish society had undergone changes. Kurdish nationalists who lived in the cities, a generation or more removed from village society and its tribal structures, developed a new set of leaders, among them a young lawyer named Jalal Talabani. When Barzani returned from exile, he was treated as a hero, but this did not hide the tensions that brewed between leaders of the new generation. As Iraqi governments came and went, toppled by coups and countercoups, the one constant of domestic Iraqi politics was the effort by Arab politicians to exploit the tensions among the Kurdish leadership.

In 1974 the Kurds rose up again, this time in the most

concentrated rebellion of Mullah Mustafah's life. For one year they fought against the Ba'ath regime, but in March 1975 Barzani's rebellion ended in humiliating defeat. Jalal Talabani had had enough. He set up his own party, the Patriotic Union of Kurdistan. The PUK became the party of choice for those who had moved on from village customs, or those who simply came from clans that were not close to the Barzanis. Mullah Mustafa Barzani died in exile and, as tribal custom dictated, he was succeeded by his son, Massoud.

For the next two decades, the PUK and KDP both fought with each other and united against Saddam; then they betrayed each other with Saddam. The two parties made individual pacts with Iran, Turkey, and the United States, then reneged on those same pacts.

In August and September of 1996, the decades-long tension bubbled up into the final burst of fighting. Massoud Barzani asked Saddam to send in the Iraqi Army and the PUK was routed from Erbil. Parts of the city were wrecked. Frantic diplomacy involving America, Iran, and Turkey got Saddam to withdraw. Then the two Kurdish factions were dragged together by the Clinton administration and forced to make peace. As ever in American foreign policy, the carrot was money. A comparative stability, firmly planted in soil watered with American money, began to grow in Kurdistan. Ahmad's family began to build their new lives in Erbil just as this stability took root.

Ahmad knew this history intimately. He had, after all, spent his first months of exile in a PUK jail suspected of being a spy for the KDP's ally of the moment, Saddam. He thought all the alliances that had come and gone had less to do with tactical arrangements along the road to independence than with consolidating the power and wealth of the individual leaders of the

KDP and PUK. He believed they had brought disaster after disaster to the Kurdish people. Yet, despite his history with the organization, he had an affinity for the PUK. Within that party a member could advance if he had talent. Your fate wasn't determined at birth by what clan you were born into, as it was in the KDP. Unfortunately for Ahmad, the PUK's headquarters were in Sulaimaniyah, a three-hour drive eastward into the mountains. Afrah did not want to move that far from Mosul. In Erbil, at least she could enjoy occasional visits with her grandchildren.

So Ahmad was stuck in Erbil, a place dominated by the KDP. He had no family connections with them, and as the months went by he still couldn't seem to find the simplest common ground to talk to their officials about his plight. He wanted to set up a branch of the Democratic Liberator Party in Erbil. Perhaps he could get some funding from the KDP or from whoever was handing out money to Iraqi dissident groups. But the KDP refused him for reasons he couldn't understand. He explained that he could use the funding to set up a small press and write prodemocracy articles. The KDP suggested he visit their ministry of culture. They offered him a job editing articles for a Kurdish magazine. "I don't write in the Kurdish language," he told them. The man at the culture ministry said, "That's okay. We will still pay you a salary of five hundred dinars a month as our brother and our guest." To Ahmad the sum was an insult. He had six children and a wife to feed. It was impossible to do that on five hundred dinars a month.

Eventually, he was offered a larger sum to translate a book— *West Kurdistan: Syria, the Silenced Kurds*—from Kurdish into English. He took the job. The book itself, published in 1999, was dull, but its subject was not. It was a documentary account of yet another country, Syria, in which the Kurds are systematically discriminated against, their culture denied them, their lives scarred by state abuse. While working on the book, he took time to research his own Kurdish ethnic subgroup, the Shabak. There are around twenty thousand Shabak. They are Shi'a, unlike most Kurds; and in researching their history, Ahmad began to wonder if the Shabak were Kurds at all but a distinct ethnic group, one more tile in the mosaic of peoples in northern Mesopotamia. When he brought this point of view up with KDP nationalist ideologues, it provoked serious arguments—for the nationalists, the Shabak were Kurds without question. The arguments further alienated him from the KDP.

A year passed, then two. The children learned to speak Kurdish and began to make friends and do well in their classes. The exile life took on its own rhythm. Occasional bursts of translation work came Ahmad's way, but there were even longer periods of unemployment. There was never enough money. He had too much time to think about the disaster into which he had led his family. When the guilt and social constriction of Erbil became too much, he would go to Sulaimaniyah to visit with friends and look for work through the PUK. But then time and money would run out, and he would have to return to Erbil. He hated the city. An old Arab proverb went through his mind at least once a day: *Man tarak darah/Qualla Miqudaraht* (He who leaves his home behind/no respect will find).

He no longer provided for his family. Now, to his shame, the main support of the family was Sindibad. Ahmad had brought all his children up to have skills outside the classroom, so they could always earn a living by their hands. Sindibad was a talented tailor and embroiderer. In the time they had lived in Erbil, the young man developed a nice reputation making women's clothes—the outer cloaks known as abayas, and hijabs, or head scarves—covered with deft workings of geometrical, floral, and traditional patterns sewn along the borders in gold and silver thread.

Operating from a small shop in the bazaar, Sindibad found his work becoming very popular in Erbil. The young man made enough money to support the family. But he didn't earn enough to save so he could get married and have a family of his own. He was in his twenties now and he had to think about these things. Ahmad decided to try and help his son find more customers. They arranged an exhibition of Sindibad's embroidery and dress designs in Sulaimaniyah. Ahmad hoped the exhibition might bring Sindibad some business from that city. He also hoped that bringing the family up to the mountain town might convince Afrah to move there. He invited some of his friends from the PUK to the exhibition and also a new acquaintance, another exile from Mosul living on the Kurdish side of the cease-fire line. His name was Thair Zeki and he was a member of the spy cohort, living on the fringes of the Kurdish safe area. There were so many political groupings in Iraq and each needed to know the gossip on the others. Thair worked for the Iraqi National Accord, the political party of Iyad Allawi. His job was to keep tabs on Ba'athist sympathizers in the area around Sulaimaniyah.

Ahmad worked the exhibition on behalf of his son. He introduced his wife and children to his Sulaimaniyah friends. Roaa spent much of the evening hovering near her father. In the two years since leaving Mosul, Ahmad had grown closer to Roaa. Now fifteen years old, she was as precocious and spirited as he had been at that age. She had begun to write and was very curious about journalism. Ahmad could talk to her about literature, politics, anything at all. He looked into her face during these conversations and saw the same attentive look his students had before the Ba'ath banned him from teaching. She became his only pupil. She will be an enlightenment point for our country, he thought.

He trusted her judgment about people. As the exhibition crowd dwindled, he pulled her aside.

"So, what do you think of my friends?"

"They are nice, but I don't like that one."

"Which one."

"The big one with the beard." She laughed and nodding toward Thair.

"Why?"

"He is very rude, he laughs too loud, and he's not cultured."

"Oh, he's not so bad. It is true he is not well cultured, but Roaa, you need to be able to talk to people from every social class. "

"Yes, you're right . . . but I still don't like him. He's too fat and he should get a haircut."

They laughed.

"Why do you like him?" Roaa asked.

"He's from Mosul. He reminds me of home."

The exhibition went well for Sindibad. He sold all his work and took orders for more. It didn't work out for Ahmad, however. Afrah still refused to move to Sulaimaniyah. Ahmad returned with his family to Erbil.

The old routine reasserted itself—the same round of begging and disappointment. Ahmad came back furious from a meeting with the KDP cultural office. He had finished a novel, *The Prison of Gavar,* while he was in Sulaimaniyah. It was the first book he had ever written in the Kurdish language, and he wanted help in getting it published. The KDP cultural office had offered a token sum. Ahmad would have to pay most of the costs. He did not have the money. He stood in the kitchen fuming. Afrah tried to calm him down.

"Do you believe those donkeys?"

"This is a small thing. We will find the money."

"How? Oh, I know your answer. Trust in God. God's will."

"Yes. You know what I think. We are here. We are safe. We are alive. This is God's will."

"God has nothing to do with this. Is it God's will that I waste my life? If we lived in Sulaimaniyah I could support my family."

"If we lived in Sulaimaniyah I would never see my grand-children."

In the living room the children were watching their favorite TV show, a Syrian sitcom about a married couple who do nothing but argue, just like their own parents. Ribal was the name of the father in the comedy show, and Afrah the name of the mother. When the evening's episode ended, the argument was still going on in the kitchen. Roaa turned to Rasha, Shawkat, and Rafat and said, "Ribal and Afrah are still on the TV in the kitchen. Should we go and watch?" The children laughed and went to the kitchen. Their parents looked at them. Roaa said, "Ribal, could you please keep your voice down." For a moment there was silence. Then Ahmad got the joke and began to laugh, and everyone joined with him.

In early 2002 an ad appeared in the local Erbil newspapers. Seminars in "democracy training" were being organized at the Iraq Institute for Democracy, and people were invited to apply. Ahmad and Roaa sent in the forms. The course was led by Faleh Jabar, an Iraqi sociologist who had made it to the West before Saddam took over. Jabar had some say over who would be selected, and local authorities in the north also had input. Even at this stage there was fear about Saddam placing spies in the classroom. Faleh consulted with some locals about the applications. Ahmad's name came up. People spoke against him. Faleh was told not to let him into the course. He asked, is he a spy? Maybe, but the complaint against him was more general. Ahmad simply wasn't "one of us." That wasn't enough in Faleh's mind to keep him out of the course, however. He invited Ahmad and Roaa to attend.

The group met three hours a day. The course work covered the history of democracy, its origins not just in the United States, France, and Britain but also in ancient Greece. Faleh led talks on democracy in the Arab world and why it had failed. The sociologist offered more rarefied lectures on the role of language in identifying and clarifying political concepts. Arabic usage, in his view, did not lead to clear and specific understanding of Western political ideas.

The teacher took note of Ahmad early on. To begin with, Ahmad was much older than most of the class. The majority of students were in their twenties and early thirties; Ahmad was in his fifties. He was also sullen and negative. Occasionally, he sat in the classroom and looked as if his entire inner being was a thousand miles away. Yet when class was over, as father and daughter walked out together, Faleh could hear them discussing the day's lecture. It was clear Ahmad was taking the ideas in and, more important, reinforcing the concepts with the young woman. The sociologist was moved by this relationship between father and daughter. He was a native of this society and knew that men don't usually treat their daughters with this loving respect for their intellect. Clearly, Ahmad had modern, tolerant views about the role of women. Roaa herself dressed in a Western style and her head was uncovered.

After a few weeks Ahmad sent Faleh an angry note, asking why he had invited so many "stupid" young Kurds into the course. Clearly, he wrote, they did not understand what was being taught and they were making it difficult for those who did. Faleh took the note as an invitation for conversation. He asked Ahmad to take a walk with him after class. They walked for hours through the city, past Erbil's prison, toward the bazaar, up the long incline to the Citadel: a couple of peripatetic philosophers discussing the state of their world.

They spoke about the curriculum, how the students were absorbing it. Faleh was grateful for the feedback. Ahmad felt that his unique position in the class had been acknowledged. The two men began to spend time together. The long walks and talks eased the anger Ahmad brought into the classroom but not his sadness. Faleh and Ahmad were teacher and pupil, but also two Iraqis of the same age who had had very different lives. Faleh understood some of what was going on with Ahmad. Faleh left the country in 1978 and saw what had happened to his friends who had stayed in Iraq. They were all talented men who had never been allowed to fully realize their abilities. An entropic bitterness had settled over these friends as they reached middle age and it became clear to each that the regime was not going away and their lives would end up wasted.

Faleh also understood the importance of belonging to a group in this society. Erbil is one of those cities that is really more of an overgrown village. It is not cosmopolitan. It is a place where newcomers are kept at a distance for a couple of generations. He understood that for Ahmad, life in Erbil was just an extension of Saddam's punishment. He could never have the life he wanted in Erbil. He was part of no group and thus was suspect to all.

For as long as it went on, however, the class offered Ahmad and Roaa a chance to be part of a social circle. The young woman took advantage of this opportunity to meet new people. Through connections at the course, she got a job with a local television station. She became friendly with a young Islamic politician named Abdussalaam al-Medeni. Abdussalaam had a way with words. He seemed able to explain how it was possible to be devout and modern at the same time. Roaa found his ideas on the role of women fascinating. They spent time discussing how a woman could have a career and still walk in the path of the Prophet's message. Roaa in turn explained these ideas to her father. They had long talks about why he had lost his faith. At first he was surprised at her new interest in Islam but he never sought to impose his religious views on her. Ahmad always presented faith as a personal choice to his children. He was a trained scientist, a secular man, and he understood the need to experiment with religion—after all, he had done it himself. When Roaa turned up at class one day wearing a long skirt and hijab, he kept his surprise to himself. He told her she looked beautiful and that was that.

By the late spring of 2002, Ahmad felt despair building to a crisis point. There was no work, so he set himself tasks: attend the democracy classes; read books and articles in English every day to keep the language fresh and learn new vocabulary. Roaa had picked up some freelance work writing for a Syrian newspaper, so he helped his daughter with her reporting. He forced himself to write articles. But an essay that should have taken a few hours in the morning to write took weeks to finish, if it got finished at all. As the summer heat began to stifle the air out of the Kurdish plain, anger and guilt closed in on him again. Every morning his son went to work as a tailor. By now, Ahmad thought, he should be an engineer, a young professional man, with a good job and prospects for marriage. Roaa was earning a living from her pen. She's just a girl. Why can't I earn my living that way? I'm the man of the house. His inner turmoil showed on the surface in flashes of rage at his family. The rage was followed by remorse that went so deep he felt it would swallow him up. He became obsessed with the idea of getting out. Faraj had made it out of Iraq and was living abroad. Why couldn't he do the same thing?

He went for a walk with Faleh. The course was coming to an end. Before Faleh returned to his home in London, Ahmad wanted to ask his help in getting out of the country. They walked their usual route, past Erbil's prison and around toward the bazaar.

"I have to get out."

"Where?"

"Out of this country."

"I know out of this country. Where would you go?"

"It doesn't matter. Beirut, Cairo . . ."

"Be patient, man. Look, the U.S. is coming. A year from now Saddam is going to be gone. I'm telling you."

"Brother, I need to go now."

"Do you have money?"

"How much?"

"Man, ten thousand dollars is what the smugglers are charging. And even then it doesn't mean you'll get some place and be able to find work. Be patient."

But Ahmad couldn't be patient. Rage, shame, guilt pushed him. He walked for hours around the dusty, noisy city, plotting his escape. Even in Mechko's teahouse, where Erbil's exile community met to pass time, his few friends were talking about the Americans coming soon. It was late August, and there were reports in the Western papers that the son of Hajji Bush was going to finish the job his father failed to do. Up in the mountains near Harir and over in Dohuk they were improving the airfields so that jets and transport planes could land. Everybody knew that. But Ahmad couldn't wait. He refused to believe the United States would come. He remembered the evenings at

Junayd's in 1991 just after the Gulf War ended, how they had relaxed and enjoyed music, smug and assured that the United States would finish Saddam. But the Americans hadn't finished the job. They will find an excuse not to finish the job this time. No one cares about our suffering, he thought.

His days alternated between manic excitement—if he thought he had devised a foolproof plan for getting away—and crushing despair, when he realized that whatever he was daydreaming would come to nothing. If he could get to Lebanon or Libya he would be fine. He could find work. But how? He couldn't fly to those places. It was not as if there was an airport in Erbil with regular service to Beirut or Tripoli. He couldn't go to Syria. He was persona non grata there since translating the book on the Syrian Kurds. The Turkish border was sealed tight. In Iran he knew no one and he would be unable to earn a penny. He feared he would die in obscurity in this shitty city living off the earnings of his children.

One day, while walking near the Citadel, he bumped into a cousin, a truck driver who had come over from Saddam territory to make a delivery. They stopped for tea and a chat. Ahmad poured out his misery to his cousin and, in the course of commiserating, the man suggested a way for Ahmad to get out of the country. In two days, he was driving an oil tanker from Kirkuk to Jordan. Hundreds of trucks made this run every week. They were rarely stopped by the police. If Ahmad could make his way down to Kirkuk, the cousin would give him a lift. Ahmad saw the escape hatch opening ever so slightly. Manic energy surged through him. The danger of going back to regime territory was a risk he would take. If Bush the son is like Bush the father and loses his nerve at the last minute, I will be trapped forever. Once I'm in Amman, Cairo, or Beirut, he thought, I will find a job and send for my family. We can all be free.

He left his home in the middle of the night after everyone was sound asleep. He went without a word, telling no one of his plan. He took his passport, a change of clothes, and a small amount of money. He made his way to Kirkuk, met his cousin at the appointed place, and they set off for Jordan. It was just before dawn. They drove to Tikrit and down toward Baghdad, swung around the city on the ring road, and headed west into the desert. The day's heat had just started to build. Just as Ahmad's cousin said, Highway 1 was filled with oil tankers. Under the oil-for-food program Jordan, which has no petroleum reserves, was allowed to import Iraqi oil. Iraq also used the Jordanian port of Aqaba to ship oil to the west. The police had no particular interest in slowing down this lucrative trade. The heat and lack of sleep killed any desire Ahmad might have had for conversation with his cousin. He dozed fitfully as they drove the hours through the boring, rocky desert. He was awakened from a nap by the sound of the gears shifting down and the truck shuddering slowly to a halt. He looked at his cousin. "Mukhabarat." They were less than three miles from Jordan.

Ahmad muttered, "Oh, shit," more in annoyance than fear. Fear he could control. He had been in this situation many times. He knew the drill. Play stupid. Don't argue. Act a little nervous, not a lot. Make very little eye contact. The fools' parade began. One flunky looked at his passport, passed it to another, and the pair went off to find a third. Ahmad was left standing in the sun for ten minutes. The trio came back and they went through his little overnight bag and his jacket. In an inner pocket in the bag they found a column Ahmad had just finished writing. It called on Saddam to step down and spare his country another war with the United States. The senior Mukhabarat officer read it incredulously. The sentiment didn't surprise him, but how could anyone be so stupid as to leave something like this in so conspicuous a place?

They took Ahmad to a holding cell. The officer called Baghdad to find out more about this fellow trying to sneak out of the country. The Mukhabarat officer went into the little cellblock and said to Ahmad, "Thank you. Thank you very much. You have just made me rich." Ahmad asked, "What do you mean?" "There is a five-million dinar reward on your head." Ahmad said, "Really, five million dinars? If I knew I was worth that much I wouldn't have come all the way through this fucking hot desert. I would have gone to Baghdad and given myself up and claimed the reward. Saddam could give the money to my family."

They put Ahmad in a prison van and drove him to Abu Ghraib, the prison on the outskirts of Baghdad. There he awaited death.

In Erbil the family waited every day for news. He had left no note indicating his plan. They had no idea where he was but they were certain he was dead. They just wanted the details. Roaa alone had hope. "Papa is like a fox," she told them over and over again. "He is smarter than all of them. He will survive and come back."

In the prison, the atmosphere was like the day before Judgment Day. The guards were looking to their own salvation. It was becoming clearer and clearer that this time the Americans meant business. They were going to overthrow Saddam. Directions from the top stopped coming to the prison as the Iraqi leadership became engrossed with finding a plan to stall the war. The constant interrogations at Abu Ghraib ground to a halt; the interrogators no longer even knew what information they were supposed to be looking for. The daily routines of torture and execution became more sporadic.

In his cell with some other political prisoners, Ahmad whiled
away the days with quiet conversation and speculation about
how the regime would deal with the American army. One day in
the third week of October, Ahmad was lying on his tiny mat, half
asleep, when he heard a commotion in the cell block opposite.
Soon the noise became the sound of a small riot. One of his cellmates called to a guard and asked what was going on. The guard
told them to wait and they would find out. Eventually, a
Mukhabarat officer came to them. Saddam has declared a general amnesty for all prisoners, he explained. The mini-riot was
the sound of thousands of men rushing for the front gate before
the dictator could change his mind. When can we go? asked
Ahmad. Not yet, said the officer, who went away. Later that day
the man from the Mukhabarat came back. When do we get out?
Ahmad asked again. Tomorrow came the answer, but first you
must go and "make apologies" to Saddam. Apologizing to
Saddam face-to-face seemed an even more fantastical idea than
the improbable notion of every prisoner in Iraq being released.

But sure enough, the next day Ahmad and his cellmates
were taken out, put in a van, and driven to the palace. Ahmad
was separated from his companions and taken to a little office.
Ahmad prepared himself for death. The stories were legion of
what happened when political prisoners were taken to see the
dictator. If you meet Saddam, you die. He rehearsed in his
mind all the things he wanted to say to the monster before the
bullet went between his eyes. After an hour the Mukhabarat
officer came for him and took him to a large room. Ahmad
waited a little while longer. Than Saddam came in looking dis-
tracted, almost surprised to see anyone there. "Where are you
from?" he asked. "Mosul," Ahmad replied, and then fell silent.
All the brave words froze somewhere on the back of his tongue.
"You people in that city are always giving me trouble," Saddam

said. A door opened, an aide looked in. Saddam looked away from Ahmad toward the aide, then walked out. For a minute nothing happened, then the Mukhabarat officer said, "Get out. Now." Ahmad didn't move. He was confused. "He didn't ask me to apologize." The officer looked at him. "It's your lucky day. Go!"

In the street the fear that he had suppressed so that his execution might have a touch of dignity rose up and he began to shake. The impersonal roar of Baghdad surrounded him. No one noticed the trembling fellow outside the palace walls unless they were very near to him. Then they walked past quickly. The unwashed shit-and-sweat stench of prison on him was overpowering. Ahmad looked up into the sky and let the sun scorch his face until he calmed down. Then he shook his head, beat down the quaking fear, and headed home.

He walked to the edge of the city and at a gas station found a driver going to Kirkuk. In the oil city he met a Kurd who was going to Erbil. Ahmad rode with him until a kilometer before the last regime checkpoint. He jumped out and walked through some farmland and along an irrigation ditch past the checkpoint and then on to Erbil. He came through the gates of his home to tears and love and the words of his wife. "I knew you would be back. Never have I prayed harder. God knows your heart is good. He brought you back to me."

The old routines of Ahmad's life resumed, but it was difficult to stay focused on simple daily tasks. Now even he accepted the Americans were coming. The satellite dish on his roof brought news of the inexorable move toward war. More and more American journalists were coming to town, so there was work. But the reporters were only transient visitors. They disappeared almost as soon as they came. The work was sporadic. He still didn't earn enough to take care of his family the way he had in Mosul. The winter sky pushed down on him. The KDP and PUK hosted a summit of exile groups in late February 2003. Hundreds of journalists came to Erbil and this time they stayed. The reporters were certain the war was scheduled to start around mid-March. Ahmad tried to find work with one of them. He had a few days with a *Wall Street Journal* reporter. Then the reporter decided to base himself in Sulaimaniyah. Ahmad offered to go with him but the reporter told him no. Ahmad returned to the hotels where the journalists were staying, but while he had been working with the *Wall Street Journal,* the other reporters had all hired translators.

The war was about to begin, yet he had no work and the financial situation at home was worsening. Sindibad was now out of work as well. The bazaar had shut down as families began to stream out of Mosul, fearful that Saddam would unleash chemical or biological weapons on the city. Then came the worst news of all. The KDP stripped Roaa of her press card. They accused her of being a spy for Saddam. How is this possible? he raged. She was only thirteen when they left regime territory. Do those idiots think she was recruited at school? He went to beg them to let her have the card back. Don't punish her for my sins, he told them. After a few weeks they gave her press card back. Manifold and strange are the workings of the petty tyrants of the world, Ahmad reminded himself.

He was trapped and in despair. Why on earth had God spared him for this humiliation? Each morning he trooped to the hotels, one of the educated ghosts of Erbil, smoking, sipping chai, waiting for a nod from one of the journalists that might allow him to provide for his family. Finally! The holiday of Narooz arrived in the emptied city. The war would start that night, everyone said so. The United States was coming to kill the monster Saddam. The dream of Ahmad's life was about to come true. But he simply could not move. Depression crushed him into a corner of his furnitureless living room. He watched his sons play chess, his daughters flip aimlessly around the television channels.

In the late afternoon Roaa came back from the Internet café where she had been filing a story to her paper in Syria. She saw her father sitting in misery and went over to him. She urged him to go up to the Erbil Tower Hotel. Her friend Nada was working at the BBC office there. She said there were still journalists arriving in town. She promised to send any who needed a translator to him. "Baba, get dressed," Roaa said to him. "Please, go see Nada."

Ahmad pulled himself out of his corner. He washed and shaved and put on clean clothes, kissed his daughter and wife, and went to the hotel. He took the elevator up to the BBC's office to tell Nada he would wait in the lobby in case any journalists came looking to hire a translator. He rode back to the lobby and bought a fresh pack of cigarettes. He nodded at a few of the drivers and bodyguards watching Fox News on the television, settled onto a sofa, and noted the irony that he was the only person watching who actually understood what the American reporters were saying. He lit up his first cigarette and continued to do what he had been doing for so many years: wait.

He was lost in his thoughts when he heard Nada talking to an American. He shifted slightly on the sofa to see what was going on. Then turned back to the television. Nada called out his name. Ahmad stood up. She brought me over and in Kurdish said to her father's friend, "This man is looking for a translator."

Ahmad's Peace

Chapter Twelve
"A Role to Play"

IRAQ HAD BEEN liberated. Ahmad knew it was his time. There was a reason he had survived Saddam. It was his time to be the leader. Finally. His mind was feverish. He couldn't sleep. In the night he mapped out projects. He would write a new book on his own ethnic minority, the Shabak. He would start a political journal. Most important, he would set up a democracy institute. It was clear people needed to learn the principles of an open society.

He was still at the center of the action, observing events, because the night before I left Erbil, I set him up with Paul Watson, the *Los Angeles Times* correspondent in the north. Paul, like Ahmad, had a nose for trouble. The *L.A. Times* man was willing to get into the middle of a dangerous situation if that's where the story was. Paul was recovering from a mild stab wound to the buttock received covering the continued rioting in Mosul. He had been lucky to get away so lightly. He had been caught by a mob, kicked to the ground, stabbed, and almost torn apart before a couple of Iraqis had dragged him free and shoved him into a restaurant. His saviors were just managing to get the business's shutters down to keep the mob out when a small detachment of American soldiers arrived on the scene and began to fire warning shots, scattering the crowd.

Ahmad and Paul, with Sami in the driver's seat, immediately clicked as a team. The pair drove off each morning to a place where something important was happening. Most days it was Mosul, other days Kirkuk. Ahmad observed how the occupation was coming together. He had time to feel out the street and see how his people were responding. Each interaction reinforced his belief that he had an important role to play in leading his fellow citizens into the new era.

The day the regime collapsed in Mosul, Ahmad and I had gone to Diwassa Square, in the heart of the city. While I recorded a gunfight in the main branch of the national bank, he had become embroiled in an argument with a small crowd about the meaning of democracy. Sami and I had to drag him away from the increasingly surly group. Ahmad said then, "I see I have a lot to do. I am surprised by the way my people act." Many people were surprised—although for the war's planners, it shouldn't have been difficult to anticipate what a quarter-century of Saddam's Stalinist rule might have done to a society's soul. Beginning in 1979 Iraqis had endured eight years of war with Iran; a genocidal civil war against a group of their fellow citizens; an invasion of Kuwait overturned by a month of bombing and less than four days of combat; two major insurrections brutally suppressed; humiliating peace terms, sanctions; the looting of the country's wealth by a small coterie of Saddam's family and senior Ba'ath officials; plus the daily arrests, torture and murder of people. The surface resilience of people in the midst of these disasters belied their shattered inner lives. Survivor's guilt, suspicions bred in the mosque, and the very rational fear that Saddam would come back weighed on everyone.

With a rueful laugh, people told journalists that they dreamed of Saddam. But it was no joke. The Ba'ath had eaten away at the very heart and soul of the society. The freedom promised by President Bush was not something most Iraqis felt they could embrace openly. Not while the streets were lawless; not while the man who had imprisoned and tortured your father, son, brother, mother, sister, cousin, neighbor, was still living down the street in no danger of being brought to justice.

Since April 11, Mosul had been without order. Finally, on April 22, American troops arrived in force. The 101st Airborne, commanded by General David Petraeus, assumed responsibility for the occupation of northern Iraq. In that first month after the removal of Saddam and before the Coalition Provisional Authority was established, America's senior military commanders were given responsibility for running their particular region of the country. Each had a wide range of discretion for managing their bit of Iraq. There was no central plan for them to implement. But General Petraeus was not flying blind in a sandstorm as he set up his office in Mosul's city hall, the governorate building. He had experience of postconflict situations. Petraeus had spent five months in Haiti after the Clinton administration's intervention put the elected prime minister, Jean-Bertrand Aristide, back into power in 1994. He then spent a year in Bosnia after the Dayton Agreement brought that civil war to a close. From those experiences, he recalled for me, he had learned a very basic fact: "If you don't get things right at the beginning, you lose." He understood that the anarchy of the last few weeks threatened America's ability to ever get a hold on Iraq.

Petraeus was responsible for an administrative region that included Mosul, its outlying suburbs and villages, plus all of Iraq from the Syrian border in the west and the Turkish border in the north, up into the mountains around Sulaimaniyah in the east. His plan on arrival, knowing no one and nothing specific about the situation on the ground, was simple. The first thing to do was let the people know who was in charge. He blanketed the city with four infantry battalions. Americans were constantly on patrol, so people in Mosul would be in no doubt that the United States was in control. The looting immediately fell off. The second part of his plan was to enlist local help.

He ordered the Iraqi police and other civil servants back to work. The return of traffic cops helped ease the congestion that kept the city in gridlock all day. It put an Iraqi face on at least one aspect of the new order. But the civil servants were a different story altogether. They lacked initiative. Getting the proper permission was more important than solving a problem, Petraeus quickly discovered. "The place had been run by a five-hundred-kilometer-long screwdriver," he said. "Everything had been directed from Baghdad . . . five hundred kilometers away." He needed to break that mind-set and give the civil servants a sense of responsibility.

Mosul's economy had ground to a halt in the months before the war, and Petraeus knew he had to get it restarted. The state sector was the largest local employer, and government workers hadn't been paid for a while. If he could get money into their pockets it would kick-start the bazaar. He found out who kept the payroll for the state workers: the manager of the national bank across the street from his office. He summoned the manager. Where do you keep the payroll money? During the looting, the manager explained, the payroll cash had been placed in plastic bags and hidden in a waterlogged corner of the bank's vaults. Petraeus demanded the manager take him to the place and show him the money. Then the general ordered the manager to bring the bags of cash out of the basement and set up payments for the civil servants.

"I don't have the authority to do that," the manager said.

"Who does?" asked Petraeus.

"The Ministry of Finance has the authority."

"I don't know how to tell you this, but the Ministry of Finance no longer exists."

"Well, then you have the authority," said the bank manager. "Yeah, you're right," Petraeus remembers saying, amused at the recollection.

Petraeus recalls the manager then asked him for written authorization, which the general provided. Then the manager said he needed that paper stamped. So Petraeus summoned the 101st's lawyer, who notarized it. The next day, he sent an aide to the bazaar to find a stationery store that sold an Iraqi notary stamp.

Petraeus also understood that these Moslawis would be more productive if they felt they were working for Iraq rather than the occupying army. "Iraqis," he remembers thinking, "needed to have a stake in the success of the new Iraq." So he decided to create an interim local advisory council that would elect a mayor to oversee administration of Mosul. It was a small attempt to inject a democratic element into the occupation.

Petraeus figured out one other thing very quickly. All the intelligence he had seen about the state of the country and people was pretty much useless. None of these intelligence sources seemed to know the Iraq that Petraeus was dealing with. In the years before the war, almost all the information about the condition of Iraqi society came from the Kurdish safe area and exiles. The exiles, working with secondhand information, had an agenda of their own: to get the United States to overthrow Saddam. Money had been channeled through the CIA to some local tribal leaders and senior army officers before the war to keep their fighters out of the conflict, but that money didn't seem to buy cooperation in the immediate postinvasion operations. The idea of de-Ba'athification was a fine intellectual construct at the Pentagon and in think tanks around Washington, but the reality on the ground was that every potential local leader one way or another seemed to be connected to the party apparatus. Petraeus and his staff learned very quickly they needed new and more trustworthy sources of information on the political players in Mosul, which former Ba'athists they could trust, which ones they couldn't. Petraeus needed to find an interpreter of Mosul society.

Paul Watson was discovering the gift of Ahmad. He was more than a translator of language, he was an interpreter of his society, a guide to its very heart. As they toured around the area Ahmad kept up a running commentary on Mosul's geography as well as its social complexity and political structures. The information gave depth to the American's dispatches. Ahmad seemed to know every dissident who was left alive in the city. Many of them had reached senior levels in their work before finally giving up on the regime or simply falling foul of it.

Shortly after they started working together, approximately two weeks after Saddam's statue came down, Ahmad took Paul to meet an old friend, Shaheen Ali Dahhir, who had worked as an engineer on Iraq's missile program. They drove through the city into a compound of relatively nice houses as Ahmad continued his running commentary. This suburb had housed senior military and scientists. Ahmad described for Paul the delicate balance between serving one's country and serving Saddam's regime. Mosul had provided many senior generals and scientists for the regime, but they were not members of the inner circles of the Ba'ath. After Saddam took over total control of the party, he filled his inner councils with members of his extended family and very few outsiders. In thinking about Iraq's future, Ahmad believed, it was important for the United States to understand these distinctions.

Pesh merga were guarding the compound for reasons that Paul couldn't quite understand. The 101st was supposed to be in charge of security in the streets, not the Kurds. Sami pulled up in front of a house, and they went inside and found Shaheen sitting alone on a sofa holding an AK-47. The scientist was absolutely terrified. Ahmad asked him, "What's going on? Where's your family?" "I've sent them into hiding" came the answer. They sat for a while and talked. Shaheen had worked at the Al-Kindi weapons center and knew a great deal about Saddam's missile program. This was why he sat there in fear for his life. Saddam loyalists were already threatening scientists who had worked in sensitive areas: collaborate with the Americans and you will die. But Shaheen was quite willing to tell U.S. forces what he knew. He also wanted to lobby the American commanders about reemploying his colleagues. Shaheen feared that if they had no work they might sell their knowledge to the highest bidders. When the Soviet Union collapsed, many of its weapons scientists had done precisely that, scattering to Libya and Iran, Shaheen explained. So far, the Americans had ignored Shaheen's approaches. That seemed ludicrous to Paul.

After the interview, Ahmad asked Paul whether they might do something to bring Shaheen to the attention of the American commanders. As it turned out, Paul did have an interview scheduled with General Petraeus. The reporter wrestled with Ahmad's request. He felt the situation challenged a basic precept of American journalism: reporters are neutral observers of events. We are not supposed to be participants in the story. If we become participants, it immediately creates a conflict of interest. Paul had to consider that if Ahmad went to meet the general with the intention of lobbying him on Shaheen's behalf, his translator would have crossed over the line from neutral observer to participant. The American debated his own role in providing the means for Ahmad to influence events the two of them were supposed to be objectively observing.

The dilemma was profound. Paul believed that it was not the place of a journalist to go up to an American commander and say,

"Hey, I met a scientist who can probably tell you everything you want to know about what was going on at the Al-Kindi weapons facility. I interviewed him for an hour and I think he has really important information. This is what he told me and here is how he can be reached. If you want, I can bring him to you."

If a reporter did that, he or she would become an agent of government, a participant in the story. What is the difference then between the reporter and someone working for the CIA? In Iraq, a self-imposed pressure to share information this way existed. As General Petraeus had quickly found out, there was virtually no firsthand intelligence on Iraq. During and after the war, unembedded journalists were often the only sources of this primary information. There were many places that I and other reporters had visited before American troops arrived. We saw things with our own eyes, met local leaders, and formed judgments about who could or could not be trusted. This is called reporting. In another context it could be called intelligence gathering. That is why scrupulous neutrality by journalists is usually required.

But, Paul remembered, Ahmad was so much more than a translator. He was a colleague, a fellow journalist. He was also a citizen of a broken country, a patriot who wanted to do whatever he could to help rebuild it. If, because of Ahmad's work as a journalist, he could meet the American in charge of Mosul, why shouldn't he act as a conduit for an old friend who might have important intelligence to share? Postwar Iraq was a place where normal rules about conflict of interest did not apply. Paul concluded, "He's got a role to play. Let him play it."

It wasn't unusual for General David Petraeus to make room in his crowded schedule for an interview. He is known as one of the most media-friendly of America's senior military officers. He gives interviews without much fuss and he engages reporters in as straightforward a way as his position allows. Petraeus is also a genuine intellectual. He likes to have theoretical discussions with reporters about international relations, a subject in which he holds a doctorate from Princeton. Talking to him is like talking to the kind of professor who spends holidays free-climbing rock in Utah as opposed to touring the cathedrals of Europe.

Paul and Ahmad went to the general's office in the governorate building in Diwassa. The three sat at a long boardroom-style table. Paul interviewed the general at length on a wide range of subjects. When the subject of the search for Saddam's weapons came up, Paul brought Ahmad into the conversation. Ahmad told Petraeus about Shaheen. Petraeus was very interested in the story. He summoned an aide, introduced Ahmad to him, and asked Ahmad to give the information to the aide after the meeting. The conversation carried on. Paul remembers the general being quite engaged by Ahmad's way of talking and his insights into Mosul's political structures. Petraeus "fussed" over him. Ahmad seemed to strike the general as an informed and independent local voice, something in critically short supply. Petraeus invited Ahmad to take part in forming the council. He even ordered Ahmad to be given credentials so he could have access to the governorate building. Paul didn't have those and was a bit jealous.

When the interview was over, Ahmad stayed behind. He sat down with the general's aide and gave him Shaheen's contact details. The men made small talk. The American officer asked Ahmad about his background. Ahmad was happy to oblige with information. Then he took a piece of paper out of his pocket and handed it to the soldier. Just after Saddam's statue came down, I had written my friend an all-purpose recommendation, extolling his skill as a translator and noting his potential executive capability based on his career at the University of Mosul and his ability to organize other Iraqis. I also noted his deep knowledge of local politics and his uncanny understanding of the social dynamics of the area. It occurred to me that as NGOs came into

Mosul or Erbil, they would need a local hire to really run their show. Ahmad would be perfect. He gave my letter to Petraeus's liaison person. It read:

WBUR Group
890 Commonwealth Avenue
Boston MA 02215

10 April 2003

Dear Sir/Madam,

Throughout the recent conflict in Iraq I was based in Northern Iraq reporting for WBUR, Boston's NPR news station. Ahmad Shawkat was my translator. Mr. Shawkat had all the qualities I require in a translator: excellent English, complete reliability and a willingness to work all the hours I required from early morning until well into the night. He was also an invaluable resource for social and political context about Kurdish and Iraqi society.

I highly recommend Mr. Shawkat for any translation work, as well as work that requires a high degree of independent thinking and responsibility. If there is anything else I can tell you about Ahmad please don't hesitate to call me at my home in London. The number is below.

Sincerely,
Michael Goldfarb
Senior Correspondent
Inside Out
http://www.insideout.org

Petraeus's aide asked if he could make a photocopy of it. Of course, said Ahmad. The two continued to talk. What did Ahmad see himself doing in the new era? Was he interested in being on the council? Ahmad thought about it, but there were two reasons to say no. The first was money. To attend meetings he would have to give up working with American journalists and he desperately needed to keep earning his hundred dollars a day. The second reason came from a certain self-knowledge. He had never really been a politician in the sense of running for office. He was a political thinker and grassroots organizer but he knew himself to be too impolitic to be much good at working inside elected councils. *I argue too much,* he reminded himself.

Ahmad told the aide the best way he could serve his country would be by running a newspaper. Through commissioning articles and his own editorials he could stimulate political debate and teach people the basics of democratic thinking. The aide made a note of Ahmad's suggestion and reiterated the general's invitation to attend the meetings that would lead to the creation of the council. As they shook hands, he encouraged Ahmad to stay in touch.

Now that he had been invited into the political process, Ahmad decided to introduce Paul to some of his political friends. He took Paul to meet Isam Mahmood, an old friend from the Nasser movement. Isam had led an interesting life. For three decades he had walked the tightrope stretched between service to his country and service to the regime, rising to the rank of lieutenant general in the Iraqi Army. Then, in the mid-1990s, he fell off the tightrope. Isam was discovered plotting a coup against Saddam. He was dismissed from the army, imprisoned, and brutally tortured. This story was well known in Mosul, and in the city's new era he was seen by the Americans as a potential leader. Isam had also been invited to take part in the council and the two old friends spent hours debating their participation. They already knew who some of the delegates were. There were going to be men in that room who had served the regime up to the last minute.

Questions with no easy answers filled the space around Paul, Ahmad, and Isam. Was the council process a sham? Were the Americans smart enough to know who could really be trusted in that group? Was it democratic or antidemocratic to take part in this imperfect gathering? The country was in a state of complete anarchy. Who should have the real power in Iraq right now? Iraqis themselves or the Americans? How far down the path of authoritarianism can you go to stabilize the society so democracy can have a chance to grow? At what point does authoritarian necessity become authoritarian expedience and then become an entrenched system? Ahmad's idea during the war— an idea shared by most potential leaders of Iraq in its immediate aftermath—was that the United States should guarantee a secure environment. But this it had already failed to do. There needed to be an Iraqi component to the security apparatus or it would simply be an occupation. What should that Iraqi component be? Was any group inside Iraq capable of doing what the American army was failing to do—provide order? What to do about the Iraqi army? Isam knew that some commanders had taken bribes from the United States, and their troops had never fought in March 2003. Should the army be left in place? Could its commanders' loyalty be transferred from the party back to the nation? Isam's could. He wasn't so sure of others.

Is it possible to grow democracy under an occupation? In that respect the council would be a first step. But it all depended on who was ultimately elected to the important positions.

Paul listened to the discussion with a growing sense of admiration and also anger. Like most journalists who cover conflicts, he had developed a passionate empathy with people who had to live with the consequences of bad government. Wars almost always happen because political leaders have failed. War correspondents pick through the wreckage of this failure and every day objectively chronicle the human suffering that is its hallmark. But a war correspondent can't do the job well without feeling emotional connection to those he or she meets. It's the passion for the victims that drives a good reporter to take the risks and work the long hours and be away from home for weeks and months at a time.

Paul felt passionate anger about the impossible situation Ahmad and Isam had been placed in by the Bush administration. It was only a few weeks since Saddam's statue had been brought down and already it was clear that there was no American plan for the postwar period. Watching the president or secretary of defense spouting platitudes or making excuses for the chaos enraged him. They had no idea of the mess Iraq was in, nor would they acknowledge the mess they had created for people like Ahmad and Isam to clean up. But the pair weren't throwing up their hands, they were thinking through ways to solve the immediate problems and build a solid foundation for a democratic future. Paul felt privileged to listen.

From time to time, Ahmad or Isam turned and asked the American what he thought about the best way to bring democracy out of this chaos. Paul tried his best but felt his input was wholly inadequate. At the end of these talks, Paul thought, *What can I tell them about democracy that they don't already know? They've been talking about and practicing democracy for decades.* Paul was learning more from the discussions than Ahmad's friends were learning from him. The intensity and sincerity of the conversations astonished the reporter. They used words like *democracy, liberty, civil society,* and *justice* with an intimacy that he had never heard before. In America these terms had been bled of their deepest meanings and turned into almost meaningless slogans by politicians. He was listening to men who had already paid with their blood for speaking and thinking about these ideals and had never lost their desire for them.

Paul remembers having an insight while listening to them: "Resistance is the true spirit of democracy; resistance, not political process, is the hallmark of the democratic mind." These men—by resisting the Saddam regime, by paying a price for their beliefs— had been much more in tune with the spirit of democracy than the average American. In the United States, it seemed the democratic spirit had come down to lawyers settling elections.

Listening to these men grapple with this new situation was humbling and shaming. Watching twenty-four-hour news channels back at the hotel in Erbil, Paul listened to proadministration pundits extolling America as a great moral power because it had brought the gift of democracy to the people of Iraq. But there was nothing moral in the chaos of Iraq a month after Saddam's statue had come down.

For three hours a day, six days running, 217 delegates from Mosul met to select a twenty-three-member city council. The council would go on to choose a mayor and deputies. The mayor would have broad authority to run the government of Mosul and its environs. General Petraeus had selected the delegates from what he considered to be a representative cross section of the community in the town and surrounding countryside. The leaders of the whole patchwork of Mosul society were there: the heads of the great tribes and families; religious minorities: Assyrian Christians and Yezidis; ethnic minorities: Turkmen and Kurds. Ahmad convinced Petraeus's staff that the Shabak were also entitled to representation. There were individuals of importance, like Isam. The

Muslim religious leadership was invited, including some radical imams. And, of course, there were former high-ranking officials of the government, judged to have served their country rather than the Ba'ath. All these people represented competing interests. As the delegates argued and shouted about who should be on the council and the method by which to choose them, Petraeus sat back and watched what he had wrought. Like Paul Watson, the general was humbled watching Iraqis grapple with the immediate necessity of democratic choice. "These were the arguments of *The Federalist Papers* being played out before us," he remembers. "Of course, not at the level of Philadelphia, but it was a fascinating thing to witness."

Ahmad had different thoughts as he looked around the chamber. There was a perverse equality in the gathering. Everyone knew everybody else's guilty secrets. All the closet doors were open and each and every skeleton was clear for everyone to see. Ahmad saw men he knew for a fact had denounced people to the Mukhabarat and others he suspected of that betrayal. He also noticed something else. Mosul had got religion while he was away. Piety had grown like a weed. Saddamites spoke like Islamists. At one level they were just following a trend. People all over the Arab world had become more overtly religious during the previous decade. Secular intellectuals were getting harder to find everywhere. Roaa's and Sindibad's deepening faith was in keeping with the trend. The discovery of Islamism by the ultraloyalist Ba'athists made him laugh. These were whiskey Muslims, the kind of believers who flew to Dubai or Paris or London for vacation and committed every sin. Sometimes they didn't even leave the country to break God's law. Ahmad knew the sexual perversions with men and women that were indulged in in the torture chambers. But even as he bitterly laughed at their hypocrisy, he recognized the danger. Pan-Arab fascism and Islamic fascism coming together had the potential to undo all the good the American invasion had done.

As names were bandied about for the permanent council, he was horrified by how many delegates were backing cadres from the old regime. They are doing it out of habit, he told himself. They do it because the one thing they have in common is the Ba'ath connection, he thought. Saddam had infiltrated everywhere, but this insight offered Ahmad no comfort. Although he wasn't a delegate, he found himself arguing and shouting about some of the names. He sent messages to Petraeus warning him about some of the people coming to prominence in the process. After the day's session, he would come out and look for Paul and explain angrily what had gone on in the chamber.

With the vote scheduled on a slate of nominees for the council, he huddled with Isam. After all their agonizing, his old friend had also decided not to be a delegate. When Ahmad finally told Isam who was being considered for mayor, his old friend felt his decision had been justified. The result of the vote was no great surprise to them or anyone else. The mayor selected was Ghanim al-Basso, a former high-ranking general who specialized, in his own words, in "logistics and political duties." It was the "political duties" al-Basso had been involved in that made Ahmad and Isam despair. Isam told Paul, "In Mosul, there were many political prisoners, but none were elected to the council. But those who shook Saddam's hand to the last minute were elected." Basso had been "forcibly retired" by Saddam. Ten years previously, his brother Salim, another senior military figure, had been caught plotting against the dictator. The brother had been executed. These facts may have sanitized Ghanim al-Basso for the Americans, but for Isam it wasn't enough.

After the election, Petraeus told reporters it was a mistake to think that you could set up a new government in Iraq "without any Ba'ath party participation. A large proportion of governmental officials were members of the Ba'ath party." He had formulated his own criterion for party members to be certified as de-Ba'athified. "Was their party membership pursued in a way that was clearly contrary to the rights of the citizens of Iraq? Did they pursue that membership in a way that harmed others?" Clearly, the general felt Ghanim al-Basso had not violated this principle.

But in the mere thirteen days since they had arrived—into the anarchy and chaos of liberated Mosul—the general had not had much time to vet former senior officials. Nor had there been a way to accurately assess the former Ba'athists' commitment to creating a democratic state. This was an example of expediency in the name of establishing democracy. Petraeus was in a hurry to have a mayor in place so the people of Mosul would feel they had a stake in the new era. Besides, Petraeus had the authority to "refresh" the council if senior Ba'athists were found out. Isam took a different view. Al-Basso had never been part of any resistance group. Isam thought active resistance to the old regime was a prerequisite for Iraq's new leaders. How else to send a signal to people that the old regime and its brutal ways were never coming back?

Ahmad had other dreams for his country that he wanted to share with his new friend Paul. He took him to visit Junayd. Paul's jaw dropped as he walked into the courtyard of the riverside mansion. Everywhere he went in Iraq he had watched people hopping from the frying pan into the fire; here he felt he was walking from the fiery furnace into an oasis. Wealth is an amazing thing, he thought. He looked around the massive courtyard and up at the gallery; he could see where it led to the balcony overlooking the Tigris. Junayd came out, shook hands, and invited them to sit in the shade of one of the courtyard's trees. Chai was brought. Paul almost felt relaxed.

The group made small talk about the grand house. Ahmad and Paul had been joined for this visit by Yochi Dreazen, a young *Wall Street Journal* reporter. Yochi was fascinated by the house's link to the filming of *The Exorcist*. Junayd took him to the library, where the main scenes had been filmed in the 1970s. He told the young reporter how amazing it was to watch Max von Sydow arrive for makeup looking like a vigorous man in his early forties and then see him rise out of the makeup chair a sickly seventy-year-old. The actor had had trouble remembering his lines, which Junayd still found very funny.

The Americans listened to the Iraqis reminisce about the salon that had gathered regularly in the house during the country's slow decline after the Iran-Iraq War. They tried to imagine the desperation of clinging to a "well-cultured" life in a country that was having the culture ground out of it by Saddam's regime. Inside the courtyard, concerts and poetry readings; outside the gates, a police state presided over by a semiliterate peasant thug. Ahmad's and Junayd's situation reminded Yochi of the stories he had heard of Václav Havel and his little theatrical troupe in Prague, making plays as much to keep hold of their own sanity as to make an artistic or political statement about their totalitarian masters.

Ahmad's and Junayd's memories were told in elliptical language. They riffed on the names of absent friends. What happened to this one? Oh, he had an accident. And that person, what happened to him? Another accident. "You see how many accidents our friends have?" Ahmad asked. Yochi realized that *accident* was a euphemism for "murdered by the regime."

From reminiscing, the conversation turned to the future. Mosul, the Pearl of the North, belonged back on Iraq's cultural map again. They would organize an arts festival with local poetry and musicians. They could organize a festival of Arab cinema or world cinema. The regime hadn't killed all the cultured people of Mosul. There were still plenty of them alive who could take part. As they sat listening to Ahmad and Junayd talk about the future, Yochi and Paul had the same thought I had had during the war. These men were like us in surprising ways. Ahmad's and Junayd's dreams of arts festivals and culture bringing people together were dreams they might expect to hear in some run-down city in Europe or the United States, voiced by people committed to its urban renewal. Walking along the gallery of Junayd's mansion and up to the balcony looking out over the Tigris, Yochi tried to imagine that the situation was not as bad in Mosul as his journalist's mind told him it was. It was possible to imagine, in an act of hopeful solidarity, the Mosul Festival of Iraqi Arts scheduled for the first anniversary of the overthrow of Saddam.

But the situation in Mosul and the rest of Iraq was every bit as bad as it seemed. Not just because the Bush administration knocked over Saddam with no sense of what to do next, but because Ahmad and Junayd were among the last of a type. Their dreams for their country were the dreams of 1968. Wandering the streets, unemployed and angry, were two subsequent generations of Ba'ath-educated people. They had never learned to think about a different kind of Iraq, a society that was just, cultured, and modern. They had learned to do only what was necessary to feed themselves and their families. Their long-term thinking in this new era concerned what group they should join for protection now and to have *wasta*—influence—once the occupiers were gone.

It was time for Paul to leave. Ahmad took him downtown to a friend's travel agency and made arrangements for a car to take him from Mosul via Baghdad to Amman. Every detail was nailed down. "Make sure it's air-conditioned," Ahmad said. When he was satisfied that the comfort and security of the reporter were assured, he negotiated a price for the ride. And then it was time to go; another farewell between an American heading to safety and a local hire left in the shit. They shook hands and embraced. Paul mumbled words that were true in his heart but that could not lift his spirit. "We have a lot more work to do covering this story. I'll be back soon." Ahmad nodded and helped his friend into the car. Paul reached through the window to shake his hand one more time. "I'll be back," he said again. Paul's voice falters as he remembers the look on Ahmad's face. It was more truthful than any words. The look said no, you won't be back.

Paul's departure marked the end of a very brief era of financial security for Ahmad. He found Paul's *Los Angeles Times* replacement in the north, Carol Williams, impossible to work with. She harangued him about his smoking and was not interested in spending afternoons drinking tea with his friends. After a few days they parted company. Fortunately, though, Ahmad wasn't totally without income. Yochi needed him occasionally. And Paul had encouraged him to join the "Thuraya club." He convinced Ahmad that the investment in the pocket-size satellite phone would pay off in short order. While working with Paul, Ahmad had filed the occasional story for the BBC Arabic service, but, without a regular number for them to call, he had been missing more assignments than he was getting. The Thuraya meant he was always reachable. He could also file briefs to the *L.A. Times* and earn a little something. Now that he was on his own, the Thuraya proved worth the investment. He filed constantly back to London. But the BBC was late in paying him. Of course, they pay all their freelancers late, but the anxiety about money returned. By the standards of most Iraqis, Ahmad was in a pretty good financial situation. But he had spent so many years living on handouts from his family and the income of his children that he could not see that fact. He feared he would never have another chance to earn the kind of money he made with Paul and me.

Certainly, he couldn't earn a dinar in Erbil. He needed to move back to Mosul immediately. But Afrah refused. The mundane care of middle-class people everywhere—the school year—intervened. The family had to stay in Erbil until the children finished their exams. These were especially important for Rasha if she was going to enter art college in the fall. They would also have to sell the Erbil house to help finance a move back to Mosul, because Afrah was unwilling to incur more debt. These were arguments she was bound to win. Besides, they were having a hard time evicting the people who had moved into their old home, the house with the round bedroom window.

Ahmad spent time over in Mosul, ferreting out news, filing bits and pieces for the BBC. He worked the contacts he had made on Petraeus's staff. There was money floating around to help in democracy-building activities. Ahmad continued to pitch the idea of a weekly political/cultural journal. There seemed to be some interest in that. He was told to be patient, that it might take a while to arrange the funding. But patience had never come easily to him, and now, with his country's future in danger, it was truly impossible to sustain. He had taken a "wait and see" attitude toward the new council, but after a month his doubts about whether these old dogs could learn democratic tricks kept bubbling up. People in Mosul were gravitating toward the new men of power, hoping to be at the front of the line when patronage was doled out. This was not the way to build democracy. He needed to get his message out to the people, to start shepherding them toward the democratic mentality they so sorely lacked.

The Americans still needed guidance. They kept making fundamental errors of judgment, he thought. They fired the man they had initially put in charge, Lt. Gen. Jay Garner. This was a signal of weakness to the Iraqi population. It told them the Americans weren't sure what to do with their country. Then the new American in charge, Paul Bremer, had almost immediately disbanded the army. This quickly made around four hundred thousand more men unemployed. In a place like Mosul, where so many senior military figures had their homes, it was a potential disaster. Not all of these men had been committed to Saddam's regime. They needed to be given a stake in the new era. These officers had networks of loyal contacts throughout the ranks that had served under them. They could set up their own organizations. Who knew what the country would become in a year if they instead used these organizations to work against the Americans?

Ahmad was too busy to fall back into depression over these events, but despair finally snuffed out the embers of elation he had felt the day Saddam's statue came down. Every day he woke up thinking, *I need to get back to Mosul; I need to get to work.* Finally the school year came to an end. In mid-July the family left Erbil. They moved into a tiny flat on the second floor of the house in Mosul where Afrah grew up. All the circles had been squared. Ahmad and Afrah were beginning their life in liberated Iraq right back where they had started out as newlyweds. There were two small bedrooms. The three boys had one, the three girls slept with their parents. There was a living room with a staircase leading to the roof. Two little closet-size spaces under the stairs contained what passed for a kitchen: a small stove in one closet and a sink in the other.

A few weeks after returning to Mosul, Ahmad got confirmation the Americans would give him money to set up a weekly political journal. There was also a grant for him to set up a democracy training institute. He decided to call it Freedom House. Now his real work could begin.

Chapter Thirteen

"Salvation Has Surprised Us"

WITH THE MONEY for the newspaper in his hands, Ahmad went to work at a furious pace. The weekly took shape in his mind with instant clarity. He wanted the paper to initiate a dialogue with readers on every aspect of Iraqi society. He summoned all his friends who could write and told them he needed their work. He would provide two articles each week: one on politics, one on literature. Roaa would write about the views of youth, and her friend from Faleh Jabar's democracy course in Erbil, Abdussalaam, would write on Islam. There would also be essays on women's politics, poetry, and cartoons.

He had to set up the business, as well. In the bazaar, down by the ancient watergate of Mosul, the Bab al Shatt, he found an office in a run-down building. It was through a dark courtyard up two flights of stairs next to a dentist's suite and across from a doctor. He signed contracts with a printer. He bought another computer. The Americans had given him enough money to hire a general dogsbody, someone to drive him and run around on errands to the printer, to collect copy from contributors, and to perhaps provide a little physical protection. Ahmad took Roaa and they visited Thair Zeki, the fellow they had met in Sulaimaniyah at Sindibad's exhibition, in what seemed ages ago. He, too, had come home to Mosul after the fall of the regime and was desperate for work. So Ahmad hired him.

The paper came together quickly. It was almost the end of August. *You see how life can change,* Ahmad thought. *Just one year ago you were arrested near Jordan and sent to Baghdad to die. Today you live in a liberated Iraq and you are the editor of your own newspaper. You will help create the democratic mentality needed for your country to progress. It is for this task God has spared you.*

All that was left to do was to choose a name for the paper. He bounced ideas off Roaa, Sindibad, and Abdussalaam. He wanted people to understand that the newspaper was free from any political party. Hundreds of newspapers and weekly journals had begun in the months since the overthrow of Saddam, but they all had a connection one way or another to a political group. He came up with the name *Bilattijah,* translating it as "Without Direction." The title had a double meaning. The first, the obvious one, was that no one directed its opinions. It was independent. The second meaning was more allusive. He wanted to give a name to the post-Saddam historical era, a time when Iraqi society was unsure which way to go. The first edition hit the streets of his city on August 26. The Arabic title of the paper was written in red ink. Above it, in green ink, the word was spelled out in Roman letters: *Bilattijah.* Below, in black: WITHOUT DIRECTION—A WEEKLY FREE CULTURAL, SOCIAL & POLITICAL NEWSPAPER.

Just below the title was his first editorial. It was written with the rhetorical and allusive flourishes that characterize much Arab writing. Translated into English, this style can seem no more than a verbal torrent that doesn't aid an argument. But it is the normal style of Arabic discourse. The essay had two purposes: to announce his return from exile to a city where he had once had some notoriety; and, in the most romantic terms, to explain the poetic nature of his journal's name.

Directions have become multiple with varied colors and pathways. Ordinary men are no longer able to recognize a direction or delineate a path to reach their desired goal. In every direction they look there is a spring flood extending as far as the eye can see. They cannot tell where the ground is firm. But they must set out across the flood. Thus we have to go off without direction!

Some friends commented on the title "Without Direction" as connoting no belonging. . . . Our belonging to the Iraqi place, the Iraqi time, the Iraqi ache, deeply embedded in history, has been near to us. Even when we were going through the pain of exile. . . . Our belonging to Iraq has been nearer to us than our veins. Then, when we returned to our country we found the public was without direction!

A poetic rumination on the meaning of exile follows. There is a sense of apology and self-justification for leaving Saddam's territory for the comparative safety of exile, before Ahmad returns to his main theme: finding the right words to describe this era in "liberated" Iraq.

Salvation has surprised us because we never were expecting it. So we surrendered to our chaos. . . . If one of us turned to the other and asked: "Where to?" He would shake his head and say: "I don't know." And if the question was reformulated: "What is your direction?" The answer would be: "Without direction!"

Amidst both the absence of direction and the multiplicity of directions, we need to give this important period of our time a title that captures the literal meaning of our new historical era. Even though we are caught in the middle of this flood, that doesn't mean that we can't detect the right path for the coming time. We are the first to fight for the building of

a new Iraq and a civil society and a transparent democracy in
a time of freedom. This is our direction in the midst of a
period "without direction."

As Ahmad prepared the next issue, the direction of Iraq in the post-Saddam era took a violent wrong turn. In the south of the country, in Najaf, the first of Iraq's bright hopes for leadership was snuffed out. Muhammad Baqr al-Hakim, a leading Shi'a cleric, was blown to eternity just after midday prayers on Friday, August 29, 2003. A car bomb left outside the Imam Ali Mosque, Shi'a Islam's holiest site, killed the imam and eighty worshippers. Al-Hakim, who had only recently returned to Iraq from two decades of exile, led the Supreme Council for the Islamic Revolution in Iraq. Despite the radical sound of his party's name, al-Hakim was a moderate and had made many public statements about wanting to separate mosque and state in the new Iraq. Ahmad had his subject for the second edition's editorial.

THE CATASTROPHE OF TOMORROW

Friday awakened millions of Iraqis from a sweet dream, a
delicious dream for many wishful thinkers. . . . If Iraq's catas-
trophe can end with the spilling of Al-Hakim's blood, then it
was the act of ultimate generosity by this sage.

Iraqis should realize well that the troublemakers and
rabble-rousers are back and they are trying to divide the Mus-
lims. Al-Hakim was not the sage of Shi'as only, but he was
the sage of all Muslims. . . . He entered all their hearts
because he embraced their hopes and dreams and ambitions.
Thus, spilling his blood was a catastrophe for Islam and Mus-
lims in every corner of the earth. . . .

There can be no doubt the assassination of Al-Hakim in

this grotesque way must be considered a dangerous turning point in the current Iraqi situation and a challenge to the Iraqi consciousness in general and the Islamic one in particular. . . .

Even in anger, Ahmad looked for some hope. For all the upheavals since the founding of the modern state, there had never been a full-scale civil war. If his fellow citizens could hold fast to the idea of an Iraqi national consciousness, danger could be avoided.

It is well known that it is historically very uncommon for this Iraqi consciousness to slip into bloody sectarian conflicts. But troublemakers are back with a vengeance! They might find in weak-spirited people an easy target to establish their goals. Here it is important to gather the elements of this consciousness, rather than react emotionally, as the troublemakers seek. If this consciousness was able to give birth to someone like Al-Hakim, it can give birth to another Hakim, as long as it is fertile.

Then, obliquely, he accuses Islamist radicals of the crime and warns Iraqis to start acknowledging their true intentions.

The population needs to stop burying its head in the ground like an ostrich. It needs to raise its head up high to see the enemy coming toward it. . . . The enemy of Islam and Iraq is one. It is the same enemy of all Iraqi factions. . . . No one should mistake the wolf for a watchdog just because it appeared today to be protecting you! The enemy is clever enough to realize how to use the elements of our history, as if he is selling us back our own merchandise.

May God rest your soul, oh Hakim, Iraq's Sage . . . we weep for you and weep for our country. They wanted to

*divide us with your killing, but we are united by your
martyrdom.*

This was one of the few times that hope overrode Ahmad's skepticism. It was rewarded by a death threat. A handwritten note was slipped under the office door, with the imprimatur of God: a verse from the Holy Quran, and a fatwa from Islamists demanding on pain of death that the newspaper stop publishing articles on Islam.

That didn't take long, Ahmad said to Thair Zeki. Then he laughed sarcastically and threw it away. When he mentioned the note to Afrah and his older children, a chorus of caution began. He went to visit Sana to see his grandchildren. "Please, go slowly this time," Sana begged. "You have too many responsibilities. Be sensible, Baba." He nodded and told her not to worry. "I am just starting a dialogue with my people," he assured her. "Some of them speak more aggressively than others."

He wanted a dialogue with his people. That was true. But already his people were yelling. The dialogue had become an argument. He wrote the next op-ed still furious at the death threat. His tone is mocking and sarcastic, then pained and rueful.

BE READY FOR THEM IN EVERY CORNER

*Fight them wherever you find them, struggle, be patient, shed
their blood, terrorize them, find new means of violence and
terrorism, stab security and peace in the heart. Let's call for
Jihad!*

*Believers in tyranny and terror, may you fill our streets with
fire and bloodshed and may destruction reign over every inch of
Iraq. Don't let us catch our breath and start reconstruction. Our
palaces are awaiting us over there . . . in heavens that are as extensive as land and sky, where rivers and light flow underneath. And
condemn to hell, those who don't believe in violence, blood, and
terror. . . .*

It has been thirty-five years of bloodshed, daily mass graves, insecurity, wars, destruction and terrorism. . . . I guess one more year or a few more years are not going to matter that much . . . our destruction is ongoing. The most important thing is to kick out the invaders and bring another tyrant. . . . We have become used to being mounted by tyrants. We have become addicted to misery and we cannot live decent lives anymore . . . we have totally failed to fill up with life. . . .

O Courageous Mujahideen. . . . May God forgive you. . . . You know better than I do that Islam is a religion of peace and that God is peace. You know that the core of faith is peace and the salute of Islam is "peace." . . . If you kill peace you kill God. Meditate on that. If you kill God then what is left of Islam? I know that you need not be reminded about peace and Islam . . . because it is you, and only you, who know this fact.

Then he makes a stern accusation. Many of the organizers of the religious insurgents were Mukhabarat who went to the mosques in the first place to keep tabs on worshippers and imams.

There were some who used to go to mosques before the liberation of Iraq to bend and kneel to God almighty, but they were just there to write reports on believers to send them to secret prisons and then to mass graves. Those people are now the same who have declared jihad and are leading fools and the deceived to spread terror and destruction in the country. . . .

That was an astonishing assertion at the time. The leadership of the American occupation had not yet discerned a link between Ba'ath loyalists and Muslim radicals. Yet Ahmad made the connection sound plausible. Saddam's Mukhabarat had infiltrated the mosques long before the war; political interaction between the two groups predated the overthrow of the regime.

From his editorial pulpit, Ahmad fancifully calls out to the true Muslim radicals to stop killing and start converting the occupiers.

> *Dear Jihadis in Baghdad, in Fallujah, in Ramadi . . . and all through Iraq . . . return to the word of God . . . return to Peace . . . the killing of one or two Americans is not a jihad as long as more than half of the Iraqis want them to stay. The conversion of one American to Islam has more righteousness than the killing of ten . . . you know better than I do God's reward for such an act.*

The newspaper now took up most of his time. But he had set himself the task of writing a book on the Shabak, his ethnic subgroup among the Kurds. He snatched time to work on it when he could, dashing chapters off like a student finishing a term paper the night before it's due. And there was other business— he needed to make right the decades of suffering he had brought on his family. He finally had money again and they would live in comfort. Ahmad found a plot of land in a newish suburb on the east side of the Tigris, only a short walk from Sana's house, and decided it would be a suitable place to build them a new house twice as large as the one he had built with his own hands back in the 1980s. He took Afrah to look at the plot. It was on a corner and had room for a large house and courtyard. She approved of the site. "I am happy," he told her. "I will build you a palace." He bought the land and started on another creative project: drawing up plans for their new home. It would have a big kitchen and enormous, cool family rooms plus a big, private bedroom for himself and Afrah. No more sharing rooms with children. No more living like a "village-ian." He had earned that right.

He took Sindibad to one of the car bazaars on the outskirts of the city. They picked out a Japanese sedan, not too old, with enough room to squeeze most of the family into. He paid cash, peeling off dollars from his roll. Having money, spending it so decisively, felt good. He drove back to his brother-in-law Ayad's house. The street came out for a look. Like any man with a new car, Ahmad enjoyed showing it off: What do you think? The men on the block took a look, made automobile small talk, and went away. In the million-person village of Mosul, these purchases became the subject of gossip. The war had thrown the economy into disarray. Unemployment was high. So who was this guy who just came back from Erbil buying land and a car? Where did he get the money? The answer was easy for the gossips. He works for the Americans. They give him money to spy on us.

Ayad heard the whispers. He told Ahmad to be a little less conspicuous in his consumption. They argued briefly. Ahmad told him that everything he was doing was for his family. "Your sister has done without for far too long," he told Ayad. "She has suffered with me. She has suffered *because* of me. I cannot give her back all those years of pain but I can give her some comfort now. I don't care what these people say behind my back. If they want to talk to me, let them come and talk to my face. I am doing what a man is supposed to do: taking care of my family."

"If you want to take care of your family, then watch what you say in your newspaper," Ayad told him.

Ahmad replied, "Don't worry. This week I am full of respect for the believers. I am invoking the Quran in the most inoffensive way." He showed him a copy of his editorial. He pointed to one paragraph in particular.

We have forgotten God Almighty's conditions, as it says in the Holy Quran: "God will not change the status of a people, unless they change that which is inside them—change their soul." We haven't changed that which is inside us yet, even though He has blessed us with freedom from the despot that destroyed our land. The freedom that descended on us is a gift from God—although the Americans haven't left yet—and damaging such a gift might be a cause for its vanishing.

"You see? I know how to speak to people in their language."

There was one more pressure building up. Ahmad had domestic trouble down at the office. He and Roaa had always been close. Now the pair became intertwined even deeper, a separate unit within the family. Roaa didn't like Thair Zeki at all. Her father's friends were all "well cultured," educated in the arts, but Thair wasn't educated at all and his friends, who felt free to hang around the office all day long, were just stupid. They looked at her in a way she found offensive. Even as a bodyguard, he was lazy. He didn't seem to have her father's interests at heart. Ahmad would send him on an errand to the printer, and it would be hours before he came back—hours when her Baba was exposed to the assassins she knew were out there, waiting for the opportunity to kill him. When Thair returned from these long absences, she would demand that he say where he had been, but he was always a bit evasive.

Roaa told her father he should get rid of him.

"Why?" he asked.

"I don't trust him."

Ahmad reminded her that she had never liked him from the first time they met in Sulaimaniyah.

"That doesn't matter," Roaa told him. "Thair doesn't have your interests at heart."

"He is my 'information catcher,' " Ahmad told her. "He has many friends in parts of the city where we do not know anyone. What he tells me is useful for writing."

Still Roaa could not understand why he kept this character around, other than out of pity. There was a city full of unemployed men from different social classes. There had to be someone more suitable and more loyal than this one.

September was over and Mosul's streets were awakening from their summer torpor. Ahmad remembered that this quickening of life happened every year after the stifling heat of the summer gave way. Events in the city were gathering pace, and the signs were not positive. Slowly, steadily the old regime elements were organizing. Ahmad knew of this through what he heard from Thair and from the testimony of his own eyes. He saw people from the Mukhabarat talking to old commanders on street corners or in teahouses. While sitting in his car, waiting in traffic, in the back seat of a car in the next lane he saw people chatting away who he thought should be in prison. I wonder what they are talking about, he said to Thair, and they would speculate and gossip about it. But he knew the answer from events. The old regime elements had assessed the occupier's strengths and weaknesses and they were discussing how they could wreak havoc on the American mission.

In Ahmad's view, the Americans were not helping their own cause. They were still trusting the wrong people. They launched raids in the middle of the night on what they had been told were the homes of insurgents. But more often than not they only succeeded in scaring or killing innocent Iraqis. Every murdered innocent widened what was already an almost unbridgeable chasm between the occupiers and the occupied.

The council was turning out just as Ahmad feared it would.

Ghanim al-Basso swept around town like a potentate with goons in tow acting as bodyguards. All these ex-Ba'athists had their noses in the American trough. They were living well, showing off the trappings of their authority while most of Mosul's workers had no jobs, he thought—without noting the irony of his own situation. The city, the country, cried out for an Iraqi-led effort to rebuild, but the donkeys General Petraeus had allowed to take over were simply taking money and distributing it as patronage to their followers. Perhaps the Americans didn't care, as long as some of the council members provided them with information on insurgents. Perhaps they couldn't see how corrupt these people were and how their power offended the Mosul street. The Americans were naive and the Ba'athists were cunning. They quickly learned the language the occupiers liked to hear and became adept at lying to them in it.

From time to time since the overthrow of Saddam, Ahmad had felt keen disappointment in the Americans. But he had always been able to push that feeling aside. For all the problems, the new era remained one of promise. But now the sense of disappointment stabbed him every day. On the walls of Mosul, graffiti started to appear urging resistance to the Americans in the name of Allah and in the name of the old regime. He still had contact with people on Petraeus's staff. He urged them to nip these people in the bud, but it seemed they had made a decision to let the Islamists alone. The Americans didn't accept his assertion that ex-regime elements and the radical imams were coming together to form an insurgency. Or if they did, the Americans around Petraeus thought that they could control the situation through the people they had steered onto the council. If anything, some senior American commanders began to think Ahmad was stirring up trouble with these editorials about Islamists. In their view, Ahmad was screwing up their plan by antagonizing the Islamists with his strident editorials.

Even his young friend Abdussalaam took offense at some of his writing. In one editorial Ahmad wrote, "I have deep doubts that we are the offspring of a profound civilization, the world's first civilization. Maybe we are the offspring of stupid monkeys." In another he wrote of the muezzins' call as the braying of a donkey. Salaam had great respect for the older man and deep affection for his family, but after reading this, he told Ahmad directly, "You cannot publish this. This is offensive to everyone." Ahmad removed the phrase. But it was not the end of the conversation. Salaam felt frustrated that Ahmad, a man who understood politics so well, could be such an impolitic character. He was different from the man Salaam had known in Erbil. In the months since the family moved back to Mosul, Ahmad had become almost manic. Increasingly, he listened to no advice. It was like there was constantly a roar inside Ahmad's head and no outside words could be heard above the din in his mind. Maybe he was going a little crazy. Even his editorials were sounding manic. They were dashed off at top speed—the carefully crafted, poetic images of the first weeks' essays were replaced by whatever phrase came to mind . . . and almost all of them were intemperate.

Ahmad's response to any criticism was simply, "There is no time. There is no time to worry about hurt feelings, no time to write poetry." In a pragmatic sense there really was no time. He was organizing Freedom House. He was writing his book. He was building his family a home. In the larger sense there was no time. The prospect of a truly democratic Iraq was being lost. The Americans refused to learn from their mistakes and ignored the evidence of their own eyes as the country was slipping away from them. The Muslim world was full of criticism about the occupation but was offering no concrete help of its own to get the country back on its feet. The Arab countries were even worse. They were actually demanding Iraq pay back debts and reparations incurred by Saddam. In the second week of October 2003, the Islamic nations held a summit in Malaysia. The meeting was held in advance of a conference in Madrid of donor countries willing to assist financially in the reconstruction of Iraq. The Islamic summit ended without any financial commitment to the reconstruction of Iraq. Ahmad could barely hide his despair in the subsequent article's sarcasm.

> *I congratulate you, dear Muslims, on behalf of the Muslim World....*
>
> *The leaders and politicians of the Muslim nation have gathered recently at a summit in Malaysia to discuss the condition of our country ... none of them made a comment on Iraqis' hunger and devastation or called—even as a form of compliment or a joke—for lending a hand to help the Iraqis....*
>
> *I have a question that might sound funny, silly and even sad. ... "Why do all the Leaders of the Donor Countries come from the unbelievers? Where are the Muslims? None of the Muslims has a couple of dollars to contribute to the Iraqi Muslims? None of the Muslim nations can help Iraqis in the reconstruction of their country? Are the glowing religious sentiments and declarations of national honor that have captivated us for so many centuries, not alive in the heart of the leader of at least one Islamic nation?"*

He goes on to ask a question of the leaders of Muslim countries. Why do they push for Iraqi sovereignty when the country is in a state of anarchy?

*We don't need sovereignty when we are dying of hunger
and our conflicts are tearing us apart . . . while we have no
clue how to use this freedom that has entered our lives so
suddenly.*

Then Ahmad wants to know why the only money from Muslim
countries finding its way into Iraq is funding Islamic terrorists.

*Can't you clearly see that those who claim to be faithful are the
ones who in the name of Islam have started the fighting
between brothers of the same religion over the crumbs of this
distorted sovereignty? I congratulate you, dear Iraqi Muslims,
for the Muslim World. Oh God be my witness that I am not
saying this as a cynic, but because I am in pain.*

He took the copy to the printer. The printer read the article and
shook his head. "No, I'm not going to print it." Ahmad asked,
"What do you mean you're not going to print it?" "It is
insulting to Muslims." "No, it's not," Ahmad told him. "It's
critical of the leaders of the Muslim countries who are leaving
their brothers in Iraq to rot in this state of anarchy and violence.
It is critical of Muslim leaders because they allow the non-
Muslim countries to take the lead in providing funds for Iraqi
reconstruction."

They argued. "Don't you see what bloody hypocrites these
people are?" asked Ahmad. "Aren't you angry about it? They
speak in the name of Islam but their every action brings shame
to the Muslims." Hypocrisy was not a concept the printer could
grasp. But then, the printer wasn't just upset about this one
article. He told Ahmad the newspaper itself was disrespectful.
The printer was devout. He went to the mosque regularly. The
local imam had told him the community was displeased not
just about the anti-Muslim sentiment of *Bilattijah* but also that

its views were too pro-Western. Ahmad reminded him that the paper contained articles from all points of view. Abdussalaam wrote an excellent column on Islamic politics and interpretation of the Quran. The man was adamant.

"Is it a question of money?" Ahmad asked. "I will pay you more."

This offended the printer's pride.

"I'm not going to print it, that's all." He handed the article back to Ahmad. "I'll get to work on the rest of the paper, but this I'm not publishing."

Ahmad went to Junayd's house. He needed some time to think and also a bit of friendly sympathy about his problem with the printer. The two men sat together in the courtyard, sipping chai. Ahmad gave his friend the article to read. If he expected sympathy, he got none.

"Maybe the printer is right," Junayd told him.

"What do you mean?"

"Look, I can see how he would think this is insulting to the Prophet or those who believe in him."

"What are you talking about?"

Junayd picked up the copy and read aloud from it. " 'Why do all the Leaders of the Donor Countries come from the unbelievers? Where are the Muslims? None of the Muslims has a couple of dollars to contribute to the Iraqi Muslims?' You don't see that this is offensive? Last week you wrote 'We are the offspring of stupid monkeys.' You don't understand this angers people?"

"That is style. It is a metaphor. Is what I'm saying about these idiot jihadis truthful?"

Junayd shrugged. "What does that matter?"

"Well, when did we stop saying the truth? We said it when Saddam was in power. Why shouldn't we say it now?"

"Now may not be such a good time, my friend. Wait a while. This is not so important that it needs to be published this week."

Anger and surprise surged through Ahmad, but he controlled himself out of respect for his intimate friend.

"No, if we want democracy we cannot take even one step back. We're the only paper that is independent. We're not American, we're not jihadi. We're going to keep doing what we're doing. I'll find another printer, or pay this donkey more for his trouble."

Ahmad kissed Junayd on the cheek three times and left. He was saddened and a little surprised by his friend. When did he become so frightened of the truth? Ahmad accepted that the cancer of "dictatorism" had moved from the body politic into the soul of the nation, but he still thought there were individual cells that were uninfected. He needed to link up with these healthy bodies. He wasn't infected, and he had thought his friend Junayd wasn't. Now he had to reconsider how deep this disease had gone. Junayd, of all people, was urging him to be cautious. Junayd should know you can't let fascists get a foothold, for once they do, they are unstoppable. You make one compromise and the next thing you know, you have to make another, and another, and then you have to join the party, and then, if you dissent, they torture you—although, with Islamists, they kill you with a sura from the Quran on their lips. How sad that his friend had forgotten this or, worse, had become so afraid. He had not been so fearful back in the days of Saddam's regime.

But Ahmad couldn't see how the cancer was affecting him as well. Once again he had placed everything at risk—his life, his family, his newfound financial security—to write this article. Would it make the slightest bit of difference to the life of Mosul? Was anyone listening anymore except those who were ready to take offense? If he wanted to be al-Fatih, if he wanted to be a leader in this new era, he needed to be alive. He was on his own, so he needed to pick his fights with greater thought. He also needed to tailor his message so that more people would listen. This is politics. Perhaps he knew all these things but had reached a point where he simply would no longer be deterred from saying what was on his mind. He weighed everything he was risking against a lifetime of enforced silence and decided he would not hold back. There was nothing new in the dilemma of trying to be free even if it meant bringing pain to his family. He had made that choice over and over again. And he always chose the risk in order to get closer to freedom. No one was his master, least of all these fascists of the mosque.

Another death threat came under the office door. But death meant nothing. He had been close to it so often. If death was coming soon, he had to spend every minute that was left to him speaking what he knew to be the truth.

Chapter Fourteen
"The Gift of Freedom"

AT FREEDOM HOUSE, the construction team was finished. The last
bit of fresh paint had been slapped on. Ahmad had organized a
conference on developing the democratic mind in the new Iraq
with an opening ceremony scheduled to kick off the conference.
There was still no postal service, so the invitations had to be hand-
delivered. The responses had come back, and it seemed there
would be a decent turn out.

Ahmad looked as exhausted as he felt. The night before the ceremony, Afrah asked him what he was going to wear to the opening.
He had given it no thought. Afrah went to the place where she hid
the household money. She gave a roll of bills to Roaa, saying, "Go
with your father and buy him some new clothes." Ahmad
protested that he didn't need anything new. But his wife insisted.
Roaa and he went to the bazaar. Once there, his reluctance to shop
disappeared. They poked and prodded at merchandise, felt it and
haggled over it. He got a new jacket, shirt, and tie and even bought
American underwear. They returned home with a new wardrobe
and no change. Afrah asked, Where did all the money go? They
toted up what they spent. "Five dollars for underwear?" She
laughed. "I didn't mean for you to spend money like that."

The next day Ahmad was very nervous. He counted the crowd as they came into the space that represented his greatest dream. Ghanim al-Basso, Mosul's mayor, sent a representative. The Kurdish parties were also represented: KDP, PUK, and Salaam's Kurdistan Islamic Union. The Assyrian Church sent someone. Around forty people came in all. When everyone had taken their seats, Ahmad swallowed his nerves and went to the lectern and began to speak. He welcomed the dignitaries and thanked them for their support. Then he began to speak about his dream for this place and his country. His words echoed themes he had been writing about in *Bilattijah*.

"Freedom is a gift," he told the assembly. "Some might argue that it is a new gift for Iraqis. We are not familiar with freedom's principles. Its arrival in our midst has produced a state of chaos.

"But freedom is about order and respecting the rights of others. The first scene of this order is the practice of democracy in our consciousness. This is represented in building bridges for dialogue, accepting and/or rejecting different opinions in a peaceful way."

It had been a long time since he had stood in front of a group talking about ideas, but almost as soon as he started speaking, his nerves disappeared. It was like teaching again. Teaching was *his* gift. Saddam could take away his pupils but could not take away his talent for explaining ideas. Ahmad went on, explaining why he had set up Freedom House. "We might not achieve a democratic consciousness in our society unless we build an institution that educates people in this new way of thinking and acting."

Freedom House would be the place where people could learn this new mentality, this mind-set. "I hope that this house will graduate a leadership cadre. Those who attend our courses will take charge of building a democratic mentality among our people and founding the mechanisms of civil society, so that freedom is not misunderstood and democracy is not misused amidst the chaos that prevails in our society these days."

As he spoke, he looked at his wife and children. This moment was what he had struggled toward all his life: standing in his liberated city, a free man wanting to teach his fellow citizens how to be free. Did his family understand? He had put them through so much, did they think the pain and sacrifice were worth it now? He was not a fool. He knew that some of his children were estranged from him because of the way he had carelessly risked their happiness. Did they forgive him? Did Afrah forgive him? For her sake and, on this day, his own, he ended with a prayer.

"May we protect and maintain the gift of freedom that God Almighty has blessed us with to change what is inside us. He is most knowledgeable of our intentions to serve our country, its people and their civilization."

He introduced the guest speakers. The speeches were full of warm words for the success of Freedom House. More important, they even seemed sincere. When the ceremony was over, the meeting broke up quickly. For politicians and community leaders, liberated Iraq was an endless sequence of meetings. The guests had other appointments to keep. Alone with his friends and family, all of Ahmad's opening-night nerves returned. They assured him it had gone well. The speeches had been genuine. It was good of the mayor to send a representative, Afrah told him. Ahmad asked Salaam what he thought of the turnout. "Quality is more important than quantity," his young friend told him. "These were important people. It was a mark of respect that they came to support your effort." Ahmad did allow himself a little satisfaction in the fact that the KDP and PUK had each sent representatives. "Maybe they are happy to see me gone from Erbil," he joked.

The next day, the first conference at Freedom House got under way. Ahmad presented a lecture on founding a democratic society out of the present anarchy. Only fifteen people showed up. The following day only ten came. He could not hide his disappointment. Salaam reminded him of the situation in the city. "People have so many problems, they're too busy trying to find a job so they can feed their families. They don't have time to come and discuss democracy right now." Salaam was correct. The building of democracy was hard to discuss in a society as unsettled as Iraq was six months after Saddam's overthrow. There has to be a minimum level of security and prosperity before people could turn their minds to these ideas. The Kurdish safe area had been created in 1991, but it wasn't until 2002 that Faleh Jabar had turned up to run the democracy seminar Ahmad had attended. It took eleven years of intermittent civil war and constant struggling out of poverty before the time was right to educate cadres in democratic principles. Ahmad understood that, but it did not ease his sense of despair. He took the disinterest of people personally. Who in Mosul was better able to explain these ideas, guide people toward building this better society, than himself?

But there were other reasons people stayed away besides the fact that they were just too busy trying to earn a living and stay alive. Freedom House was already under suspicion. It was in an official building, a place connected to the new government. The rumor in the street was that the Americans were funding it and only collaborators went there. It was six months since the overthrow of Saddam, and in the unabated anarchy, the old regime's loyalists were influencing public opinion in ways the Americans could not hear or see. The idea that Iraqis who worked to normalize the situation were collaborators was taking hold in the street. In the radical mosques—and there were more and more of them as Islamists pressured moderate preachers out of their pulpits in Mosul—the imams told their congregations to stay away from Freedom House. These imams had imbibed the current Wahhabi teaching that freedom and democracy were Crusader concepts, alien to the spirit of Islam. Good Muslims had nothing to learn in such an institution. The struggle in Iraq now was to rid the country of the unbelievers and return Iraq to Muslim rule as in the days of the Prophet Muhammad, peace be upon him. The next day and the day after that the attendance at Freedom House dwindled to virtually nothing.

The night after Freedom House opened, Ahmad slept a long time. Exhaustion always brought guilt, because the urgency to do things made him ignore his family. When his body finally gave out, he would be overwhelmed with sadness and guilt. He felt the desire to say: I'm sorry. Afrah remembers: "Many times he said to me, 'I bring hurt to everyone I love. You will be better off without me. Do you want to leave me?' I always said no. I was always faithful to him."

Then she remembers something else from that day: "He was so tired. He knew his time was near."

But it is only in retrospect that we note these things. People often work themselves into exhaustion. But when the task is finished, you go to bed early, sleep deeply, and wake up refreshed. But maybe Afrah is right. Perhaps Ahmad did know his time was near. In their small bedroom the windows faced west. A desk and computer were set up by the window. Late the next afternoon, Ahmad was going through a draft of his editorial for the next edition of *Bilattijah*. He looked out the window at the sun growing fat and orange as it slipped through Mosul's pall of smog and dust. Afrah came into the room after praying. He turned to her and said, "Look out the window. Sunrise is beautiful, but so is sunset."

Afrah knew what he meant. The light is slipping away into the darkness. The day is ending, and endings bring peace.

The editorial for the next edition of *Bilattijah* reflected his despair at the state of his country and his sense of personal rejection. In the two and a half months since he had dreamed up the title "Without Direction," the society had found its course. It had chosen a direction and it was the wrong one. The wrong people had been put in charge by the occupiers, and the occupiers didn't care. They could not see that the society was being turned against them. He had tried to explain to them whom they could trust and who they could not. They never listened. He had been so busy with Freedom House and finishing the Shabak book that the deadline for the editorial was on him before he realized it. He dashed off a jeremiad with a speed that brought it close to incoherence. He was screaming at the top of his lungs at Petraeus and the two million other people in Mosul.

THE DEFUNCT REGIME IS STILL ALIVE

It is not easy to cut off a regime whose octopus-like tentacles reached into every Iraqi home for 35 years. It might be Mission Impossible. However, we are in a moment where the word "impossible" should be removed from our dictionaries. Without erasing this word we are opening all our doors and windows—if we hadn't already opened them— for dictatorship and members of the old regime to come back. The stench of administrative corruption—a well planned and thought out return—has started to spread in everyplace in the new leadership.

The Iraqi street in general, and Mosul's street in particular, has started witnessing a phenomenon of decay, indicating clearly that those who are responsible for it occupy influential positions, while no one has any influence on them. Worse is that every person who has influence knows this reality, but cannot . . . act to stop this phenomenon.

I wish that the decay was limited to the head of the fish; but it has spread to its body too. There is no government department that does not have a well-organized gang. We managed to infiltrate and get close to some of them and we were shocked by the scale of forgery and corruption that was going on—each with its own specialty. However, we couldn't approach some of these gangs because they have no mercy. This is a matter for those in power who haven't been supervising the work of these organizations since they ordered them brought back to life. Maybe, they did visit them and spoke for a few seconds with the employees, but do they have trustworthy informants to tell them the truth and reality of what is going on there? Don't they understand we are a people who have never learnt to work without someone watching over us?

Till this day we know that the head of the (X) organization is covering up for a group of people working for the Ba'athists in his organization. Mr. Bremer has no clue about how sincere the repentance is of Ba'athists coming back to work. Those repenting individuals are starting campaigns to overthrow innocent and honest people from their work places. Yes, they are working to remove innocent people from offices that have been missing them while they were in the cells of the defunct regime or living in the agony of exile waiting to get back to their homeland.

He ended the editorial with a direct plea to the Americans running his country.

We are not accusing those in power, rather we want to open their eyes and remind them that the decay has reached everywhere in their short rule. That means that the first step was not successful. . . . Many members of the previous regime have infiltrated this group that promised they would correct their path and lead us out of the decay that was prevalent during Saddam's regime. However, if the Americans knew who these people were, then our disaster is most grave.

Tuesday, October 28, five days after Freedom House opened, Ahmad went to the office with Roaa. He gave her a copy of his finished editorial. They didn't talk about it much. If she felt it went too far, she never would have told him. Thair Zeki came as usual. For her father's sake, because he seemed so tired, Roaa was polite to Thair. Just before noon, one of the contributors came by. He had an article on a floppy disk and asked Roaa to run down the street to the Internet café and print it out.

The three men sat around chatting while Roaa went to the Internet café. The Thuraya beeped, indicating a call was coming in. Ahmad picked it up and raced up to the roof to get a clear signal. He told everyone who called him via the Thuraya that if he didn't answer immediately to call back in two minutes. That would give him enough time to get upstairs. He pushed open the heavy metal door and walked out onto the flat rooftop. The roof was surrounded by a sea of concrete balconies and twisted telephone wires, and there was only one small space where the satellite signal could find its way through. From experience Ahmad knew precisely where it was. He went to that little space. The phone rang again, and he answered. Sometimes on a Thuraya there is a delay as voices bounce back and forth from earth to space. His back was to the door as he concentrated on listening for the caller's voice, so he never heard the footsteps coming up the stairs. From just inside the doorway, he was shot in the back.

Ahmad collapsed to the ground amid the detritus of the roof: discarded needles and ampoules of drugs from the doctors' offices below; cigarette butts and soda cans and little swirls of concrete dust. The killer removed the Thuraya from his hand and took out the SIM card, the digital engine that makes the phone work. The person also lifted the flap on the right breast pocket of his shirt and removed the three hundred dollars in cash Ahmad had stashed there.

The shot had been heard all over the bazaar, and Roaa raced back to the building. Nobody had done anything to help her father. She screamed at Thair Zeki to call an ambulance, then ran down the block and around the corner to the police station.

Three floors below the roof, in the bazaar, the street is three and a half cars wide, that half lane offering false hope to drivers anxious to move faster. It entices them to try to drive through space that doesn't really exist. Traffic flows at speeds from crawl to full stop. It was almost twenty minutes before a police car could make it around the block to the entrance of the building. Thair Zeki helped the police pick Ahmad up by the shoulders and legs and bounce him down three flights of stairs, through the courtyard, and into the backseat. Roaa jumped into the front. The hospital was only a few miles away, but it took more than half an hour to get there.

Ahmad lay in the backseat of the police car, stuck in the gridlock, life oozing out of him. As he fell in and out of consciousness, Ahmad looked up at Thair and said, "I'm dying." The bullet had entered his body above the right kidney and exited just under the left lung. At Jumhuriyah Hospital the doctors told Sindibad they needed to wait for his father's condition to stabilize before they could begin to repair the damage the bullet had done. But Ahmad had already lost too much blood. At 2 P.M. he died.

When the children broke the news to their mother, she was calm. No surprise. No tears. He should have been dead many times before.

The body was released by the police late in the afternoon. The family took the corpse and prepared it for burial. Word spread speedily among friends and the extended family, and by seven o'clock they had gathered at a cemetery east of the city on the road to Erbil. The body was laid in the ground. Even fewer people turned up for Ahmad's funeral than for the opening of Freedom House. The law of Islam calls for a body to be interred as soon as possible after death, so not everyone who knew him could get to the cemetery in time. But people were also afraid to come. Saddam was gone, but the default setting of Iraqi society remained fear. A man who has enemies prepared to kill him is a dangerous person to be associated with, even in death.

The grave was prepared and the headstone painted with an inscription, chosen by Roaa, from the Quran: ALLAH'S PROMISE IS TRUE. It means that God's promise to the living that someday they will die holds true for everyone. She had the word SHA-HEED—martyr—painted underneath the verse. The few mourners stood around the grave, their palms in front of them turned upward as if holding an imaginary book. The gesture is called *dua*. They offered their prayers to Allah to take Ahmad into paradise. Then one by one they prayed for their own souls and, as they finished, wiped their faces with an imaginary white powder, the powder that will distinguish them from non-believers on the Day of Judgment.

Chapter Fifteen

"Please Do Something for My Father's Blood"

WHILE HER FATHER'S body was being prepared for burial, Roaa went to the police station and gave her statement. She immediately raised a question about Thair Zeki. He was supposed to be her father's bodyguard. Why had he not gone up to the roof with him? The police should detain him and find out. She asked a detective to go look at the murder scene himself. The next day, the detective did this. Then the criminal investigation ground to a halt.

Justice is the foundation of society. Without it there is nothing but vengeance and blood feuding. Ahmad had known that. He taught his children that. Now all his grieving family wanted was justice, an investigation by the police that would lead to the arrest of their father's murderer. But confronted by the weight of indifference, they quickly resigned themselves that the killer would never go to jail—all except Roaa.

In the extended family the mourning period oscillated between a sense of resigned sadness and anger. It had been bound to happen, they thought. He would not slow down or temper his message when he should have. And he had no sense of responsibility to his wife, children, and grandchildren. Ahmad put us in danger, they whispered, and it was not his right to do this.

Life didn't come to a halt inside the little flat. The comfort of Islam guided Afrah: *Allah gives life; only Allah can take it away. When it is your time, he will take you. It had been Ahmad's time.* Afrah was still in her mid-forties; though the days of widowhood stretched out before her, they did not hold much fear. *Zainab is still young and needs looking after; Sindibad will fulfill his duty as the oldest son and will not leave me alone.* There was money to finish the house. The world did not stop because of Ahmad's murder, and this fact eased the sense of loss.

In those first days after her father's death, Roaa alone was inconsolable. But it was a dry grief—she was determined no one would see her tears. There was work to do. First, the next issue of *Bilattijah* had to be brought out, and Freedom House had to remain open. Then she would return to the police. Her father must have justice.

"Who killed my father?" Roaa asked over and over.

"Let it go," her family told her. "Rest, you are exhausted."

She looked at her family settling back into routine. "How can you act as if nothing has happened? Don't you want justice? Who killed our father?"

"Roaa, be patient," they told her. "It is dangerous."

"No." She demanded, "Who killed my father?"

She went to the police station again. This time she demanded the police arrest Thair Zeki. She called the next day and the day after. The police told her: "We are looking into this, be patient. We cannot be certain he is involved, there are procedures we have to follow when we investigate."

Yochi Dreazen drove up from Baghdad to pay his respects to Ahmad's family. To justify the trip to his editors, he pitched them a story on how so many potential grassroots leaders of a new Iraq were being murdered—men like Ahmad. He went to see one of the senior policemen involved in the investigation. The detective, named Jabar, told him nothing was being done about Ahmad's case. Yochi expressed surprise. He was an important newspaper editor, he told the policeman. Jabar replied, "If he has an American asking questions about him, I can see he must be important. But if he's that important, why does no Iraqi care?"

Yochi left Mosul and the situation carried on as before—still no investigation. And there was no one to bring pressure on the police to do anything. Every minute of the day Roaa thought of seeing her father's murderer brought to justice. But she could not pursue him full-time. Sindibad had returned to university after his seven-year hiatus in Erbil and had no intention of dropping out again. So Roaa had to earn money and help support the family. She took over Ahmad's freelance strings with the BBC Arabic Service and the *Los Angeles Times.* As a combat zone, Mosul had calmed down since the first days after the war, but there was still enough activity in the north to keep a reporter busy. Police stations were being car bombed in Mosul and Kirkuk. There were bodies to be counted, investigations to be made into who was responsible.

With Ahmad's commanding energy gone, the dream of *Bilattijah* soon ended. Roaa could not take it all on. She had no time, and she was not experienced enough to write about her country with the same deep understanding as her father had. Issue number ten of the weekly was the last edition. Ahmad's photo, taken in the Kurdish mountains near Dyana the day we went looking for Iraqi prisoners of war, took up half the front page, surrounded by facsimiles of his book covers. Then there was a headline and an obituary written by Abdussalaam in the imagined words of his dear friend.

WE ARE CONTINUING . . .

You were used to having Ahmad Shawkat writing this op-ed. And he wrote unlike he had done before. He didn't write it with his pen and the fingers of his hand, rather dictated it with the echo of his soul and colored it with the blood of his heart. This time, it is written in a different language; a language spoken by all those who see their ideas living after them like a fine tree that has deep roots and branches reaching the sky; becoming taller than the midgets who cannot look high up, throwing stones on it and as it becomes out of their range, they shoot it down.

I am a father of eight and have a caring wife. I spared nothing to bring them up on great principles and values and made sure that they become loyal to religion, learning, the nation, and people. This was my way in this life. My only weapon was my pen....

I have roamed the world and lived dreaming to see humanity at its paramount. However, my share of it was persecution, imprisonment and torture. For at least thirty-five years, we have suffered repression and oppression. Those who resisted had their tongues thrown eternally into prison. Then, we were filled with hopes that this era had passed . . . forever. However, reality shocked us and we realized that this mentality still exists.

My message had been always to stand up against darkness and injustice, defending the freedom and humanity of the human being. That is why I decided to build a ship, without direction, with my own efforts and capital, along with the efforts of loyal friends around me, embracing this message, to direct it to safe shores. In the midst of this, I didn't spare effort or struggle to deliver my message. Some of this effort came at the cost of my health and the health of my family and children. Then we set off "In the name of God, blessing its sailing and setting to shore." There it was; a newspaper without direction; a nucleus for an institution without direction that made a promise: to serve this country. . . . We sailed, hitting the waves of an angry sea; believing that the word is a trust, the pen is a responsibility, and what the author and the writer do cannot be achieved by armies.

Because of that, some have tried to break our pen and sink our ship. They tried and thought that they succeeded, but actually they failed. They could have come to talk with us to find common grounds for dialogue, but they chose the law of the jungle. They might think that they have killed me, but I am not dead. After me there are buds, flowers and a message that doesn't die. In fact, my spilled blood is now watering these buds and flowers and is nourishing this message, giving it a new life.

You did not scare us with what you did—my cowardly killer. You made us stronger and more courageous. You made us more determined and we realized that the ink of our pen is stronger than the bullets of your gun. You should know that, for more than ten years now, I have been living in "overtime"! You poor thing, you didn't surprise me. I am like the poet Di'ibil al-Khuza'i who said about himself: "I carry my gallows on my back, waiting for someone to hang me."

Please do accept my brotherly advice: Search for another weapon, a stronger, more effective and cheaper one.

I am not sad about what happened to me. What makes me hurt are the tears pouring from the eyes of my wife, children and friends; and the wondering that will overcome them when my six-year-old daughter, Zainab, asks: Where is my father?

Finally, when Omar al-Mukhtar was arrested, he said to the officer who delivered him his death sentence: "My years are going to be longer than my executioner's." I say what Omar al-Mukhtar said, "My years are going to be longer than my killer's."

Freedom House was closed forever. One man had a dream for his country; his countrymen did not share it. There was no one who could commit the time or energy to making it work. More important, local people thought the place had been funded by the Americans, anyway. The Americans came for oil, they said, not really to bring democracy. Rumors spread from the mosque to the bazaar through the medium of the same old Ba'ath loyalists: Freedom House was a CIA front. As Ahmad had written, the Ba'ath had never been neutralized—they had lost all their political power but not the brutal power to terrorize.

The overthrow of Saddam did not lead to a change in the work habits of Iraqi bureaucrats. Doing nothing slowly was how they worked. Roaa kept calling the police, chasing around from place to place, giving her statement again and again on the events of the day her father was murdered. She was told to wait, be patient. But she could see any possibility of justice slipping away.

When I returned to London after the war in late April 2003, I had stayed in sporadic e-mail contact with Ahmad and was able to gauge the mood in Mosul by the tone of my friend's messages. At first his e-mails were desperate. "The events in Iraq—in general—tend toward the worst, especially in Baghdad and south . . . the Americans lacking serious plans for perfect control. I expect that they are going to face a lot of troubles. Simply, they don't know upon whom they can depend." The Coalition Provisional Authority had virtually no Americans who were Arabic speakers working for them. They were wholly reliant on local translators whose loyalties weren't necessarily to the CPA. Ahmad added, "Excuse me friend I may feel sad to tell you that. But this is truth: that I have been disappointed. I have often despaired."

Sometime in the summer that despair had begun to lift. He wrote, "I know that you will be very happy when I tell you I have now a cultural, social & political Newspaper of 12 pages with all equipment required to produce it weekly." He asked for help in finding contributors. "I need you now so much to write some articles about democracy, civil society and social development in general. I will translate your reports into Arabic to be published in my newspaper. I'll be grateful for you if you can send me some American poems especially those are written in modernism style or concerned with modernity. If you know of poets and writers, try to send me their writing." He also asked for help in getting in touch with civil society think tanks like Freedom House in Washington, D.C. "I'm planning to establish an institution for democracy studies in Mosul to build a democratic mentality for cultured Moslawis. . . . This project is my great dream."

He wrote, "I anxious to hear your voice, to feel your breath, so please try to call me." But Thuraya contact was not easy, and it was expensive for me. I called him on the July day when the sons of Saddam, Uday and Qusay, were trapped and executed in Mosul. Ahmad took the call just outside the house where the shoot-out took place. He had been filing reports for the BBC Arabic Service. It was not far from where we had been on the day the regime collapsed. I reminded him of what we were told by his brother-in-law in Mosul that day: Saddam was hiding in a mosque in the city. We had mocked that rumor; maybe we had made a mistake. We joked about the big scoop we missed by not checking the rumor out. We could have interviewed Saddam . . . and then arrested him! But other than that call, we did not speak often.

My plan when I left Iraq had been to return in the autumn. We both thought it would take maybe six months for the situation to settle down, and the north of Iraq is beautiful in the fall. It would be a good time for a visit, and we would finally be able to have our fish lunch by the banks of the Tigris. In mid-September I went to Saudi Arabia to report on the increasingly violent opposition to the House of Saud. The trip was supposed to last for three weeks. I packed my flak jacket and helmet. The thought was to knock off an hour's worth of material in Saudi in about ten days and then fly to Kuwait and hitch a ride to Baghdad. I called Ahmad as soon as I got to Riyadh and told him the plan but included the caveat that it all depended on my getting enough tape in Saudi Arabia. This he understood—work always came first. Then I asked him if the road from Baghdad to Mosul was safe.

"Yes, yes. It is safe, there is no problem. When you reach Baghdad, call and I will send a car for you."

We made some small talk about the paper and his family. He sounded positively manic. Then with great seriousness he told me to be careful, Saudi Arabia was a very dangerous place for Americans. I was sitting outside in the ultraclean Saudi Arabian capital with the towers of Riyadh glistening in the distance. He was sitting in the unreconstructed anarchy of Iraq, telling *me* to be careful. The moment had its irony. I laughed and told him he was the one who needed to be careful. "I not afraid," he said. "What they can do to me else?" I reminded him that bad guys were starting to kill people they thought were too close to Americans. He protested again that he was safe. I said I would call when I got to Baghdad.

But Saudi Arabia proved to be the most difficult place I've ever worked. Earlier, an American diplomat had told me the natural sound of Saudi Arabia is silence, but silence does not make good radio. The diplomat was right. It took every waking minute of the three weeks I was there to scrape together enough sound for my documentary. I never did make it to Baghdad and I never called to tell Ahmad what happened. I figured he would know I got stuck in Saudi. We would catch up with each other later.

I came back to London the second week of October and began putting together the sound I brought back from Saudi Arabia. One morning, reading the papers online, I saw a sub-headline on the daily wrap-up piece from Baghdad in *The Washington Post*. A newspaper editor had been murdered in Mosul. I knew who it was even before reading it. The murder merited a single paragraph in a couple of Western newspapers. Journalists can squash the basics of life and death into a very small space: Ahmad's name, his occupation, who was suspected—radical Islamists—and a single quote from Roaa: "They have destroyed this family."

Death has not been a frequent visitor to my life. This was one of the things that made Ahmad so compelling a friend. His life had been steeped in gore, with those around him dying in the most violent ways. And yet the things we had in common—humanism, a sense of irony, a love for literature, a hatred for tyranny and political cynicism—trumped all the memories of the deaths he had seen. There really was something adolescent in the way we became friends. We admired the things the other had done, admiration that fell short of jealousy. I particularly admired him for his toughness and courage in the face of so much pain and death. Not having known death much, I was surprised by my reaction to the news. Rather than feeling burdened with shock and loss, instead I was filled with a surge of energy. I wanted to do what was possible: contact the family, make sure they weren't all under threat, take care of them financially. I also wanted to do what was impossible: time-travel back a month to Saudi Arabia and, as planned, fly to Kuwait, go to Baghdad, then drive to Mosul to meet with my friend. I could have talked sense to him, told him to slow down, and he would have listened. I *was* his intimate friend.

I buzzed around for the rest of the day. Called Mosul on the Thuraya, left a message. Sent an e-mail to Roaa. E-mailed Anna and David and others from the Dim Dim. Contacted the Committee to Protect Journalists and Freedom House, both in America, then wrote Ahmad's obituary for *The Guardian.*

Several days went by with no word from Iraq. I sent more e-mails. Eventually a reply came. Roaa wrote in desperation that the police investigation into the murder was going nowhere. Could I help in some way?

I tried to use what little *wasta* I could muster with the American authorities to find out what was going on. By chance, the week after the murder, I had to fly to Boston to guest-host on WBUR's program *The Connection.* One of the guests that week was New Jersey Superior Court judge Donald Campbell. The judge is also a general in the military reserves and had just spent five months in Iraq advising the Coalition Provisional Authority, the occupation's administration, on how to reconstitute the Iraqi courts. Judge Campbell gave me some names in the CPA and the military. When I returned to London, I attended a briefing by Sir Jeremy Greenstock, British prime minister Tony Blair's man in Baghdad at that time. Greenstock's senior aide, a helpful fellow named Simon Shercliff, took an interest in Ahmad's case. E-mail chains were started on the American and British sides of the CPA, and by the end of November, a month after her father's murder, I was able to give Roaa the name of someone in Mosul who might be able to help.

President Bush claimed to have brought "freedom and democracy" to the people of Iraq. But these things were worth nothing without the rule of law. An independent legal system had to be grafted onto the totalitarian system that the Ba'ath had put in place. A judiciary needed to be retrained and police practice needed to be altered. But the Bush administration underestimated just how large a program was needed to effectively create a new criminal justice system. The retraining program they did set up completely underestimated the effect of Iraq's justice system being held hostage by the Ba'ath Party for three and a half decades. Besides, even after the looting stopped, there was so much crime in occupied Iraq that any nation's courts would have been overwhelmed. Murders, kidnappings for profit, extortion all flourished in the new era of *bilattijah*.

The American military was the CPA's interface with the justice system in Mosul and the Nineveh region. Captain Gary Masapollo was assigned to liaise with local police and judges, monitor their performance in the new era, and report back to the CPA with suggestions about how to make the justice system work. I was told to pass his name on to Roaa, that he was the man who could push an investigation into life.

Roaa made contact with Captain Masapollo and arranged a meeting. On the day of the meeting she dressed up a little, put on makeup that emphasized her beautiful eyes, and took a taxi to Captain Masapollo's office in the Nineveh Palace Hotel. The cab pulled up to the hotel. The usual groups of old-regime loyalists were loitering about, noting who was going in to see the Americans. They knew who Roaa was. She was a familiar figure around Mosul: the pretty, jockey-size Muslim girl, hijab wrapped tight, fighting her way to the front of the crowd at scenes of mayhem, demanding information about what had happened. They all knew she was the daughter of that trouble-making collaborator. They hissed threats at her as she paid the cab, whispering cruel things about her father as she walked by them into the hotel without a glance.

The Nineveh Palace is an amalgam of 1980s Soviet-style/third world three-star luxury, with a chrome and marble lobby filled with sofas designed for killing time while waiting for important men to see you. Roaa went up to Captain Masapollo's office. A translator came in, and yet again Roaa went through the story, although now she could add details about how little had been done since the murder. As she unfolded her tale, Masapollo was struck by her fierceness and determination to get justice. He was also a little confused. There were many interfaces of incomprehension between American forces and the people they had liberated. Of all of these, women were the most puzzling. More than the climate, the architecture, or the sound of the street, what let the soldiers know how different this world was, was the sight of all these women, most of them wrapped from head to toe in clothes that got progressively less colorful and shapely the older the women were. The troops came from a world where stylish female dress meant provocative female dress. In the malls and hangouts they left behind, female flesh was on display everywhere. There was no flesh to be seen as they patrolled Iraq's streets. None. It was weird to them. And the women in Iraq seemed so deferential, so often willing to accept their second-class status.

Captain Masapollo was trying to reconcile those impressions with the young woman telling her story. If he saw Roaa in the street, he would have thought: Typical Iraqi female, second-class citizen of a third-world country. But now that she was sitting talking to him, it was clear Roaa was as assertive as any modern American young woman. Roaa reminded him of the young women on the campus of the University of Notre Dame, where he teaches military science and history as part of the ROTC program. He could see her as a law student or journalism major—feisty, confident, heading toward a big career.

The captain listened to her story and took notes. In his time in Iraq he felt he hadn't had much opportunity to make a personal difference in people's lives. If he could help the Iraqi police find the killer of this young woman's father, that goal would be satisfied. When Roaa had finished her story, he told her he would have an American military policeman look into the status of the investigation. He suggested Roaa come back the following week and also gave her a series of contact numbers to call in case she found out any new information. He rose and put out his hand without thinking that some Muslim women would not shake it. Roaa did. He told her his office was always open to her. He was not just being polite. Then Captain Masapollo began working his system to find out what was going on in the murder investigation of Ahmad Shawkat.

The investigation had been assigned to Captain Hamza of the Iraqi Police Service. Masapollo went to see him. It was one of twenty-five murder cases on Hamza's desk, a massive load for any investigator, but virtually impossible to clear in the postwar situation. The first problem was that there was no technical database. That was another point of incomprehension between the Americans and the Iraqis. For more than a generation, police departments in the United States have used computerized databases to access records and share information among law enforcement agencies and throughout the justice system. Most police procedures are now based on the assumption that computerized databases hold the information needed. But in Iraq there were none. Police practice was more like it had been in the United States in the 1950s. And the written records of the last few decades were patchy at best. Most of those files had gone up in smoke or turned into the confetti that filled the sky in the rioting that followed the overthrow of Saddam.

Masapollo asked Hamza about procedures. Hamza explained

that there were twenty-nine police precincts in Mosul, and each had its own homicide squad. None of their activities seemed coordinated. Ahmad wasn't the only high-profile figure to be murdered in recent months. Judges, lawyers, and doctors, the potential leadership cadres of a new Iraq, were being gunned down all over the city. Masapollo posed a hypothetical to his Iraqi colleague. Suppose there was a series of murders taking place across the city, each with basically the same type of modus operandi. What would happen? Would the homicide detectives compare notes, at least? Hamza answered, "*Inshallah.*" God willing, they would compare the cases. Masapollo was flabbergasted.

He asked for a copy of Hamza's notes. They were handwritten. He shook his head. Who could read these notes besides Hamza? The judges' permissions were also handwritten. "You guys need computers," he told his Iraqi colleague. Hamza nodded. The American sent an e-mail to Baghdad: Obviously, there is a great need to procure automation for the IPS; train the IPS in automation and how to use it effectively; and to provide an effective automation support package in support of any automation initiative.

Another problem blocking a thorough investigation was the aftereffects of what Ahmad had called "dictatorism." No one in the Iraqi police knew how to take initiative—everyone was waiting for the proper permissions before taking action. The CPA was aware of the need to retrain the police not just in procedure but in opening their minds to independent thinking. A "best buddy" program was set up, in which American military police were assigned as mentors to the Iraqi police. But mentoring was only one of the MPs' assignments and not even their primary task. Even so, eight months after the overthrow of Saddam, they were becoming frustrated with the inability of the Iraqi police to get with the program. The MPs were reaching the conclusion that the Iraqis simply could not solve anything.

They gave numerous classes on modern police work. Teamwork and cooperation were emphasized along with the idea of pooling information. The Iraqi policemen would listen attentively. It was clear they were getting the concepts being discussed, because they passed written tests on what was being taught. There were practical training exercises as well. Yet back in the station house, all of that went out the window. The police did not incorporate any of what they had studied into their work routines, according to MPs. Investigations were a nightmare to follow. The Iraqis simply wouldn't share information with those they did not know. They had lived too long in a totalitarian society where an unguarded word to someone who was not an "intimate friend" could land even a policeman in prison. Sharing rumors, however, was no problem. Rumors spread like wildfire, but factual information—descriptions of suspects, vehicles, license plates—was still not being shared.

Then there was the problem of the old chain of command left over from the Ba'ath regime. Under Saddam, a local magistrate had to give written permission for each aspect of a police investigation. In liberated Iraq, that had not changed. An Iraqi judge's permission was even required to show Ahmad's file to Major Al Kabakov, the MP whom Gary Masapollo assigned to follow the case. Getting these permissions was a time-consuming process. Judges were not always available. They didn't work terribly long days and didn't always answer their mobile phones. The investigation into Ahmad's murder was hampered from the beginning by this fact and others. A file on the homicide wasn't started until the next day. By then the crime scene had been picked over and contaminated. Once on the roof, none of the cops took the initiative and put together a crime scene sketch or took photographs of the area where the murder took place.

Major Kabakov reported his findings to Gary Masapollo. It

was a very brief report. Because of the delay in opening the murder file, there had been no neighborhood canvass until the day after the murder. Some witnesses claimed to have seen two suspects fleeing the scene, one wearing traditional Arab dress, the other with a burn on his face. Beyond that, there were no other physical details noted: not height, age, hair color, or other distinguishing features.

Sindibad had met with Kabakov and some Iraqi police officers and told them they should look into Thair Zeki's behavior. According to Sindibad, Thair Zeki had taken the SIM card from his father's Thuraya. Ahmad's son had also heard that the bodyguard's wife said a few days after the murder, "I know my husband is involved, and he might have killed him." But so far the police had not even interviewed Zeki. They claimed this was the first they had heard about the wife's statement. Kabakov wasn't sure whether the report of her statement was true or just one more rumor floating around the investigation.

"Is there a motive, at least, for the murder?" Masapollo wondered.

"There are a few plausible motives for the assassination," answered Kabakov. "The victim allegedly violated religious taboos by questioning: 'Where is Islam?' "

Masapollo nodded. "That could get a man killed in this part of the world. Anything else?"

"He seems to have offended many people, and that may have something to do with his murder."

"That's it?" asked Masapollo.

"That's it," replied Kabakov. "If the Iraqi Police Service solves this one, it will be amazing."

As scheduled, a week later Roaa returned to the Nineveh Palace Hotel. Again she ran the gauntlet of thugs who kept up their harassment of people visiting the CPA. Masapollo relayed Kabakov's findings. Roaa nodded when Thair Zeki's name came up. We have been begging the police to arrest him, she said. Masapollo promised to bring this up with the investigators.

In mid-December 2003, Saddam was dragged out of his spider hole, and for a moment everyone in the CPA and the U.S. military thought this might be the turning point. All the resistance to the new order might fade away with the physical proof that Saddam was never coming back to power. It didn't work out that way. In Mosul, the military-civilian team at the CPA continued its various outreach programs, trying to mentor an entire society in the processes of democratic thinking. Ahmad, who spoke the languages of the local people, had attempted this and been murdered for his trouble. The Americans, who needed interpreters such as Ahmad, didn't fare much better.

Roaa continued to visit the Nineveh Palace. Every little rumor she could ferret out from the street she brought to Masapollo. The captain and his staff looked forward to her visits. By trying to help Roaa get justice, they felt like they were actually making a difference in the country. The meetings with leaders, the liaison discussions with cops and judges, all these were impersonal and routine. Masapollo had spent the first part of his tour in the Sunni Arab heartland, in places like Baquba. He had also spent a bit of time at Abu Ghraib. He came away from that experience thinking that he hadn't been able to make a dent in changing the mind-set of Iraqi society. But in Mosul things were different, and much of his feeling that he was helping to build something better for the Iraqis crystallized around his efforts to help Roaa. When she left the office the guys under Masapollo's command would joke about marrying her and getting her to America, where she would be safe. Masapollo found himself thinking from time to time about fate. If she had been born in America, what a life she would have had. If she could just get out of Iraq, he thought, she could be living in London working for CNN. The possibilities for her would be endless.

For Roaa, the relationship was also important. Someone was taking her seriously. At home now there were arguments with Sindibad all the time. They lived in a society where a young woman's reputation was everything, and Roaa's was now the subject of gossip. She worked in a world of men. Traveled to stories with them unchaperoned! She took taxis around the city unaccompanied! Sindibad, as the man of the house, argued with her about this. She was ruining her prospects for marriage. Her mother sided with Sindibad in these arguments. In the little flat Roaa was a traditional Arab woman, helping her mother to cook and serve. In the streets of the city she was a modern career woman and crusader for justice. That was how she was seen by the soldiers in Gary Masapollo's office.

The winter sky lowered around Mosul. A new year had begun. Thair Zeki was arrested and interrogated, then released after a few weeks. There were no new facts unearthed by his detention. So an old suspicion floated around as a theory of the crime. Islamists from the mosque ordered the killing. But there was no way to prove it. As Roaa went around the city, reporting on the increasing attacks on the police and private citizens working with the United States, she was developing a different theory. She thought the murder might have been organized by Ba'athists, who were developing a sustained campaign against those who worked with the "occupiers." But suspicions are not facts. Bring us facts, the police told her. She didn't even point out to them that it was their job to find the facts, not hers. The investigation was going nowhere, and her hope of continued pressure on the Iraqi police from the Americans began to fade. Gary Masapollo's tour of duty was coming to an end. Roaa knew what this meant. In January, he had a couple of weeks' leave. Before he left, he gave Roaa a contact name on the CPA staff. Dr. Mike would handle the case, Gary told her; she should feel free to contact Mike the same way she contacted him. But it hadn't worked out. She sent Masapollo an e-mail.

> Today I met Dr. Mike. I told him that the judges are not helping well with us and do not do any thing for our case. But he was very cold in his response. Please do something with him or by yourself because I am helpless with the Americans, Iraqis, every one.
>
> Plllleeeeeeaaaaaaaasssssssseeeeeeeee,
>
> please do something for my father's blood.

> yours,
> Roaa al-Zrary

Gary Masapollo left Iraq in late February. As Roaa feared, with him went the personal interest needed to keep the CPA pressing on her behalf. As the anniversary of the war to over-throw Saddam approached, she was still searching for justice for her father's blood.

Chapter Sixteen
"Don't You Work for the CIA?"

A YEAR AFTER Saddam was overthrown, spring came early to Kurdistan. By March 2004, in all the countries where the Kurds live, the fields were lush and the mountains' snowcaps had begun their summer retreat. The borders were all open. I chose to return to Mosul via Turkey. The familiar route was a comfort. I flew to Diyarbakir, the de facto capital of the Kurdish region in southeastern Turkey. There, an old friend arranged a car and driver. We set out on the four-hour drive along the great plain—the northern reach of the Fertile Crescent—to the Iraqi border. In ancient times, for merchants returning from China this plain was the wide homestretch of the Silk Route, the first extended flat space they encountered as they emerged from the mountains of central Asia. We were driving the opposite way, deeper into beauty and poverty, to Silopi and the Habur Gate, the border crossing into Iraq.

When I had been here the month before the war, in February 2003, the entire region was on edge. Turkish Army convoys rumbled up and down the two-lane blacktop. All economic activity, except the black market, had ceased. Now everything seemed calm and normal. The Turkish Army was hardly visible. As we approached the border, the single greatest sign of the resumption of normal service was the queue of trucks waiting to cross into Iraq. The line of vehicles, two and sometimes three abreast, stretched back maybe six miles from the customs station. This time the trucks were laden with consumer goods: refrigerators and air conditioners and hundreds of satellite dishes.

As we pulled into the border-crossing compound, a local cabdriver ran up to our car. For twenty bucks he agreed to get all my papers stamped on the Turkish side of the border and drive me over into Kurdistan. The Turkish formalities took less than half an hour to complete. On the other side, I was met by a friend of Abdussalaam's. In the months since Ahmad's murder, Salaam had become my link to the family. His English is very good, and Roaa, Afrah, and Sindibad all trusted him to speak on their behalf with me. I piled my stuff into his friend's Mercedes and headed for Erbil. My original plan had been to stay in Mosul so I could visit Roaa and the rest of Ahmad's family every day. But the American NGO I was supposed to bunk in with had pulled out of the city for security reasons the previous week. Their landlord had received death threats because he was renting the American group a house. This was considered collaboration. Fearing for his life, the landlord told the NGO staff they had to leave. The group had moved en masse to Erbil, so I was left with no choice but to do the same.

Knowing about the danger to American civilians, I was surprised when Salaam's friend didn't make the turn toward the mountains but headed for Mosul along a four-lane highway originally built for the Iraqi military. This road would cut the driving time in half, but it did seem risky.

"Isn't it safer to go through the mountains?" I asked.

"No, this is safe and much faster," Salaam's friend said.

Well, much faster, anyway. The drivers along the old Saddam

highway were absolutely heedless of life. I buckled up and we made small talk while narrowly avoiding death.

We got to Mosul and took a ring road around the city. Everything was familiar and different. The city was no longer the setting for anarchy; it had somehow settled back into order. A year after General David Petraeus had blanketed the streets with American soldiers, the American military was now conspicuous by its absence. Nor was Mosul the hellhole that reports in the press had led me to expect. There was clearly a lot of normal economic activity going on, if the number of cars in the street was any measure. The rush-hour traffic jams around the major intersections were awe-inspiring. Hundreds of cars were backed up in each direction. It was not a happy feeling at first to sit in this gridlock. If violence was to be aimed at me, I'd be trapped. There was no way out. But after the fourth epic bottleneck, my anxiety lifted. I was as anonymous as any other person on the road in this city of close to two million people.

I relaxed enough to make more small talk with my driver. He was a businessman. The next day he was going to the Syrian border, then flying to Damascus and on to Dubai to make a deal—another sign of normal economic activity resuming in Iraq. We were at an intersection that looked familiar and I wanted to ask this fellow about the place, what kind of neighborhood it was, who lived in it, but though he spoke English, it was not good enough for sustained conversation. I had only been in country for an hour and a half and the realization hit me: Mr. Key was gone. Ahmad would have opened the door and explained everything. Now I would only be able to see Iraq like any other journalist.

For the three weeks I was in Iraq, that is how I approached the country: as an ordinary journalist, skeptically and mechanically acquiring the building blocks for my next radio documentary. I was prevented from seeing things through Iraqi eyes by the imperative of getting my material quickly and safely. *Intimacy,* as Ahmad meant the word, had nothing to do with it. The only intimate moments came while visiting with Afrah and the children, and there were simply not enough of these.

We drove through Mosul and turned east toward Erbil. The Khazer bridge had been repaired and we zoomed over it, but it took almost a half hour to get over the Kalak bridge. The pesh merga had set up a checkpoint, although they weren't dressed like pesh merga anymore. They now had proper uniforms and were part of a national police service.

I arrived in Erbil in the late afternoon, checked in at the Dim Dim, and the very next morning drove back to Mosul to see Ahmad's family. Abdussalaam arranged a different driver and translator to accompany me this time. When we got to the city the traffic jams had not diminished at all. As we sat at the first gridlocked intersection of the morning, near the ancient walls of Nineveh, a ten-year-old newspaper boy knocked on the window. My translator bought a copy of the paper he was selling: *Shehad,* "The Witness," a pro-Saddam weekly newspaper. The boy tried to sell us a poster of Saddam's sons Uday and Qusay, pictured wearing the head scarves of Muslim martyrs. We took a pass on that offer. The translator asked if I read Arabic. I said no. He gave me the paper anyway and told me to look as if I were reading it. A useful bit of camouflage.

Roaa was waiting for me at the Nineveh Palace Hotel. She had written me in January: "I want to tell you I am running out of patience waiting for you to come back in March. . . . I want to see you so as to reduce missing my father because when I look in your face I see him. . . . You are the only person that I can talk open heartedly with about him and cry in your presence. . . ."

We embraced, and true to her word, she began to cry. She

cried until my shirt was soaked through. Her crying did not slowly shudder to a halt. Instead, she turned her tears off in one second. They were the only tears I ever saw, even as we spent the next few hours retracing her father's murder step by step. She took me to the *Bilattijah* office building in the bazaar, to the rooftop where he was shot, past the police station, to the Jumhuriyah Hospital so that I could see for myself her father's last journey. Roaa was not confident enough in her English to speak with me directly. Zeto, my translator, was a stranger. Before we set off, I asked Roaa if she would be okay talking through him. "Ask me anything, I will tell you all I know" is how he translated her reply. But, Zeto added, there was one matter Roaa could not talk about. She would wait for Abdussalaam. At each place we visited she explained things with forensic dispassion, but the story was highly confusing. When I asked her for clarification about who gave her father the money to start the paper, she said, through Zeto, this was the topic she could not talk about in front of a stranger.

We went to the flat for lunch. Family life had reestablished a sense of routine. The middle boys, Shawkat and Rafat, came back from school and relaxed with some TV. Zainab, so much younger than everybody else, clung a bit to her mother's skirts. Rasha came home from art college more silent and withdrawn than she had been the previous times we had met. Sindibad was over at the house his father had started building, overseeing construction, and lunch waited on his return. While we waited, Afrah and Roaa prepared the meal. They moved in and out of the tiny kitchen, more a closet with a small stove, just adjacent to another little closet that had a sink where they drew water to wash vegetables. When Sindibad came in, Roaa and Afrah put the meal out. It wasn't quite on the scale of our lunch in Erbil during the war, but it was still massive, a triumph of flavor and logistics considering the coordination required to prepare something of this size in rooms so small.

When lunch was finished, we exchanged mementos of Ahmad. The family gave me a bound copy of all the issues of *Bilattijah*. I gave Afrah a photo of Ahmad I had taken in Mechko's tea shop. It showed him in profile, smoking, looking intense and poetic. I also gave them a copy of the *Guardian* obituary I had written and a CD with my radio program, *Ahmad's War: Inside Out,* on it. Ahmad's family would always be able to hear their father's voice.

Then Zeto and I accompanied Roaa to a television studio on the edge of Mosul. She had become a bit of a celebrity journalist around town and was invited to do a weekly talk show as the voice of youth. As we pulled through the gates into the television station compound, two American military vehicles were pulling out. There had been a mortar attack on the station the previous day and one person had been wounded. The army patrol was doing a cursory security sweep. It was the first time during this visit that I had seen the U.S. military anywhere in Mosul.

The cemetery is not far from the television studio, and when the program was over we ended the day with a visit to Ahmad's grave. While Roaa and Zeto, the translator, prayed, I stood quietly. My friend and I had shared the same skeptical relationship with religion and the same understanding of the rites of mourning: cultural expressions that comfort the living rather than do anything for the souls of the dead. While we stood around the grave, a widow was grazing a flock of sheep among the tombstones. I could see the evening sun illuminating Mount Maqloub, which guards the horizon to the north. Halfway up Maqloub there was what looked like a white scar gouged out of the mountain—it was Mar Matte, the monastery we had visited during the war. When Roaa and Zeto finished praying, they wiped their faces with the imaginary white dust. I reached down, picked up a big pebble, and put it on his headstone. I doubt they understood that that was a Jewish tradition. The day had been liberating and confusing. Liberating because of the rituals of grieving; confusing because Roaa had been unable to explain satisfactorily who had killed her father. Her initial thought was that he had been murdered by radical Islamists, but now she wasn't so certain. Maybe it was Ba'ath remnants, she said, but maybe it was any number of groups who had taken offense at her father's writing. Maybe it was the Americans. He had criticized them as well. This was liberated Iraq, a world where no one, not even the liberator, could be trusted.

A couple of days later, Salaam took a day off from his work leading democracy training seminars for an American NGO and drove with me to Mosul so we could delve deeper into the mystery of Ahmad's death. We went to meet Gary Masapollo's replacement. The army's military–civilian affairs office had recently relocated from the Nineveh Palace Hotel to Saddam's actual palace. We parked on the far side of a four-lane highway and walked to the security gate. Despite the car bombings and occasional mortar attacks, there was a queue of cabs waiting for Iraqis as they emerged from their business behind the walls. Inside, at the security checkpoint, we were processed by a combination of military and private-company clerks. We waited for a driver to take us up to the civilian affairs office. Periodically, well-built men wearing tight polo shirts with the logo KBR (for Kellogg, Brown and Root) came to the gate to pick up other visitors.

Inside the walls were crisp order and silence. Outside was the din of a city veering from normalcy to war and back again in the space of an hour. Inside the walls was the imperial space. Outside were the barbarians. It must have been like this in Roman times. When locals stepped through the gates of the

Roman army's camp on official business, they moved from a world of sudden violence and disorder to a world of uniformity and calm, of comfort. I felt safe.

Eventually we were driven to the civilian affairs building in the complex. It had been a dormitory for some element of Saddam's retinue. The 101st Airborne had departed the previous month, along with the 431st Civilian Affairs Battalion. They had been replaced by the Stryker Brigade and the 416th Civilian Affairs Battalion. These new soldiers had only just gotten their feet under their desks. We met with Allan Haight, who had taken over Ahmad's case from Gary Masapollo. The meeting was polite and brief, a getting-to-know-you session for Roaa, nothing more. Gary's interest in the case had been personal. The new unit in Mosul was still figuring out what its priorities should be. Uniformity in the American military presence didn't extend beyond security at the gate. New commanders with different ways of doing things meant that as units changed, so did relationships with the local community. This was not the moment for the newcomer to commit to continued special interest in a single case.

When the meeting was over, I went outside to soak up the spring sun. My Iraqi friends stood in the shade. We were not at liberty to roam around the acres of quiet, manicured landscaping. We stood around waiting for our lift back to the gate, speculating about who had killed Ahmad. Salaam was certain it was Islamists. On his own journey from "Islamist" to "Islamic" politics he had come to know well the mind-set of Islamic fascists. Salaam said that what Ahmad wrote was as good as asking Mosul's tyrants of the mosque to send out a hit squad after him. Roaa reiterated her view that her father had been murdered by Saddam loyalists who saw her father as a tool of the Americans.

"But he wasn't," I said. "He was independent."

"But he was close to them," Roaa said.

"I know. He told me the CPA funded the newspaper," I agreed.

"No, he actually worked for them."

"What?"

"You got him the job," she added.

"What are you talking about?"

"You wrote a letter to General Petraeus telling him to hire my father."

"No, I didn't."

Now I was really confused, but Roaa was insistent. She thought that the contact had been made intentionally, that I had been some kind of recruiter for the U.S. government.

"Don't you work for the CIA?" she asked. Salaam translated her question and I shouted, "No . . . *no, no, no, no!*" Salaam did not have to translate that.

"Where did she get this idea?" I asked him. Then I turned to her. "Who told you that?" But before Salaam could translate my question, the penny dropped.

"Oh no . . . oh God. . . . Just before I left"—I nodded to Salaam to start translating—"I wrote your father an all-purpose recommendation letter and he must have shown this to one of the Americans."

Roaa nodded. "He did."

We were all silent for a while. I felt nauseous. I got him killed. I wrote him that letter so he could find work after I was gone. He was so concerned that he would be unemployed again and wouldn't be able to pay off his debts and take care of his family. But the recommendation could be taken a lot of different ways. A civil society NGO recruiting a local manager would read it one way; David Petraeus's chief of staff might read it another; a CIA field officer looking to build a local network would read it in yet another way. Is that what happened? Did Ahmad actually work directly for the CIA, or was he just the recipient of funds the Agency had allocated for democracy building? My first reaction was that it was crazy for a journalist to be directly funded by the Agency. My second reaction was, What else could he have done? To whom could he turn? He needed the money to start *Bilattijah* and Freedom House. That was his dream from the first minute Iraq was liberated. He would have taken money from anyone to realize it. But the news that he may have been in some way connected to the CIA still shocked me, and I knew how this connection would look to outsiders if it ever became public. It was certainly enough to get him killed if the wrong people in Mosul had found out.

We returned to the flat for lunch, then Afrah accompanied us to Darawish to meet Khalil, Ahmad's older brother. The peasant life was written all over Khalil's weathered face—one eye white with a cataract—and in his swollen, gnarled hands. We sat and drank Pepsis while Khalil reminisced about his brother. He told the story of their mother's vision that Ahmad would be a great man, and pointed out the little hill where he used to go to read and write. The older man had a reverence for his younger brother that was moving. There was a small disagreement between brother and widow over the detail of a trip abroad that Khalil had paid for. The old man said it was for study; Afrah said it was for political reasons. Nothing was settled, but as we stepped outside Khalil's compound for a tour of the village, Afrah said through Salaam, "Don't believe Khalil. He had to flee because of politics. I know everything."

"Do you know who killed Ahmad?" I asked.

"Ba'athists," she said without hesitation. "For thirty years they made his life misery, and in the end, they killed him."

We walked around the mud buildings. The village had barely been modernized. Water was still drawn from Alyas's Well. The living room of the house where Ahmad lived after his father's death was now the home of an enormous cow. The visit gave me another reason to admire my friend. He had not just traveled an enormous intellectual distance to his worldview but had time-traveled from a nineteenth-century boyhood to a twenty-first-century death. I joked about how primitive the place was. Roaa and Salaam jabbered at each other for a bit. Then Salaam translated.

"Roaa says you haven't seen just how primitive."

I could already guess. "The outhouse?"

"Yes." Roaa giggled. "I stayed here once, and for three days I did not go to the toilet."

Then we drove back to Mosul and visited the new house. It was payday, and Afrah was paymaster on the project. The tiny woman, wrapped in widow's black, inspected the week's work with eagle eyes and, satisfied with its progress, precisely counted out cash for each worker.

After a week of shuttling between Erbil and Mosul, it was time to get down to business. I traveled all over the north before going to Baghdad and the Shi'ite south. My assignment was to put together an hour-long documentary on the state of the country as the United States prepared to hand over "sovereignty" to the Iraqis. The idea, as the year before, was to report on how Iraqis were experiencing this process. Too much of the Western reporting from Iraq following the overthrow of Saddam had been from the point of view of America, the occupier. I was more interested in reporting from the point of view of the occupied. I had arrived in Iraq wanting to "see" the transition process through Iraqi eyes. I knew now that would be impossible. After Ahmad, there was no interpreter who could take me that deep inside the society. But it was possible to focus exclusively on the words of Iraqis. I decided I would have only Iraqi voices in my piece.

The situation in Kurdistan left me confused and giddy. I had never seen it so prosperous. On my first visit in 1996, the poverty in the street was almost like what I'd seen in Africa. Now Erbil felt more prosperous than the Kurdish towns over in Turkey and it was a lot safer as well. In Mechko's I drank tea with a businessman who was importing fine Italian tiles to fit in the new houses springing up in the city's sprawling suburbs. Now that Saddam was gone, exiles were returning home with cash saved from their jobs driving cabs, waiting tables, and working as casual labor in the cold, damp cities of Western Europe. In their time away, the wealthier returning exiles had started their own businesses everywhere from London to Hamburg. They could afford a bit of luxury, and my tea-drinking companion was happy to provide it.

Across the street from Mechko's, in the massive covered bazaar, the section of the market where the goldsmiths and jewelers had their shops was crammed with peasant women putting their families' new prosperity into the tangible form of bracelets, anklets, and chains, all worn underneath their abayas.

I had been back in Erbil for a few days and was trying to make contact with Sami Abdul Qader, my driver during the war. Sami had taken me to his brothers' jewelry shop a year earlier and I thought I would leave a message for him there. But I couldn't find it. Then, as I was walking out of the bazaar, someone called out "Mr. Michael." It was Sami's son Kharzan. He took me to his uncle's shop, and I was invited to sit and drink chai. I spent an hour drinking more tea, smoking cigarettes, and watching, astounded, as thousands of dollars changed hands; then I left a message for Sami and headed off for Kirkuk.

Down the road, in the region's oil capital, the situation was very different. Zeto and I stopped in at a police station that had been car-bombed the previous month. Ten people had been killed that day. We went into the office of the station's commander, who was talking to the mother of one of his cops. The young man had been injured in the blast, and she was begging the commander to let her son have a few more weeks off. The chief seemed to be saying no: he comes back or he loses the job. The woman seemed to accept his judgment and left. The chief gave me a brief interview, all very official patter, very boring.

The suicide bomber had detonated himself just outside the chief's office, and as we chatted, workmen were fitting a new window into his office. The glass had all been shattered, the fireball from the explosion leaving scorch marks on the ceiling that were in the process of being painted over. The commander had been sitting behind his big, heavy desk, which had saved him from serious injury. I asked the chief why he would do this job. He shrugged. He had been a cop for thirty years and had learned a long time ago that people don't like the police. "These things happen," he told me.

Then I asked the commander about Arab/Kurdish tensions in the city. Saddam's Arabization program had been particularly aggressive in Kirkuk, and in the new era many Kurds who had been displaced were demanding their homes and land back. The Arab families, some of whom had been in these formerly Kurdish homes for a quarter of a century, were refusing to leave. The previous day, the leading advocate for Arab rights on Kirkuk's council had been shot dead. I asked the commander if he knew anything about the case. He sent us to another police station to find out about the investigation.

I thought I might join the cops on a house-to-house canvass. But there was no canvass under way yet, as the murdered man's family had taken his body back to Najaf, in the south of the country, for burial. It would be a week before they even returned and could give their statements. The police shook their heads. There was nothing they could do about this. Another high-profile murder in Iraq would go unsolved.

Zeto took me to the bazaar. Kirkuk may be the center of the oil business in the north, but the city itself derives very little tangible benefit from the wealth it generates. It is a poor, polluted place. The bazaar reflects this. The goods all seemed to have fallen off the back of the proverbial truck. Kids were reselling packages of cookies from World Food Programme stores. The crowd wasn't hostile as we wandered through, but it was aggressively curious. There were no Americans in the streets of the city, no Westerners at all. One boy carrying a live chicken poked its beak at my hand and it took a nip; someone else came up and whispered "Saddam, Saddam" in my ear. I tried to organize some fake-spontaneous conversations about the future among Arab, Kurdish, and Turkmen merchants. Everyone said there's no problem in Kirkuk: "We all get along like brothers." The Arabs said they would be willing to leave the city if they were properly compensated.

After about fifteen minutes, Zeto whispered to me that we should probably get going. I had enough sound, so I agreed. We went back to the car. As we pulled away he apologized for making us leave, but he said he had become concerned for my safety. The remarks people were making were getting more aggressive and hostile the longer we wandered around the market. People had been murmuring threats to my life.

My reporting in the north completed, I needed to go to Baghdad, so I renewed my search for Sami. I didn't trust anyone else to get me there safely. It turned out that Sami was working for the same NGO where Salaam worked as a democracy trainer. I went to look for him at the group's compound in Ain Kawa. He saw me before I saw him. He shouted out my name and ran over. We hugged for a very long time. I told him I needed a ride to Baghdad and he said he wouldn't let anyone else drive me.

On the drive south, once again everything felt familiar yet everything was different. We left at sunrise, as we had the previous year, and for the same reason: security. Sami needed to be back in Erbil well before sunset. At night a man alone driving a nice car would be an easy target for thieves. Sami would be lucky to be left on the side of the road to hitchhike back to Erbil; more likely, the thieves would kill him and just take the car.

We drove along the very route we had taken the previous year—the same fields were still being cleared of mines—but this time the road was crowded. Trucks similar to those I had seen at the Habur Gate, stacked high with consumer goods, were cruising toward Baghdad and Baquba. Rather than riding in a beaten-up cab, we were cruising in a five-year-old Mercedes, part of a small fleet of cars Sami had been putting together. The new era had been good to him. Steady work for American journalists brought cash. Sami was using the cash to buy late-model cars that he hired out to NGOs for even more cash.

We spoke about Ahmad. The pair had become close during the war and remained good friends afterward. Sami had helped the family move back to Mosul, although he had begged Ahmad not to go. "I told Mr. Ahmad, don't go back," Sami remembered. " 'Why go back, it is very dangerous for you. Stay in Erbil.' But he won't listen."

As we cruised out of Kurdistan into the date palm plantation areas of the Sunni Arab heartland, I had a "what's wrong with this picture?" moment. Something was missing along this road. We slowed down to a crawl for what turned out to be the one and only checkpoint. Some American soldiers were having a training session for the Iraqi police, showing them the right way to do a stop-and-search. The people being stopped and searched were invariably Arabs in traditional garb. "Village-ians." As the minutes ticked by, I grew increasingly nervous and began running my eye over every car, looking for a potential suicide bomber. Then I figured out what was missing from the picture. In every conflict zone I have ever reported from, the highways are filled with SUVs and supply trucks from the UN and the major NGOs, like the Red Cross, CARE, Save the Children, and Doctors Without Borders. But there were no vehicles in this queue with those logos. These organizations were not currently operating in Iraq, or if they were, they were staying away from the Sunni Triangle. Danger was one reason, but it had been dangerous in Bosnia, and those outfits had still operated there during the Balkan War. Their absence was a key measure of how isolated the United States was in its regime-change operation. This was George Bush's show, the NGOs seemed to be saying by their absence, and he could take care of the mess himself.

The only dangerous moment on the trip to the capital came as we entered the outskirts of the city. We were on a wide boulevard with three lanes heading into Baghdad. Traffic ground to a halt for no particular reason other than there were too many cars and too little road. Across a small concrete divider, three lanes were leading out of the city. Traffic on that side had also crawled to a stop. Immediately opposite us, on the outbound side, was an American convoy, two semis carrying construction equipment guarded by three Humvees. The convoy was a sitting duck for anyone with a rocket propelled grenade launcher—and there were thousands of folks who had them. I was a sitting duck if the RPG missed the convoy or if it hit someone's fuel tank and started a conflagration. For five minutes I sat with Sami, wondering if I'd done enough in my professional life to warrant a small obituary in *The New York Times*. Then, as traffic jams are wont to do, for no reason at all we began moving forward again.

The Bush administration had turned Iraq into the wet dream of radical libertarians. It was a country with minimal public services, where no one paid taxes, there were no business regulations, and a well-armed citizenry looked after its own. The naked capitalist struggle for survival made Baghdad manic. People were out and about doing business, looking for work. Men who had no money stood on street corners with whatever construction tools they had and waited for a day's work on a building site. There were acres of brownfield sites around the city that had been turned into used-car lots. People with a bit of money bought the cars in bulk in Jordan or the Gulf states, transported them into Iraq, and sold them to people with even less money. An automobile is a tool; if a man can't find work, he can always take the car into the street and be a driver.

Initially, the energy and economic activity conveyed a sense that the country was moving forward. I had the same first impression in Baghdad as I'd had in Mosul: things aren't as bad as news reports led me to believe. But that impression didn't last for long. Every day I went out to look for sound and a sense of the place. Sami had gone back to Erbil, and my current driver and translator knew the city well. We drove from al-Mansour to Khadamiyah to the Green Zone to the outskirts of Sadr City in a red Kia that had somehow made it to Baghdad from the American South. A Georgia State Patrolmen's Benevolent Society sticker was still on the windshield. Everywhere we went, fear and anger were palpable. No security and no jobs were the main reasons. In al-Mansour, the wealthy part of town, a money changer specializing in foreign currency—a man for whom business couldn't have been better—complained bitterly about the lack of safety in the city. He asked, rhetorically: What kind of freedom is this? What kind of democracy is this, when you have no one to protect you from criminals?

Near a bus station in downtown Baghdad, a group of men from Sadr City were watching another day slip away without work. They had been standing on the corner since 5 A.M., hoping to be picked for a day's casual labor on a building site. They had the same rhetorical question: What kind of freedom is it, what kind of democracy is it, when there are no jobs, no work, so a man cannot even feed his family?

From the wealthiest to the most impoverished, everyone had the same sense of resentment. The Americans did not stop the looting after the war; they have not brought security; nor have they rebuilt the bomb-damaged buildings of Baghdad. "They are only here for our oil" went the common refrain.

The frustration in the street was echoed inside the walls of the Green Zone. Diplomats from other countries in the "coalition of the willing" felt that the Coalition Provisional Authority had been turned into an extension of the Bush-Cheney '04 reelection campaign. Other nations' professional foreign-service officers found it shocking that senior CPA figures attended meetings with their Bush-Cheney lapel pins on. Didn't these people understand, they wondered, that they were supposed to be above partisan politics? Didn't they know they were representing all Americans, not just the president's supporters? Men with decades of experience in the Arab world who spoke Arabic fluently—something no senior American could do—found their advice ignored. Every decision taken by the CPA seemed to be framed not by what Iraqis needed but by what would impress American voters.

After almost a week in Baghdad, I was reaching the conclusion that the Bush administration had lost the country. The confirmation of this came in Karbala, a city to the south of Baghdad with two massive Shi'ite shrines. A month before I arrived, the city had been packed with pilgrims for the Shi'a festival of Ashura. Under Saddam the pilgrimage had been forbidden. It was the first time in more than a decade that the Shi'a were able to celebrate Ashura. Pilgrims from all over the region flocked to the city, from Iran and Saudi Arabia as well as from Baghdad. Tens of thousand of people were congregating in the streets around the two mosques when, in a coordinated attack, two suicide bombers walked into the crowds and blew themselves up. Around a hundred people were killed.

In Islam, the dead are commemorated forty days after their passing. The ceremony is called an *arbayeen*. I went to Karbala to interview the city's senior cleric, Sheikh Muslim al-Tai, who suggested we meet at the main police station, where he was scheduled to attend a planning session for the *arbayeen* to commemorate the dead of Ashura. Muslim al-Tai is known in the city as the representative of Iraq's supreme Shi'a cleric, Grand Ayatollah Ali Sistani. The deference Sheikh Muslim was shown was mind-boggling. Walking with him through the police headquarters, I had the feeling of what it must have been like to walk with a medieval cardinal along the battlements of a town under siege. Tough-looking, well-armed men gave him hopeful glances, as if a look from the religious leader might bestow a blessing to survive another day. If he had had rings to kiss, they would have reached for his hand, but as this was Iraq, they leaned forward toward him in the hope of a kiss on the cheek.

We settled into the chief of police's office and began a tortured, elliptical conversation about the current situation. The windows of the office were open to the warm spring air. From a loudspeaker in a nearby mosque the entire noon prayer ceremony was being broadcast. The chanting from the Quran was lovely.

The interview was going nowhere, so I told the sheikh a story. Just before our conversation, I had wandered around the area where the bombs had gone off a few weeks earlier. There was a broad pedestrian avenue leading up to the golden-domed shrine of Abbas. In the center of the avenue, a desultory bazaar was set up for pilgrims, who, ever since the atrocity, had been staying away from the city in droves. I had begun talking with some of the merchants hanging around, and we spoke about the bombings that had taken place there. I asked the obvious question: Who did they think carried out the attack? I was shocked by their answer: the Americans had done it. It was utterly preposterous, but the men all piled in with their claims that the United States had set off the bombs. One man claimed to have seen a rocket come out of the sky. Another claimed he had seen soldiers taking pictures from American helicopters in the days preceding the incident. I didn't have time to ask him if they were "black helicopters," and besides, the man wouldn't have understood the poor joke.

I turned to my translator. "Are these guys crazy?"

"No," he said. "This is what people are saying in Baghdad also. They ask: Who benefits from this violence? The Americans."

"Ask these men: Why would America do this? What is the benefit?"

The translator did. There was a bit of conversation.

"They say: America wants to make Iraqis fight Iraqis, so we will ask them to stay and protect us."

When I had finished telling this story to Muslim al-Tai, I asked him what he said to his worshippers who share this opinion. The religious leader couldn't or wouldn't say how he defends the United States.

"This is what people say in the streets," the sheikh said. "People's opinions, what they see with their own eyes, is airplanes opening fire."

I repeated my question. "But, Sheikh, if someone came to you and said that U.S. planes bombed the crowd, what would you say to him?"

"I wouldn't tell him that he's wrong, but that there's no solid evidence. But then, I don't know missile types or to whom they belong."

Then the religious leader added, "Only time will tell who is with us and who is against us; who is coming to serve and who is coming to ruin."

My time in Baghdad had its ironic moments. I was supposed to meet with Thamir al-Dulaimi, to whom Ahmad had introduced me in Erbil. He had been yet another internal exile waiting for Saddam to die so he could return to his home in regime territory. Thamir came from one of the great tribes of Iraq and had more status than Ahmad's other exile friends. He was from Ramadi, the son of a senior general who had attempted to assassinate Saddam in the mid-1990s. We arranged to meet at a seminar on forming political parties conducted by the International Republican Institute at the Babylon Hotel. When I arrived with my translator and driver, we were handed a sheet of paper saying that owing to a credible security threat, the meeting had been shifted to the Baghdad Hunting Club. We drove over the river to the place. The Hunting Club had been the personal playground of Uday Hussein, and its grounds were green and pleasant. Several large tents had been set up in the perfect spring sunshine to accommodate the crowd of tribal and community leaders who were there to learn about forming political parties. A young American man was addressing the group with a lecture that managed to be naive and condescending at the same time.

"I'll give you some technical ways to think of a political

party," he told the group, pausing strategically to let a translator put each and every phrase into Arabic. "A political party exists to channel political power. . . . Once you have political power, then you can create, you can do what you want with government, right?"

To people who had survived the Ba'ath, a political party that *really* knew how to channel power, the lecture must have seemed ridiculous. At least if they looked across the lawn they could see the lavish luncheon buffet being set up.

By now I was full of a slow-burning anger. My friend Ahmad had died for this? So some kid could stand inside a privately guarded compound, explaining that "a political party exists to channel power," on a street guarded by American soldiers in a city where, one year after the overthrow of Saddam, the original meeting site was so insecure that local police could not defend it? This was bringing freedom and democracy to Iraq? The most powerful nation in history had rendered itself utterly powerless here.

Ahmad would have preferred to live to see his country transformed into a democratic society. If he had to die to bring that society into being, he would have given his life for it happily. But that liberal democratic society was not even close to reality, and the arrogant political careerists running the CPA seemed hellbent on making sure the Iraq that Ahmad envisioned would never exist. The ways in which the Bush administration bungled the postwar period will occupy historians for a century. It might occupy historians for longer if the war to overthrow Saddam proves to be the event in which America's moment as the world's imperial force begins to unravel, or if the war's aftermath forces the United States decisively away from republican democracy to authoritarianism and dictatorship. America, like Rome, is a republic that became an empire. Sometimes, listening to the rhetoric of the Bush administration's loyalists in Congress and the media demonizing those who dare to question the conduct of the war, it is possible to imagine that, like Rome in the time of Augustus, America has turned decisively down the path to authoritarian rule.

The Iraq War will certainly occupy historians trying to understand what could have been done after the Cold War to dismantle the human infrastructure of tyranny created by America and the Soviet Union as their third-world proxies fought for world domination. It's a cliché that in the truce that ends one war the seeds of the next war are planted. And though the Cold War ended without a written peace agreement, political leaders should have seen the seeds of the next conflict scattered in front of them. The breakup of Yugoslavia was an object lesson in what would happen when America's and Russia's little monsters were left alone. Yet in the decade after the Soviet Union disintegrated, governments and their partisans on the right and the left were reluctant to deal with the armed thugs the superpowers had sustained in power. These dictators were like land mines left in a Kurdish pasture, primed and waiting to go off under the foot of any child running carefree after an animal. Saddam was only one of these thugs left in place, the Taliban regime was another. Africa is honeycombed with them. The policy that wasn't formulated in 1990 is causing death and destruction today.

Who knows if Saddam would have survived for even three years of the Iran-Iraq War if every great or formerly great power hadn't kept him propped up as a bulwark against the Iranian theocracy? Perhaps the Ba'ath might have imploded. But certainly the international community should have forced him out when it had the chance in 1991. If the United States and its allies had carried on to Baghdad or bribed the military not to fight, as it did in 2003, Saddam could have been removed. Perhaps Ahmad would have been able to resume teaching. We would never have met. But he would be alive, possibly even content, and contributing to a civil society.

Chapter Seventeen

"Always Disasters Befall the Iraqi People"

THROUGHOUT THE WEEKS in Baghdad and the south, my work was standard reporting. *Look at this. Look at that. Record it.* It wasn't lived in. I had many voices and sounds but nothing "intimate" to bring my documentary alive. I returned to Mosul, and on my last day in Iraq, I took Roaa downtown to Diwassa Square to interview her. I thought taking her to the place where my documentary about her father had ended might provide an intimate conclusion to this new one. An interview in Diwassa would give a true measure of the state of the country one year on. I would tell her about her father, my "intimate" friend Ahmad, and how he got into an argument about democracy even as a gunfight was going on in the National Bank. Then I would ask her whether she thought the overthrow of Saddam had been worth her father's life. Salaam came along to translate. Sami found us a driver, a former pesh merga called Haidar, who bore more than a passing resemblance to Lee Van Cleef in *The Good, the Bad, and the Ugly.* He was a scary-looking dude, and given the security situation, that was a comforting thing.

Diwassa was just as I remembered it, except that the

scorched shell of the National Bank was now covered by scaffolding and the governorate building was surrounded by concrete blast barriers. The shops were open and the streets teemed with people. I took out my tape recorder to start talking with Roaa. Before we could get very far, a small group of men surrounded us and began to give their opinions on everything. She tried to shoo them away, but they just ignored her.

"Does the American understand the mess his government has made?" one of them demanded.

"Does he know about the two girls killed here yesterday?" another asked.

I nodded yes. The previous day someone had fired a rocket propelled grenade at the governorate. The grenade had bounced off the concrete barriers and exploded on the sidewalk. Two schoolgirls walking by at that moment had been killed.

"But let me ask you," I said, "if you knew who did this, would you turn him in to the police?"

The men shook their heads no.

"Why?"

"We don't know who did this," said one. The other fellow told the truth. He said he wouldn't go to the police because the people who organized the attack would find out about this and kill him.

The conversation was getting a bit loud. From just a few men, a small crowd had grown around us. A cop came over and moved us along. Roaa led us toward the governorate's entrance. We stopped by the splotches of the schoolgirls' blood, congealed overnight from crimson to brown with the help of Mosul's dust. We entered via a side street, were searched, and walked past police recruits getting desultory training in martial arts. They looked bored, but not as bored as their instructor. In the governorate building itself, there was the anxious hubbub of people on police business: looking for information on family members who had been arrested, making reports on thefts and other crimes.

In the courtyard, Roaa saw someone she knew from attending press conferences. It was Colonel Mukhadem, chief of security for Iraqi officials in Mosul. She called out to him. He stopped and introductions were made.

At this point in the occupation, there were three main groups who caused security problems: local insurgents, still loyal to the old regime, who regarded any attempt to normalize the country, such as setting up a government, as a form of collaboration; jihadis hoping to foment the war for control of Islam all over the world by striking against American targets; and ordinary murderers and thieves. I asked the colonel which of these three groups had attacked the building the day before. He gave me the party line: "Iraq is open three hundred and sixty degrees to the world. Foreigners enter Iraq and do these things." He added, "It was America's fault for failing to secure the borders." I had heard this from every policeman I had spoken to. No Iraqi would kill another Iraqi; all the violence was caused by foreign fighters.

It was, of course, untrue. I pressed the colonel about specifics. After ten months of occupation, surely he must have an idea of who in Mosul might do something like this. The colonel retreated into the mind-set that had frustrated Gary Masapollo and Al Kabakov as they tried to help Roaa find her father's murderer. The colonel's job was security at city hall. "If anybody make some kind of operation I cannot make any accusation because my job is simply security. Not to chase people." I pressed again. He must have some sense of who did this. But if he did, he had no intention of telling me. While we spoke, across the courtyard a couple of cops were vigorously shoving a young man toward a jail entrance.

As we left the governorate we heard the unmistakable *whoosh* of a rocket propelled grenade passing overhead. Dozens of idlers heard it as well, and we followed the crowd chasing down the sound at a fast shuffle. We came to a park and asked if anyone had seen anything. No one had seen a thing. The police had already cordoned off the green space. Someone said he thought the missile had landed in the park but hadn't exploded. The sky began to swarm with American helicopters. All over the city the tiny, daily incidents that made liberated Iraq into a terrifying place were unfolding. We turned around and walked back to Diwassa, followed part of the way by another bunch of idle men who caught sight of my equipment and chanted *"al-Jazeera, al-Jazeera"* after us. They want to be interviewed, said Roaa. Yeah, right.

When we got back to Diwassa, the car was gone. The driver, Haidar, had been standing in the square when we went chasing off to find out about the RPG. He and Salaam had exchanged a few words. Now he was nowhere to be found. I turned to Salaam. "Where is he?"

"The driver told me the police were making him move the car."

"Where?"

Salaam didn't know.

"I don't like this," I said to him. "This is not safe."

Now Diwassa felt exactly like it did a year before. There was an atmosphere of impending violence like an electrical charge in the ether just before a springtime thunderstorm. I turned on my tape recorder in anticipation of something happening. It picked up the sound of cop cars racing by, sirens blaring, and American helicopters darting overhead.

There was a general sullenness in the crowd and among the police trying to control traffic in Diwassa Square. I turned around 360 degrees. I was the only American. Hatred was coming at me in waves. "I do not like this," I said aloud. "I do not like this at all." I called out my driver's name, "Haidar,

Haidar." Someone in the crowd mocked it back at me. I got a grip on myself and walked over to Salaam and Roaa. Salaam said he would go find the driver. I had to stop him. Today he was my translator, all that stood between me and an assault by a mob or being dragged away by cops wondering who the fucking American is standing there by himself. I turned around again. Then Roaa tapped me on the arm and said quietly, "Look."

Three plainclothes policemen had surrounded a young man and one of them was demanding his papers. The youth was mouthing off. The policeman in charge gave him a tremendous open-handed slap across the face. Then the young man kicked one of the other cops in the shin and broke free. The police chased him past us and caught hold of the youth on a little traffic island about ten feet away. Suddenly the whole picture fell into place. The young man had a wispy beard. Unlike any other twenty-year-old in Diwassa, he was wearing neither jeans and T-shirt nor dishdasha. He was wearing a baggy Pakistani shalwar and a very loose-fitting shirt to cover what I immediately assumed was a suicide bomber's belt. *He's wearing the belt* flashed through my brain. *He's going to blow himself up.* I pushed Roaa back and slowly began to step away from the confrontation. As we moved back, I saw him reach into his pocket and thought, *This is it, he's going to push the detonator and I am going to die.* Instead this kid, no more than twenty, pulled out a grenade. I called out to Salaam, "Grenade. Get back. Get back." As I said this, the kid pulled the pin and threw it at the cops' feet. I was already diving to the pavement as the grenade went off. Luckily for us, the bulk of the explosion was on the other side of the little traffic island. The cops emptied their guns into the young man for what seemed like several minutes, though in reality it was only for about twenty seconds.

I lifted my head to look for Roaa. She had run behind a wall. Then the shooting started again. I lay in the open street until this fusillade ended, then quickly ran over to her. Salaam was lying motionless in the street. I called out to him; he lifted his head and then the cops started shooting again, spraying the rooftops indiscriminately, endangering more people than the wannabe jihadi who nearly killed us had. When the shooting stopped, Roaa and I sprinted ten yards across the road to a little teahouse. As we went in, the police were carrying one of their comrades past us. He was unconscious and bleeding heavily from shrapnel wounds along his side. Salaam still hadn't moved; he was lying facedown, one leg akimbo, his body ominously relaxed. I was now frantic. I had already gotten one person killed in this fucking city. Now it looked like I had caused another one to die. Then he got up, dusted himself off, and came over to us. "Man, don't do that to me," I shouted at him. He put his hand on my shoulder. "No problem, Michael," he said. "I am a Muslim. If it is my time. . . ."

The police kept us locked inside the teahouse for about twenty minutes. Sporadic bursts of gunfire could be heard in the neighborhood. Then, like water after a spigot opens, normalcy flowed through the streets. It was as if nothing had happened. We were allowed to go. Before I could stop him, Salaam went off to find our driver, Haidar. We watched him go down the street, and as we lost sight of him, Haidar came wandering out of a shawarma joint, working a toothpick around his mouth. He'd been having lunch the whole time.

At the Nineveh Palace we washed up and had lunch. Colleagues of Roaa's came in with footage of the day's big events. In a brutal foreshadowing of what was to happen in Fallujah a few days later, a convoy of SUVs carrying Western engineers to a power station on the outskirts of Mosul had been attacked. One vehicle's gas tank had exploded and the engineers inside had been incinerated. In a separate incident, an American armored personnel carrier on patrol in a suburb had been turned into a similar inferno. The U.S. military spokesman in town said no one had been killed. The Iraqi cameraman simply refused to believe it. Later that day, a member of the Mosul city council survived an assassination attempt, though her bodyguard wasn't so lucky. By the end of this typical day in liberated Mosul, our near-death experience wasn't even worth a line in CNN's wrap-up. The only reason anyone knows about the rocket attack on the governorate building or the jihadi's death just outside its gates is because I happened to be there. If an atrocity takes place in a war zone and there's no journalist there to record it, do the dying people make a sound?

I didn't have time to interview Roaa at length. She was filing a summary of these incidents to her outlets. The sun was fading and we needed to get back to Erbil before dark. I only had time to ask her if she thought, with all she had lost and with the continuing chaos, whether Saddam's overthrow had been worth it. Her answer in English was swift. "Of course."

The next day Sami drove me to the Habur Gate. He did not go back through Mosul. In the three weeks I had been in Iraq, the security situation had declined dramatically and it was about to get worse. As we went through the mountains we heard a report on Radio Sawa, the American-backed station: Ambassador Paul Bremer had closed down the newspaper of a young radical Shi'a cleric named Moqtada al-Sadr.

"That's stupid," I said to Sami.

My driver, ever loyal to Hajji Bush, disagreed. "Moqtada is a bad man."

I nodded. "I know. But there are better ways to start a fight with Moqtada than to close a newspaper." Sami's English is not bad, but I don't know if he understood what I said. In any case, the conversation ended there. I stared into the mountains and started up a conversation in my mind with Ahmad. I said to him, "Do you believe this shit? How stupid can they be? If they want to start a fight with Moqtada, why close his newspaper? Don't they know that in every bazaar, people will be saying, 'The Americans promise us freedom of the press but what do they do when we write something they disagree with? They close down the newspaper. Just like Saddam.'"

And in my mind's eye, I saw Ahmad nodding. I heard him say, "Always disasters befall the Iraqi people. Americans are just the latest."

I wish you were here, Ahmad. Every day I have questions about the situation in Iraq. You are the only person who could answer them. I also want to know with certainty who killed you, not just who pulled the trigger, but who paid them and why. You would know. I have my own theory. I believe it is as you wrote in Bilattijah: *former Saddam regime elements have joined up with radical Islamists, the people they once spied on in the mosque. They are allies against a democratic Iraq. They hated you for what you wrote, so they organized your murder. How they knew you were on the roof talking on the Thuraya is a question for Thair Zeki to answer. But he never has and he probably never will.*

I wish you were here, my friend. There are important things I need to tell you. I wanted this war. I have wanted this kind of war since 1968, the year you and I started our higher education. We set out on such different paths that year and ended up in the same geographical place, although my journey was easy and yours unbearably hard. Just once in my lifetime I wanted my country's government to do the right thing and remove a tyrant from the neck of a people and set their nation free. I say that still to everyone who was against the war. They spout so much rhetoric about peace and justice without realizing that sometimes you have to wage war for those ideals. They would have let you die in exile or be tortured to death under Saddam, your story never to be heard. Not one of them has your courage and not one of them understands how precious your months—mere months—of freedom were.

But I must also tell you how angry I am. My government betrayed you and the thousands like you. In the months before the war, in public and in private I argued that the war was worth fighting, not for their reasons but for our reasons. On human rights grounds alone it was right to remove Saddam. When circumstances allow, it is always right to remove a tyrant. When people spoke of the potential for violent anarchy after Saddam was toppled, I argued back that failure was not an option. The Bush administration was too attuned to the domestic political risk of the war not succeeding. They would have a plan to organize Iraq and open up the society to people like you, Ahmad. But they didn't. And they did not even have to pay a political price for their failure. I want to tell you how sorry I am. I want to "make my apologies," as you had to do with Saddam, for the arrogance and stupidity that led Hajji Bush and his advisers to celebrate before the victory was won. They were busy celebrating as your murderers were planning your death.

The Americans in Mosul should have protected you. You were the best translator, the best interpreter of the society they had conquered, but they left you out there exposed to all your enemies. Everything the Americans feared came to pass in your murder—Ba'athists and jihadists making common cause. The day will come when they slaughter each other, but they are in charge now in Mosul, though the

Americans don't know it. They have the power to protect your killer and so he walks free.

I also want to tell you about your daughter Roaa. At the end of the day we went to Darawish to meet your brother Khalil. She got a call on the Thuraya. There had been a roadside explosion near an American installation. The injured and possible dead had been taken to Jumhuriyah Hospital. With Salaam we raced over there so she could get the details.

Roaa knows how to do her job. When we arrived, she went straight to the hospital's security office to find out what ward the injured had been taken to. There were half a dozen men sitting around smoking, rough-looking characters of a type you knew very well. This was not a room for a woman to visit. They looked at me when we walked in, completely ignoring your daughter, her hijab wrapped tightly around her head. And then she got their attention. Pushing forward to the desk of the man in charge, she asked him where the injured were. He ignored her question and carried on talking to his friends. She raised her voice. The one behind the desk snarled back a question. It must have been something like, Who the fuck are you? She didn't give an inch. She took her press ID out and showed it. She spoke evenly but raised her volume and gave him just the right look to get something out of someone in authority. She didn't deploy any feminine charm or get flirtatious with these guys. That would only have brought disrespect. She looked at the brute behind the desk directly but without challenge. She put in her voice a quality of stubbornness, making it clear to this man that she would not move until he told her where the injured had been taken. Don't get angry, just be stubborn. It took me years to figure that out. Your daughter does it like a veteran. She found out what she needed to know and left the room.

Outside in the parking lot, the local Reuters television news crew was pulling in. Roaa waved to them. The bodies inside the hospital were not bodies I needed to count. But for Roaa this was the day's news. She had to get the story. She looked at me. "Go to work," I said. She walked over to the crew, and I watched her go through the rituals of our trade. Standing with the Reuters producer, notebooks flipped open, sharing information on the event, making a plan on how to get the facts they needed in a place where they were not welcome. I told Salaam to wait before leaving, and we watched them disappear into the hospital where you died. I was on the verge of tears. I wish you could have seen her.

I know you would have felt what I felt: love, concern, worry for this young woman undertaking something you know is difficult, and then the sheer relief that the kid can do it, followed by the flood of pride that brims up with tears when you see she can do it brilliantly. Then the final bittersweet emotion: you want the moment to continue, to remain connected, praise is on your lips, but she has already turned away and left you behind. She no longer needs your praise. She knows she's good at what she does. Roaa went into the hospital to get her story without looking back. She is her own person . . . but through her, my friend, you speak to me.

Author's Note

In a better world I would have written a book *with* Ahmad rather than about him. We would have waited a decent interval to see what kind of Iraq was taking shape, then looked back at the war and its aftermath. The book would have been about the hopes the Bush administration's overthrow of Saddam brewed up and how they were dashed through partisan carelessness and—Lord, help us all—sheer laziness. Instead I have had to write this book alone, with the help of a small network of his family and friends.

The physical sound of Ahmad's voice was in my ear during its composition. I still have the tapes that I recorded during the war and listened to them frequently while writing the book. I also have the tapes from my trip to Iraq a year after Saddam was overthrown. In the first and last sections of the book, wherever I am present, any dialogue that appears in quotation marks is taken from those tapes or very directly from notes I made at the time. This is not just dialogue spoken by Ahmad, but the speech of Captain Pat and the other Green Berets, the little bespectacled man in the Mosul mosque who assured us there were no weapons of mass destruction long before the Iraq

Survey Group figured that out, and the words of Roaa and Abdussalaam the day we almost died. Also, sound effects like the B-52 strikes rumbling through his house at precisely the moment Ahmad was reminiscing about being arrested at the Jordanian border and sent to prison are taken directly from the tapes. If you are curious to hear my friends' voices or the sound of battle, you can listen to them at http://www.insideout.org. Click on the banners that read *Ahmad's War* or *Fear and Anger, the View from Iraq.*

The middle section of the book is an imagined biography. I had planned to move to Mosul for a while to do research, and I would have, if Mosul had been safe enough for me to live in for an extended period of time. But it is one of the triumphs of the Bush administration's Iraq policy that in overthrowing a hideous tyrant, they managed to create an environment in which Americans, rather than being thanked, are likely to be abducted and decapitated if they walk alone down the street. Instead, I had to engage in extended e-mail conversations with his friends and family, none of whom write English with fluency. They all have the circumspection born of living in a totalitarian system about putting details in writing, so it was a long process to draw out information.

However, the resulting biography is not fanciful. It is built from the stories Ahmad told me and those memories his family and friends were able to share. No man can wholly know another, but the circumstances in which I became friends with Ahmad were extraordinary. We both had waited a long time to find someone we could open up to. I think I came to know him well enough to fill in gaps in his story faithfully. The dialogue and thoughts I ascribe to my friend are as I imagine them, although much of the dialogue is taken from stories told by his family. The key incidents: the riots in Mosul in 1959, the visit to Mar Matte monastery, the murder of Mothana Kasmoola, Ahmad's trip to Poland, his year of exile in Egypt, his hounding into "retirement," his failed attempts to get to the West, meeting Saddam, and so on, all happened.

The quotes from Ahmad's writings are based on translations he and others provided. I then worked through them to make them grammatically correct and reshaped those sentences that were not comprehensible. They are faithful renderings. I missed my friend most when working on these pieces. We would have had wonderful arguments about language and meaning as we prepared the essays and stories for the book we never got to write.

To firmly grasp the history of Iraq, the Ba'ath, and Kurdistan, I relied heavily on the following books and URLs. They provide an excellent syllabus for anyone who wants to know more about the country the United States conquered and the prospects for a decent outcome for the people of Iraq.

Books

The Modern History of Iraq, Phebe Marr, Westview Press.

Republic of Fear, Kanan Makiya, University of California Press.

After Such Knowledge, What Forgiveness?: My Encounters with Kurdistan, Jonathan C. Randal, Westview Press.

The Old Social Classes and the Revolutionary Movements of Iraq, Hanna Batatu, Princeton University Press.

Churchill's Folly: How Winston Churchill Created Modern Iraq, Christopher Catherwood, Carroll & Graf.

The Longest War: The Iran-Iraq Military Conflict, Dilip Hiro, Routledge.

War Stories of the Green Berets, Hans Halberstadt, Zenith Press.

URL

http://www.parnassuspoetry.com/Ormsby.htm
http://www.kurdistanica.com/
http://middleeastreference.org.uk/iraqiopposition.html
http://www.padfield.com/1996/nineveh.html
http://mcadams.posc.mu.edu/txt/ah/Layard/
http://www.aina.org/
http://www.sanskrit-
  sanscrito.com.ar/english/linguistics/origin5.html

Index

Acknowledgments

THIS BOOK COULD not have been written without the help of the family of Ahmad Shawkat. I am particularly grateful to his daughter Roaa Ahmad, his wife, Afrah Abdulrazak, and his oldest son, Sindibad Ahmad. Abdulfaraj Shawkat Alyas was invaluable in providing background on Darawish and insights into his older brother's character. Faraj's own life was blighted by Saddam's tyranny, and I hope some day he can return to the United States to join his son and enjoy life in a stable, free society.

Three translators were needed to tell the story of my singular interpreter. Omar al-Dewachi translated Ahmad's editorials from *Bilattijah* with skill. He also added helpful notes on changes he adduced in Ahmad's mental state from these essays during the period leading up to his murder. Zeto Siany took me around Kurdistan a year after the war was over. Bilal Sayd Ahmed translated some of my detailed inquiries back to Ahmad's family during the year I was writing this book.

There was a fourth translator: Abdussalaam al-Medeni; but Salaam is much more than that. He is my dear friend. He is also someone who gives me hope that Iraq may yet have a good future.

Faleh Jabar shared his memories of Ahmad and reminded

me that I first heard the name of Ahmad Shawkat from him. In September 2002, I was planning a trip to Kurdistan to report on the Kurds' view of the upcoming war. I visited Faleh, and he gave me a background briefing on the situation. I asked him if he could suggest any translators in Erbil, and he gave me a few names, among them Ahmad's. In the end that trip never happened and I inevitably lost the list. The fact that I found Ahmad anyway makes me think that our meeting was fated.

Paul Watson of the *Los Angeles Times* and Yochi Dreazen of the *Wall Street Journal* racked their memories for details of their time with Ahmad. I hope they feel my representation of them is fair. David Filipov of the *Boston Globe,* Anna Badkhen of the *San Francisco Chronicle* and Lynne O'Donnell of the *Irish Times* were also helpful.

Jonathan C. Randal, formerly of *The Washington Post,* took me under his wing on my first trip to Kurdistan in 1996 and continued to help me with insights into the place as I wrote this book.

General David Petraeus helped me with his recollections of his time in Mosul. Captain Gary Masapollo was completely open with me about Roaa, her father's murder, and the problems of trying to shepherd the new Iraq toward stability. Frank Antenori, one of the Green Berets in action at the site of the friendly-fire incident at Debaga, thoroughly answered questions about that day.

Ornithologist Brayton Holt offered advice on Kurdistan's birds of prey.

This book grew out of my reporting for Inside Out, the special projects unit of WBUR, Boston's NPR news station. My executive producer, Anna Bensted, first dreamed up the title *Ahmad's War,* and encouraged me to write this book after Ahmad was murdered. It is thanks to my studio producer, George Hicks, that Ahmad's voice lives with such clarity.

My editor, Philip Turner, taught me how to write for the page rather than the microphone, which required a great deal of patience on his part.

My agent, Ron Goldfarb, sold the book in a disturbingly disinterested market.

Finally, my wife, Christin Cockerton, has held her fear in check for years while I followed my need to observe history at its violent epicenter. She is always my first reader and my best reader.

About the Author

For almost two decades, Michael Goldfarb has been public radio's most familiar voice from London. He is currently senior correspondent for "Inside Out," the award-winning radio documentary unit of WBUR Boston. He has covered major conflicts from Bosnia to Iraq to Northern Ireland. In 2003 he was awarded broadcast journalism's highest honor, the DuPont-Columbia Award for his report "Surviving Torture." He also won British radio's highest honor, the Sony Award, for his series of essays about the American Midwest, "Homeward Bound." In 2005 he won the Lowell Thomas award given by the Overseas Press Club for his report, "British Jihad: Inside Out."

Since September 2001, Goldfarb has reported extensively from the Middle East. His "Inside Out" documentaries are heard on more than 150 public radio stations around the country. Goldfarb's radio documentary on the Iraq War and Ahmad Shawkat's return to Mosul, "Ahmad's War: Inside Out," won the Radio Television News Director's Edward R. Murrow Award.

A regular commentator on American culture and politics for BBC television and radio, Goldfarb was also the regular host of the BBC World Service flagship arts program, "Meridian," the only American who has ever held that position. He has also been a Shorenstein Fellow at Harvard's Kennedy School of Government.

Michael Goldfarb has been living in London since 1985.